A FEW WORDS OF

Comfort

FOR THE GRIEVING

The One-Year Companion
for the Brokenhearted

A FEW Words Of Comfort For The Grieving
Publishing Coordinator: Kimberly Joy Krueger

Volume 2 of the "A FEW Words" Series from FEW International Publications

Contributing Authors: Kimberly Joy Krueger, Reji Laberje, Annabelle Ahlers, Susan Brozek, Karen Bruno, Neesie Cieslak, Jessica Chase, Lisa Danegelis, Victoria Dreckman, Rebecca Faye Grambort, Linét Lewerenz, Luanne Nelson, Maria Christine Notch, Amy Sikkema, Heather Taylor, Traci Weldie, Ava Olivia Willett

Contributing Editor and Interior Layout Design: Reji Laberje, Bucket List To Bookshelf, www.bucketlisttobookshelf.com, reji.laberje@gmail.com
Associate Editors: Amy Oaks, Kimberly Joy Krueger
Cover Design and Interior Layout Graphic Elements: Mike Nicloy, Nico 11 Publishing & Design, www.nico11publishing.com, mike@nico11publishing.com
Author Photos and Marketing and Publicity Footage: Kimberly Laberge, labergekimberly.wixsite.com/thedramaden, Laberge.kimberly@gmail.com; additional photos supplied by contributing authors

Bible translations of all scriptures are noted and taken from www.biblegateway.com. © 1995-2017, The Zondervan Corporation. All Rights Reserved.

ISBN-13: 978-1949494020
ISBN-10: 1949494020

Categories:
Religion & Spirituality/Christian Books & Bibles/Literature &
    Fiction/Collections & Anthologies
Religion & Spirituality/Christian Books & Bibles/Christian Living/Devotionals
Religion & Spirituality/Christian Books & Bibles/Christian Living/Death & Grief

Dear Reader,

The journey of grief can be isolating and unpredictable. Everyone will experience grief and yet, so often, we feel alone and as though our situation of loss is unique. It is so important that we are patient with ourselves when we walk the path of darkness, because finding the light can seem impossible. But I believe that every dark Good Friday ends in a bright Easter morning.

Loss is a very important part of life and needs to be courageously embraced so healing can transform us. The greatest Biblical miracle was performed at the grave by our Almighty God so we can rest in His comfort, sovereignty, and promise of hope that no loss is too great to go unanswered by God.

The grief journey is an invitation. Bless your own soul by receiving the gift of companionship that is offered by the seventeen authors who open their hearts to you in these pages. They give a peek of what redemption looks like through their tender stories of loss. Choose your pace and be encouraged by the hope given as you journal through the prompts in each entry. Let peace fill you as you reflect on how God has met everyone in a very personal way.

Say "Yes!" to the path of grace and mercy that has your name on it as you walk hand-in-hand with your Savior in the new places of understanding His love for you. God has healing, light, and hope for you as you trust Him to carry your broken heart. He doesn't just want you to survive grief, He wants you to be filled with a new JOY!

You are loved, you are not alone, and you are known.

"Even the darkness will not be dark to you; the night will shine like the day, for darkness is as light to you."
~ Psalm 139:12

~ Linda Znachko
Founder of: He Knows Your Name Ministry – heknowsyourname.org
Author of: "He Knows Your Name –
How One Abandoned Baby Inspired Me To Say Yes To God"

Table of Contents

About Your Grief – About Your Companions   6

Denial   8

Pain   22

Guilt   46

Anger   72

Bargaining   98

Depression   112

Looking Back   134

Loneliness   150

Transition   178

Rebuilding   198

Acceptance   220

Hope   246

Meet Your Companions   272

An Invitation To Receive The Comforter   278

Other Great FEW Books   280

"A FEW Words Of Comfort For The Grieving," the second release in FEW International Publication's line of devotionals, is more than a book to simply read.

- → Each devotion is followed by introspective questions to allow you to reflect on your own journey of grief.
- → Inspirational quotes will encourage you as you work your way through the stages.
- → Seventeen different authors share multiple grief experiences, allowing you to relate to loss of many types.
- → Choose to read from front to back or focus on the area in which you most struggle.
- → Choose to work your way through the devotional at your own pace.
- → Most FEW authors are available to present to your ministry, group, church, or organization. Like what you read? Consider inviting one of our authors to present a teaching on her devotion(s).

A FEW Words . . . MANY ways to use them on your own faith journey

About Your Grief . . . About Your Companions

From FEW International Publications Owner, Kimberly Joy Krueger
And FEW International Publications Coach, Reji Laberje

Kimberly started it all . . .

One of the perks of owning FEW International Publications is getting to hear hundreds of women's stories! Over the course of the last four years of listening to so many extraordinary stories, a common theme began to strike me: women suffer great loss of all kinds. Women know pain and women know grief. It began to stir in my heart that, since this is true and will continue to be true, then there needs to be a FEW resource that will provide comfort to women's grieving hearts. And who better to write this book than women who have grieved, lost, and bled, but have come out on the other side. After all, grief is real, but so is healing. The Lord gave me the following scripture and off to work I went collecting the stories you will read about in this beautiful and powerful book.

> *"Blessed be the God and Father of our Lord Jesus Christ, the Father of mercies and God of all comfort, who comforts us in all our affliction so that we will be able to comfort those who are in any affliction with the comfort with which we ourselves are comforted by God."*
>
> *~2 Corinthians 1:3-4 NASB*

Although this book hosts 120 devotions, grief is rarely a 120-day process. In fact, most say the first year after a great loss is the most painful and arduous. Our book acknowledges that, as well as the fact that grief is not only caused by the death of a loved one. Our hearts are grieved when we lose a friendship we treasured, a business we poured into, the marriage we dreamed of, or our very own health. If any of these apply to you, or your own reasons for grief, then you are sure to find comfort in these pages. I intentionally sought stories of loss of all kinds so that this book could be universally comforting to women. I proposed the idea to Reji, and in true "Reji" form, her creative juices started flowing!

Reji's turn . . .

I remember being in basic training for the military more years ago than I care to admit. Make no mistake; it was hard. It was physically hard, as we pushed our bodies to do more (on less) than we'd ever done before. It was hard emotionally, because we had been broken down to weak states of fragility; we could find ourselves crying in frustration over tasks as simple as making a bed. What we had, though, was a graduation date. No matter how difficult life got and no matter how insurmountable a struggle seemed, we could look forward to that finish line. We knew that, if we could just push through these couple of months, it would be over and we could celebrate.

Wouldn't it be nice if grief worked that way? It sure would be awesome to say, '*Yep. This "guilt" phase really stinks, but I'll be done with this in another three weeks. Then, I can just move onto the next grief stage and be done with that. I'll have this thing whipped by summer.*'

When Kim and I started working out the plan for this book she was inspired to, we (or, at least, I) thought we could structure it in a clean and organized fashion. We expanded on Elizabeth Kubler Ross's famous five stages of grief (denial, anger, bargaining, depression, and acceptance) to include a number of "substages" inspired by work on life transitions that I had done with Christian authors and leaders, Evelyn Johnson and Dr. Alan Forsman on their #1 Bestselling *Crescendo – An Ascent To Vital Living.*

'Perfect! We have twelve stages of grief; we could go through a stage of grief each month. Let's find fifteen women who each do eight devotions. We will guide them such that all of the areas are covered, ten devotions per month for one year is 120 comforting devotions inspired by God's Word. In one year, everybody who reads this book will be healed of their grieving!'

Yes. I know how convoluted it sounds when I read it back. The science of book structure and layout was going to turn out to be much less . . . well . . . scientific, for this theme.

Would you believe that the women did *not* experience grief in a nice orderly fashion? Crazy, right? Alright. Even the organizational side of my brain agrees this isn't so crazy, after all. The stages of grief get mixed up and sometimes revisited. You may spend longer in one stage than another and skip other stages completely. Our "perfect" concept didn't come together, as you'll see the stages represented in chapters of . . . *gasp* . . . different lengths! Some of the devotions turned in could have gone in several of the "stage" chapters because the emotions were all mixed up together. I get it, now. Grief is messy, unordered, and illogical, but it's relatable and—in the sharing of those relatable experiences—there is healing from it, albeit not in the perfectly scientific structure that I had planned. The book on grief *should* be messy and unordered; I believe that's what God ultimately put together in these pages.

Mind you, we did keep some of the organizational tools necessary to helping those on their grief journeys, including, not the fifteen authors we had planned on, but seventeen writers, or, as Kim realized, your companions . . .

Kimberly brings it home to you . . .

As we pieced these beautiful stories, quotes, and journaling questions together, it became apparent to me that we had not just created a resource for the grieving, but a companion. We envisioned our readers being able to open up this book and turn to the section she may need the most. Or she may go through it chronologically and find that these stages of grief have mirrored her own journey. We imagined that the temptation of feeling alone in her grief would be more easily resisted with the many examples of God's comfort written about here, along with the Scriptures, quotes, and definitions of the stages of grief. We aimed to validate the grieving experience, not rush anyone through it! We were confident that not only would our book be a comforting companion to our readers, but the seventeen authors who have chosen to share their deeply personal and harrowing stories will be their willing companions on the journey, as well. And we saw to it that the journey can be as gentle as our readers need it to be.

Our 120 Devotions need not be tackled in 120 days. Each entry is followed by three journaling questions to ponder. If so desired, readers can read each devotion, answering only one of the journal questions each day. For example, after reading the devotion the first day, the "Picture This" question can be answered. That may be enough for one day for a hurting soul. The following day, after re-reading the devotional entry, the "Ask This" question can then be considered. On the third day, readers can review the devotion and pour it all back to God in the "Pray This" section. In so doing, each devotion can be a very gentle, three-day process, allowing this book to guide its readers through one year of grieving.

We implore our readers to set their own pace and be as gentle with themselves as need be. After all, Jesus, Himself said, "*Blessed are those who mourn, for they will be comforted.*" (Matthew 5:4 NIV)

Our prayers for you have been and continue to be just that.

Be A Companion

Instead of,
*"You just need to accept
your new situation,"*
Try,
*"I know this is really
hard for you."*

With Words Of Comfort

*You may not understand their denial.
But you can love them through it.*

The First Stage

DENIAL *(noun) – according to your companions*
[de - **ni** – *uh*l]

1. Choosing to believe a fairy tale you or someone else has made up, in an effort to avoid the painful, dreaded truth
2. The act of pushing truth away to avoid pain
3. Avoiding or not accepting what is real or true
4. Refusing to admit the truth about something unpleasant
5. Refusal to accept your reality
6. Anything that blinds you from seeing truth
7. Avoidance of reality realized

What does "denial" mean to you:

The Shrapnel of Truth

→ Ava Olivia Willett

"But I am afraid that just as Eve was deceived by the serpent's cunning, your minds may somehow be led astray from your sincere and pure devotion to Christ."

~2 Corinthians 11:3 NIV

When I was eleven and just beginning to develop my own thoughts and opinions on life, I chose the church. Everything about the mysteries of God drew me in deep waters. As I branched out and joined a youth group, I was quickly crowned a "leader" to become an example and teacher for my peers.

I had always sensed my pastor's favor upon my head. I saw it in her eyes the first day I stood up and spoke in front of the sea of faces, explaining a scripture I carefully interpreted myself. I saw it when I danced around during service, expressing my love for God to anyone who asked me.

The feeling of favor changed the day Pastor said, "Ava, I am very disappointed in you."

I felt my heart swell and a lump formed in my throat. The words ripped like shrapnel through my soft skin and organs.

In the middle of developing my thoughts on how magnificent God is, the teenage side of me developed thoughts on how interesting a certain boy at the youth group was. I was crazy about him, following him around and obsessing over how funny and adorable I thought he was. My youth group leader saw my behavior as wrong and banished me from my leadership role.

The loss of this leadership position broke my heart. I wrestled in my faith after I was torn down from that leadership and, as I watched my childhood youth group crumble before my very eyes, I turned away from God a bit, feeling like the calling on my head was too much of a burden for someone my age to carry on. I realized many years later that my outbursts and deep-rooted heartaches were stemming from the day my leadership role was cut. I felt ashamed and unworthy.

I denied that I was heartbroken about my loss for a very, very long time. Reflecting on this denial of grief, I learned how to recognize which situations are tearing me apart and face them bravely instead of cowering away in sin, hoping the pain would eventually dissipate.

Jesus, walk with me. Walk with my broken heart in Your hands. Reveal Your truth about the situation as tall as a mountain ahead of me. Your goodness will spin me on my heels to walk on the path I'm called to tread. Uncover my heart that I hide under a basket from You. I am vulnerable, but I'm safe with You. Amen.

Picture This - What situation are you facing that might be a road-block in your healing process that you may not recognize?

Ask This - What options do you have, through God, to deal with this road-block?

Pray This - Lord, help me to face my obstacles and come to the reality of my situation. Open my eyes to Your Solutions and guidance in this slow and dry season.

Words of **Comfort** for Denial:

"God's delay is not his denial."

I Have No Right

→ Heather Taylor

"Instead of your shame you will receive a double portion, and instead of disgrace you will rejoice in your inheritance. And so you will inherit a double portion in your land, and everlasting joy will be yours. "For I, the Lord, love justice; I hate robbery and wrongdoing. In my faithfulness I will reward my people and make an everlasting covenant with them."

~Isaiah 61:7-8 NIV

The two candles, one blue and one pink, were lit and ready for him when he walked in the door. The table cloth was bright pink but he wasn't observant so he wouldn't notice. He walked in the door, I held my breath.

"Wow! What's all this?" My husband asked, looking for an explanation. I shrugged and handed him two presents. "Okay?" he said reluctantly taking them. "Are we celebrating something?" He asked. I picked up our two-year-old daughter and watched. He unwrapped the blue wrapping paper to discover the blue rattle. looking at me with confusion he began unwrapping the pink paper. My husband finally got it and grabbed us and gave us a big squeeze. "We're pregnant?" he said.

"We're pregnant!" I said.

That was the happiest day of my life; unfortunately it didn't last.

Just eight short weeks later, I started bleeding which led to a night of complete emptiness in the ER. My husband was away on business and Brooke and I were visiting my mother-in-law so she was watching Brooke while I suffered the loss of not one, but two babies, alone, in a bleak hospital with strangers. TWINS! That would have been the happiest news ever just one day ago. But I wasn't able to feel the excitement or disbelief of two, just the loss. I was mad at how upset I was. After all, I was only a couple months pregnant. This happens to women who are much further along than I was.

I have no right to grieve. The women in my life were good at picking up and moving on and that's who I was, but all I wanted to do was feel this loss. I was torn between needing to move on and wanting to hurt. I was overwhelmed with the need to stop and feel the bad feelings—the pain of losing them – but thought I couldn't because of timing or my right. I didn't deserve to grieve. I tried to fight back the tears, the pain, the anguish my heart felt. I would never hold, nurse, kiss, smell ,or rock my babies. I knew I shouldn't be so upset, but I was. I continued to tell myself, "Get over it, Heather! You have no right to feel such loss!"

But I couldn't. All I could do was hide it. I hid it well enough that everyone thought I was fine. I was a trooper. I had moved on. The pain and I were secret friends. Unfortunately, pain is a terrible BFF! What I truly needed was permission to grieve.

I finally received permission from a knock at my door. As I answered there wasn't a person but a note stuck between my screen and the door. I grabbed it and began reading: IT ISN'T YOUR FAULT! YOUR PAIN IS REAL AND GOD WANTS YOU TO HAVE JOY AND HEALING.

I remember laughing uncontrollably and grabbing my Bible. Isaiah 61 gave me permission. I started to cry as I finally stopped denying my pain and surrendered to the loss that was consuming me. God wants us to have joy, not pain, blame, shame or sorrow. What the devil steals God will restore. Your pain is real. But God will restore what the devil has taken.

Lord, I pray You will bring healing to everyone that reads this devotion. Let them confess out loud that You hate robbery and wrong doing. Let them know that You are a God of hope and Restoration. Amen.

Picture This - Picture someone telling you it's okay to grieve your loss. Imagine them saying, "It's okay to feel the pain." How will you respond?

Ask This - Have you allowed yourself the proper time to mourn your loss?

Pray This - Father, I pray that you will restore what the devil has taken from me and replace the joy that I have lost. Heal my broken heart.

Words of **Comfort** for Denial:

"I should know enough about loss to know that you never really stop missing someone – you just learn to live around the huge, gaping hole of their absence."
~Alyson Noel Evermore

I Will Receive You

→ Jessica Chase

"Though my mother and father forsake me, the Lord will receive me."

~Psalm 27:10 NIV

As a child from a broken family, you dream of being like everyone else. Not extraordinary or super, just normal. You long for family memories and listen with envy as others share theirs. Anxiety causes a lie to be planted that says if anyone knows that you aren't normal, they won't accept you, so you live behind an "acceptable facade." There are so many masks to choose from nowadays: overachieving, drinking, drugs, materialism, power, obsession with outward appearances, and even religion can be masks. The mask may work for a while but—inevitably—a trigger event overwhelms the soul and the facade crumbles; the pain won't be denied forever.

I didn't have just one mask, I wore many: overachieving, alcohol, drugs, obsession with my looks.

I would cry out to God: "I cannot carry this pain and I cannot hide behind this facade anymore, it's too hard . . . HELP!"

In the midst of my masquerade, God met me and said, "Release your grip, these choices are leading you into more pain. Have faith little Lamb, My grace is enough, My strength is made perfect in your weakness. I will be there when you fall, even if everyone else leaves you, I will not, because I am your Good Father".

Then, one day it happened, an answer to my cries for help came in the form of my trigger event: my drinking got the best of me, the police were called, and my facade was shattered. My livelihood, my relationship with my children, and even my freedom were threatened.

From this low point, God asked me, "Are you ready to choose differently my Beloved Daughter? It's time to step out from behind the facade and deal with the pain."

A resounding, "Yes!" echoed from the deepest part of my soul.

It hasn't been a cake walk but I am here to testify it is better to be real, feel the pain and heal then to deny, hide and be dying inside.

Lord give us courage to trust in Your ability to carry our pain and comfort us in our darkest most painful places, the places we'd rather ignore. Heal us to the uttermost the way only you can do: one-on-one, face-to-face, and heart-to-heart. Amen.

Picture This - What are the masks you wear? Do you remember when you put it on for the first time, what did it feel like?

Ask This - What do you think would happen if you chose to take off your mask; what would you lose- what might you gain?

Pray This - Pray the following scriptures aloud to remind you of Your true identity in Christ:

Genesis 1:27

Jeremiah 1:5

Ephesians 1:5

John 1:12

Colossians 2:10

1 Corinthians 6:17

Galatians 3:27

Words of **Comfort** for Denial:

*"What screws us up most in life is the picture
in our head of how it is 'supposed to' be."*

The Truth Is Always Your Friend

⇒ Kimberly Joy Krueger

> *"The heart is deceitful above all things and it is extremely sick; Who can understand it fully and know its secret motives?"*
>
> *~Jeremiah 17:9 AMP*

Denial is just a fairy tale we tell ourselves to avoid the truth. I should know; I have mastered this "skill" since I was a young girl. By the time I was married with kids and experiencing loss after loss in a marriage to someone who struggled with chemical addiction, it sounded like this: *'He loves us. He really does. If his life wasn't so hard and he wasn't under so much stress, he would be there for us more often.'*

See what I did there? Or better said, see what denial did there?

'No, no, Kim, the reason you're raising your large family mostly alone isn't because he is stressed, and his life is hard. His life is hard, and he is stressed because he's using drugs and alcohol to numb his pain and he isn't doing a thing to change it.'

Jeremiah nailed it when he said the human heart is deceitful above all things. We lie to ourselves simply to avoid the pain of our reality. I thought I was living in faith when I held to the belief my husband would magically wake up one day cured of his alcoholism. (*'Oh, thank You, Lord! He's cured!'*) IT was actually denial, because it was a complete disregard for reality . . . for the TRUTH. When I realized that I had mastered the art of deceiving myself, it actually scared me. This revelation was the catalyst for a decision to consciously move out of denial and toward the truth . . . no matter how painful it may be.

I had to look in the mirror and say, "He is an alcoholic. He is not choosing to face it. He will not be a part of my children's memories of these events and there is nothing that can change that. Your kids will be children of divorce. They will not have the security and stability of two loving parents who love each other." Ouch. None of that is fun – but I will move towards all of it.

"The truth is always your friend."

That is what my mentor, Sue, tells me every time life delivers another blow. Denial is not an effective weapon against those blows. It's like going to the front lines of our battles with a squirt gun! It doesn't protect us, it makes the situation worse, and makes us more vulnerable.

Make a decision to move away from denial, no matter how "comforting" it might seem, and surround yourself with friends who help you do that. Choose to embrace the truth because, you will know the truth and the truth will set you free. (John 8:32)

God, thank You that "(I) will know the truth, and the truth will set (me) free." (John 8:32) Amen.

Picture This - The term reality check simply means facing your reality, head on. Take a good look at yours. Write it down here. Take your time, but don't gloss over anything. Get real.

Ask This - What is the most frightening about your reality? Why?

Pray This - Write a prayer offering your reality to Jesus. Tell Him what your fears are and that you will release them to Him, trusting Him to take perfect care of you.

Words of **Comfort** for Denial:

"We try to hide our feelings, but
we forgot that our eyes speak."

Two Truths We Can Count On

» Traci Weldie

"I have told you these things, so that in me you may have peace. In this world, you will have trouble. But take heart! I have overcome the world."

~John 33:16 NIV

I read the paperwork repeatedly: "George is such a smart, sweet boy. He really wants to be adopted and have a family."

Proudly I thought, *'It's just like God to bless us with a smart boy!'*

I immediately began dreaming of watching our son graduate from high school, or better yet, getting a college degree and hearing him say, *'Thanks, Mom and Dad, for saving me!'*

However, that is not what God gave us in George. The day we picked him up from the sweltering hot orphanage in Ethiopia, we knew something was not quite right with this six-year-old boy. George did not seem sweet at all and he surely did not want to be adopted later that week, as he screamed, kicked and spit on us on the airplane ride home. All my dreams, all my expectations of what adoption looked like, were suddenly shattered. My hopes for George's future came crashing down a few years later when we received the news that he is significantly intellectually disabled and has several mental health disorders. What? Are you joking, God? You clearly called us to adoption and you decide to give us a child with such severe disabilities that he will be with us, like an eight-year-old, for the rest of our lives? No way. This cannot be true.

Jesus has a wonderful discourse with his disciples in the book of John where he teaches that as a follower of Him, trouble is inevitable. The Message translation says, "In this godless world you will continue to experience difficulties." Growing up, this was the kind of verse I easily memorized to earn a gold star in Sunday school class. Nevertheless, the reality of living this out is something entirely different. Jesus clearly draws a distinction between two truths we can count on; in this world there will be painful messes and in Christ there is peace. We can all too easily focus solely on the "peace" part forgetting the assurance that we will face trouble. Even when coming face to face with calamity, Jesus calls us to look up because he has conquered sin, death and so much more…even intellectual disabilities and mental illness. His work on the cross crushed all tribulations; even my complete denial of what I was truly called to as an adoptive mother; to embrace my new normal.

Lord, You told us that we will face troubles. But You also gave us the victory over all our heartaches in this world. Help me to lean into Jesus who promises an unshakeable peace. Amen.

Picture This - How does it feel to know Jesus told us to expect trouble in this world?

Ask This - Describe how peace can come by trusting that Jesus has overcome the world in his death and resurrection.

Pray This - God, teach me what it means to "take heart" and allow me to do so in You.

Words of **Comfort** for Denial:
"Three things cannot be long hidden;
he sun, the moon, and the truth."
~Buddha

Grace And More Grace

→ Victoria Dreckman

"My grace is always more than enough for you, and my power finds its full expression through your weakness. So I will celebrate my weaknesses, for when I'm weak I sense more deeply the mighty power of Christ living in me."

~2 Corinthians 12:9 NIV

Have you ever been in denial? The kind that says, "No way is this happening!" You watch as a bizarre situation unfolds before your eyes. Your heart sinks into your stomach, the lump in your throat grows larger, and the tears fall freely.

My daughter, six months pregnant with her first child was in labor and rushed to the ER. We found our way to the birthing floor where a nurse came to speak with us. "Your daughter came into the ER dilated at 10 cm and the baby is breach. They are prepping her for a C-Section. I will come back as soon as I have more information for you."

All the color drained from my face. I had no strength. I couldn't speak as tears streamed down my cheeks. I could feel the empathetic stares of the other grandparents in the waiting room.

My heart cried out to the Lord, *'Is this really happening?'*

It was through my heart's cry that He reminded me, *'My grace is always more than enough for you, and my power finds its full expression through your weakness. So I will celebrate my weaknesses, for when I'm weak I sense more deeply the mighty power of Christ living in me.'*

My grandson quietly passed from the arms of his mamma into the arms of Jesus. In times of grief, we want to deny what is happening. However, we need to stop, pray, and listen…with our spiritual ears. In our inability to grasp or understand what is happening, God pours His love and strength into us. He says, My grace is more than enough, rest into Me and sense My power within you.

We must open our hearts, minds, and hands to Jesus and say to Him, "I am weak, cover me with your love and strength".

God, You are the God of all comfort and we ask You to overwhelm us with Your strength, compassion ,and grace as we walk through the steps of our grief. For, in the midst of our weakness, we sense Your mighty power. Be with us and give us Your peace in our life. Amen.

Picture This - What words come to your mind when you read 'my power finds its full expression through your weakness?'

Ask This - In what ways can you turn your denial into trust?

Pray This - Turn your 'ways to trust' answer into your request to the Lord. Write that request into a prayer, here.

Words of **Comfort** for Denial:

"Denial helps us to pace our feelings of grief. There is a grace in denial. It is nature's way of letting in only as much as we can handle."
~Elizabeth Kubler-Ross

Be A Companion

⩗

Instead of,
*"I know how much
you're hurting,"*
Try,
*"This must be very sad/
scary/difficult/painful."*

⩘

With Words Of Comfort

You may not understand their pain.
But you can love them through it.

The Second Stage

P A I N *(noun) – according to your companions*
[pān]

1. The cry of the heart in both physical and emotional areas In which words are not able to express
2. The Lord's tool of refinement
3. The aftermath reality of a very adverse and horrible event

*What does "**pain**" mean to you:*

Purpose For The Pain

» Amy Sikkema

"But I am afraid that just as Eve was deceived by the serpent's cunning, your minds may somehow be led astray from your sincere and pure devotion to Christ."

~2 Corinthians 11:3

Purpose for the pain: it seems unnecessary and ill thinking. Why do we suffer illness? Why do we have to struggle through infertility? Through death? Divorce? Through this broken world? For many, it may feel that these questions will never be answered on this side of heaven. I believe if we let Him, God will reveal things about Himself through the pain; immeasurable, and invaluable parts of who He is that can only be discovered through pain.

The day I followed my husband's casket down the aisle with our baby girl in my arms and our two boys at my side, was one of the most (if not the most) painful moments of my life. A breeze hit me as we opened the doors to make our way toward the flowers that would be with him at the front of the church. *"I Will Rise"* was playing overhead, but not loud enough to drown out the crying of the people around me. From sniffles, to wails and moans, the only sound was sadness. My whole body felt heavy and my throat was closed with a lump that throbbed with my racing heart. My sons were beside me and I carried my daughter tight against me, feeling the contrasting softness of her silk dress against me in this dark moment. Knowing that this would be the only aisle our daughter would walk down with her dad; the pain literally numbed all my senses. Complete disbelief had taken over. With both of the boys looking to me for comfort, I winked, and mouthed, *"I love you."* It was all I could do in that moment. The storm that was raging in me suddenly grew quiet. I had no other option but to be still and assure them that I loved them. As a mother caring for her young children, I wanted nothing more than to hold them and take the pain away; I imagine God feels the same for us.

In those moments, He is holding us and saying *'I love you, I know this hurts. I hung on that cross and know pain.'* I also imagine him saying *'It's not finished, my child. Let me comfort you. Let me reveal to you the purpose for this pain.'*

Since my husband's death, I have been able to walk alongside many widows in this pain. Sometimes, it's pain that brings people together. To be able to say, *'I get it,'* or *'I've been there,'* are sometimes enough comfort for the pain.

I pray that the pain that you may be experiencing today will not compare to the joy that will be felt tomorrow. Amen.

Picture This - In what way might God be using your pain to further His Kingdom?

Ask This - Do you have a friend or family member experiencing pain? If so, how can you walk with or reach out to them (sometimes the deepest healing comes in helping others)?

Pray This - Dear Lord, thank You for being a God who heals and restores. Thank You for being my helper through this pain. Help me to know that there is purpose for my pain. Show me how to use this to further Your Kingdom. Help me to lay down my own desires for Your will in my life. May Your goodness and light shine as a bright beacon through this season. Calm this painful storm so that Your light will shine brightly through me. Amen.

Words of **Comfort** for Pain:
"The darker the night, the brighter the stars,
The deeper the grief, the closer is God!"
~Fyodor Dostoyevsky

Poured Out

⇀ Annabelle Ahlers

"Trust in him at all times, you people; pour out your hearts to him, for God is our refuge"

~Psalm 62:8 NIV

I wish I'd received sharing in the comfort of the Holy Spirit a while ago, yet I did not. Instead of pouring my heart out, as the psalmist directs, I did the very opposite. I stuffed it all down. Used by many other humans to avoid pain, the effects of this strategy are the same: not good.

As I decided not to connect with the pain of childhood traumas that I had gone through, it became hard to emotionally connect with anything; I felt numb. Yet, I continued on living in deep fear of pain. This led to the explosion. For me, it was not a single event that let it all out. It was multiple events. Starting with small irritations, that led to me having a complete meltdown. I would yell, cry, and emotionally attack people I loved.

I would become so upset with myself afterwards and cry out to God, "Why am I doing this?"

I felt completely on my own and hopeless, until—one day—I was reading the Bible and I saw this: "Pour your hearts out to him, for God is our refuge".

The truth of The Word set me free. I began to weep and realize that I did not have to sort through these emotions by myself. No. I had a God that cared about what I was feeling. And so it began. I poured myself out to God. I did not just give a summary of the hurt, I delved into the memory of the pain with him. It was the first time in my life that I was authentic about my pain, because I knew someone cared. By the end, I felt like a deflated balloon as I released years of emotional pain.

The Lord is asking you to be poured out to receive the healing he has for you. By pouring out your heart to God and inviting him into your pain, you allow Holy Spirit to come and do the healing only He can do. Jesus died on the cross, so His spirit would dwell within you. He wants to come into all the places of pain, so He can begin to heal. Yet, the healing starts when you invite him into your pain, past and present.

I pray that the Lord of all comfort would come into your pain and begin to heal you – completely. Amen.

Picture This - What areas of your life do you keep separate from the Lord?

Ask This - Do you believe that the Lord cares about your hurt? In what way do you see God expressing His care for you?

Pray This - Holy Spirit, I trust You and invite You into my pain with me. Heal me and restore me fully. Bring to mind the places I am shutting You out of because of the pain. Give me the strength to open up old wounds and to touch the ones that are still fresh. Amen.

Words of **Comfort** for Pain:
"Sometimes, the people around you won't understand your journey. They don't need to, it's not for them."

Unless God

Karen Bruno

"He heals the broken hearted and binds up their wounds"
~Psalm 147:3 NASB

Pillows replaced my make-up and decided my hairstyle; blankets replaced my clothes; my leg hair was comparable to my sons. The only reason I could muster the energy to leave my bed was when my bladder refused to comply with my need to lay in bed all day. My heartache was so severe that I wasn't sure I had the energy to stand. I was consumed with pain and my grey-striped comforter was my daily comfort.

In my state of grief, I recalled counseling a young woman about her broken heart and wounded life. I asked her to picture a thin glass vase dropping onto a hard marble floor and shattering into a million pieces. She was so broken it wasn't hard for her to envision. The analogy went on as I described the process she would need to take to painstakingly glue these pieces back together and how the repaired vase would finally appear, but it would never truly look the same again.

UNLESS!

With God there is always "unless."

Unless you give your broken heart to Him. Unless you give your wounded places to Him. Then He can bind up your heart and heal your wounds. Then you will be truly whole again. Day after painful day I began to choose the unless and pulled off my grey-striped comforter and found true comfort in the One who would heal and bind me.

Lord, it is only with You that I will find true healing of my broken heart. Amen.

Picture This - What places in your life seem shattered?

Ask This - Can you pull off your false comforter and allow Him, The Comforter, to bind and heal you?

Pray This - Lord, You are my true Comforter. I put my broken pieces into Your hands, knowing you will bind them up and heal me. Amen.

Words of **Comfort** for Pain:
"Those scars you have accumulated are the markings of a warrior."

God Is Near

» Linét Lewerenz

"Why, Lord, do you stand far off?
Why do you hide yourself in times of trouble?
In his arrogance the wicked man hunts down the weak,
who are caught in the schemes he devises.
He boasts about the cravings of his heart;
he blesses the greedy and reviles the Lord.
In his pride the wicked man does not seek him;
in all his thoughts there is no room for God."

~Psalm 10:1-4 NIV

I think to myself, '*How can my story be part of a book on devotions about grief? Surely my story does not belong here. I am blessed with loving children and grandchildren. My husband has been with me over forty years. We love one another, we love our family, we are secure in the knowledge they love us.'* Then, I think again. '*What else would you call what is inside me, has always been a part of me, and has influenced my entire life . . . but grief?'*

It's a grief brought on by loss . . . a loss of my childhood.

God was included in my upbringing, but he never intervened to stop my abusive father. He, in fact, had years to do so. This gave rise to the thought, the idea, the almost certainty . . . that God had abandoned me. I would not raise my children with God's influence only to have that faith shattered. This is a hard story to tell.

Child abuse is the devil's perfect playground. He relishes it, takes away our love of self, and creates within us a hole that he fills with anger, sadness, and depression. Some of us grow up to abuse, others continue as victims of abuse, and then others, like myself, fake ordinary lives, but that hole filled with anger, sadness, and depression still lies within.

All these years, I've blamed God for the devil's designs. The struggle of good (God) versus evil (the devil) does not mean God has given up and abandoned me. The offer was there; he was never hidden from me. I was not ready to accept Him.

God has waited patiently for me while the devil, always impatient, always greedy, used me and robbed me of my self-worth. I was blind and could not see the devil's puppet strings. His work with me is done. I will look to God, for He is near me. I can choose for the hole inside me to be filled with peace, happiness, and abundance. I am worthy in God's eyes.

Today I pray – may all children of abuse find God's love and know they are worthy and He never abandons them. God is near! Amen.

Picture This - Imagine life with trust in God, a life where your heart is not shattered, but instead is filled with peace, happiness, and abundance. What do these traits look like to you?

Ask This - Find a Bible verse revealing trust in a God who never abandons us.

Pray This - Lord, help me to trust and know You are present in my life and always have been; you have never abandoned me. Amen.

Words of **Comfort** for Pain:

"When you can't look on the bright side,
find someone who will sit with you in the dark."

New Beginnings

→ Lisa Danegelis

"In the shadow of His hand He has hidden me, and made me a polished shaft."

~Isaiah 49:2 NKJV

Heart surgery? OUCH! Did God really just say He was doing heart surgery on me? His voice was clear; His intentions? Not as much. I was scared.

I had given Him all of me (or so I thought) years before as a young believer. In His perfect wisdom, He waited well over a decade to fully embrace that sacrificial prayer of surrender. He knew I needed time to dance with Him on mountaintops before descending into the valley of suffering. Life had taken unexpected sharp turns and I saw no end to the looming hill in front of me. Depression and anxiety were consuming that hot summer afternoon as I sobbed, pouring my heart out to God. I surrendered everything . . . again, wondering where my life's "dance partner" had gone. He seemed elusive, even indifferent.

I reminded Him of all "our" dreams for my future in continued sobs; dreams I was sure were His heart for me too. In a life changing instant, I became keenly aware that these dreams in themselves had become an idol. It shook me to the core. In the next breath, I surrendered them, as well. My heart felt shredded. As the tears continued to flow, I had a vision that God told me to record, because it was the "beginning of my new life." It was the solid rock bottom God is still using to rebuild my life. In the vision, I laid down the broken pieces of a mosaic platter. Jesus came, picked them up, smiled at me, and walked away. I was emptied of myself that day.

I later had a vision of my heart tearing, expanding, then healing. Surgery was underway; the new heart was now being prepared to more fully embrace others and bring healing from my own pain.

The polished shaft referred to in Isaiah 49, is the Israelites. God is referencing their return from exile; a whole new beginning. The pain of melting, shaping and polishing that silver shaft speaks of vibrant life; a new beginning. Pain is a catalyst for growth, and our Surgeon's steady hand of love will never fail us.

Hold me tightly in Your hand Father, as You mold and shape me. I know You will perfect all that concerns me as I surrender to Your plans for my life. Amen.

Picture This - Imagine the things in your life that you have not yet surrendered to God. How does it feel when you hand those things to Jesus?

Ask This - What holds you back from surrendering everything to God?

Pray This - God, thank You for polishing the broken pieces I bring to You and making me into something new. Please help me to bring every piece of me to You. Amen.

Words of Comfort for Pain:

"Grief is not weak. Or weird. Grief is not shameful. Or embarrassing. Grief is real. And raw. Grief is necessary. And unstoppable. Grief is, love."

~Better not Bitter Widower

"It's Alright. Cry."

→ Luanne Nelson

"Jesus Wept"

~John 11:35 NIV

Jesus wept with compassion seeing Mary and Martha grieving the loss of their beloved Lazarus. Jesus was aware of the predicament we were all in with death. He wept with his friends in their misery (Romans 12:15); he wept because of our mortality in death brought on by human defiance in the Garden of Eden (Genesis 2:16-17).

In His humanity, Jesus wept for Lazarus. In His Divinity, He raised Lazarus from the dead.

I was a crying mess. I had lost three of the most important people in my life. My Dad, my dear Nana, and my former husband all died within a few short years of each other. Toss in a stint in a local women's shelter after being battered and you get enough of the picture to know I was weeping often and much. I felt defeated and alone.

We can cry. We can weep. There IS life afterward and God will tell you. For me, he sent Maryanne to remind me that all was well. *'I brought Lazarus back. Here's Nana. Cry. It's okay. You need to cry in the end, but there is joy after this.'*

God saw fit, though, in His infinite love and mercy, to send an angel. (Hebrews 13:12). Maryanne led my children and me to safety away from the hands of a very abusive man in the midst of all of this sadness. My children and I spent a few weeks at a women's shelter.

One evening, a few months after moving out of the shelter and into a cute little rental house, Maryanne called me. Maryanne calmly told me my beloved Nana, who had died a few years earlier, had just appeared to her with a message for me. The message was a very personal one. Maryanne would not have guessed this information in a million years on her own. I was stunned. Nana's message to Maryanne for me gave me the strength I needed to get through some serious immediate pain and a tragedy that had yet to unfold.

Maryanne went to her rabbi to discuss what had happened. Her rabbi reassured her, "Yes, this has been known to happen to people who have a deep bond of love between them in extreme times of need. It's mentioned in many old Jewish writings." I visited my clergyman and told him what had happened. He repeated almost verbatim what the rabbi told Maryanne.

Maryanne never knew Nana. They lived over six hundred miles from each other and had no occasion to ever meet each other. I brought my wedding album over to Maryanne's house, she immediately recognized Nana in a group of elderly women.

Maryanne died a few years later. I'm certain she and Nana are both in heaven kibitzing over coffee. I am looking forward to seeing them both again someday.

Dear Lord Jesus, thank You for allowing me share this lovely story so others know – yes – there is life after this just like You promised us. We will see our loved ones again because of You. Amen.

Picture This - Imagine feeling completely safe and secure in the eternal forever life we are promised through Jesus' Resurrection!

Ask This - Have you experienced a strong, almost palatable remembrance of a loved one who has died? Have you considered journaling about it as a way to keep the memory alive?

Pray This - Dear Jesus, Lord God Almighty, forever change my heart from being a doubting Thomas to a true believer in Your Promise of eternal life! Amen.

Words of Comfort for Pain:

"Learning how to keep going, when there is no light at the end of the tunnel, is going to be the best skill you ever had."
~Derek Halpern

My Heart Physically Hurts

Maria Notch

"My God! My God! Why have you abandoned me?"

~Psalm 22:1a NLT

Scientific studies show that when a woman is pregnant, maternal cells cross over to the baby and fetal cells cross through to the mother. So when a mother who has lost a child says, "it feels like a part of me has died," there is physical reality to what she is experiencing! The excruciating emotional pain that a mother feels when she has lost a child truly exhibits itself physically in her being.

I remember my arms literally aching for months-on-end after carrying a child in my womb that I would never carry in my arms. There were days when the pain was so intense, I could hardly breathe. Sometimes the pain was triggered when hearing a friend was expecting or seeing a mother with her new baby who was born around the same time as our child was due. Baby showers, gender reveals, and birth announcements constantly plagued my surroundings on social media and in social circles, simply because we were in that season of life. Other times, the trigger disguised itself and caught me off guard, like being at a shopping store and seeing the baby aisle, or going to hear a speaker . . . who just happened to be pregnant. The constant reminders of our losses pierced my heart daily.

I've been through the process of miscarriage four times. Yes – four times. The best way I can describe it is it that grief comes like labor pains. Don't think I don't recognize the irony of the metaphor, but the pain comes in waves and you have to breathe deep, let the pain wash over you, and trust it will wane. It's the exact same process physically as it is emotionally. The trouble with grief is that it hits at unexpected times without warning. This is again where the patience comes in; I've found that I need to be patient with myself and allow myself the space and time to grieve when the waves come.

I am reminded of our Lord, Jesus Christ, on the cross. He suffered despite obeying the Father's commands and following His law. I felt I had been obedient, but I was left sobbing, crying out to God, "have you forgotten about us? Have you overlooked our faithfulness? How can you bless others while forsaking your faithful servants?"

What I realized amidst my pain, is that the Lord wasn't inflicting it. He was weeping alongside of me. We live in a fallen world with broken bodies, and sometimes awful things like miscarriages just happen.

God doesn't will His people to suffer, just like He didn't want His Son to suffer on the cross. But God, in His infinite wisdom, can bring goodness in and through our suffering.

Heavenly Father, please hold us close and help us as we suffer through this time together. Remind us that You are weeping with us and not the one hurting us. Give us Your peace and help us trust that You can work good through each and every situation. Be our Healer here and now and bring us to joy and new life just as You raised Your Son from the dead. Amen.

Picture This - What emotional things in your life have had a physical manifestation? Put your hand on your heart while praying. Put your hand on your head while praying. Put your hands out in front of you, opened and facing upward. In each situation, focus on what you physically feel while praying and try to carry that physical manifestation of your faith into and through your journey of grief.

Ask This - How do you believe God shares in your suffering?

Pray This - Read Job 6:10 and write a prayer that comes to mind as you reflect on a pain in your life.

Words of Comfort for Pain:
"When it was dark, you always carried
the sun in your hand for me."
~Seán O'Casey

No Pain Wasted

→ Neesie Cieslak

"Thou tellest my wanderings: put thou my tears into thy bottle: are they not in thy book?"

~Psalm 56:8 NKJV

Pain is real. Jesus knows the reality of our pain like no ever can or will. I'm prone to avoid pain at any cost. I don't like pain; physical, mental, spiritual, or emotional – I would rather do without it. Our reality is that pain has a vital role in every human being's life. It simply cannot be avoided.

For years I acted like nothing could touch me. Nothing could really "hurt" me and no one was going to see me cry; I'm a strong woman, I'm tough. That didn't work very well for long. I came to a place where the Lord showed me that I must get intimate with my pain, like Jesus did, and feel it.

Growing up I heard words such as; *"You better stop that crying or I'll give you something to cry about,"* or, *"What do you mean your back hurts, you're too young to even have a back!"*

When I was nine years old, I was pushed on the ice, which busted open my right eyebrow. I was at school. They called my grandparents to let them know of the situation, then rushed me to the hospital. At the hospital I had to be stitched up. My grandparents never came. I was taken back to school to complete the school day.

When I returned home that afternoon, I was greeted with, "So I heard you busted your head." That was all. Thus, I learned to stuff all of my pain.

Pain and the tears that so often come with it are never wasted. God knows the pain. He knows why the tears flow. Science has proven that the tears we cry are structurally different under the microscope depending on the reason those tears were shed. He knows why they flow and even keeps account of them. He preserves them in His bottle and writes each down in His book!

The pain of loss sometimes feels like wasted time or no one sees nor cares. Sometimes we may even feel foolish for our weepiness. That's okay. We need not fear this, because the Lord tells us that each tear that falls from our eyes because of our pain is of great value to Him. He will not let them fall without his remembrance. That is a promise that comes with remarkable comfort.

Let your tears flow. let your pain be felt deep in your soul as you lean on the arms of Father, God. He's catching you and your tears.

Father God, thank You that You catch my tears of pain. Help me to remember Your promises contained in this scripture. My tears are never wasted. You keep them for Your good purposes. Help me to let them flow and trust You in my healing. Amen.

Picture This - Do you have a pain that you know have not looked in the face? Write it here to recognize it in your life.

Ask This - Ask yourself if you've gotten intimate with each of these painful places.

Pray This - Father, I need You to help me in my pain. Help me to face it, get intimate with it, and heal. Amen.

Words of Comfort for Pain:

"Take chances, make mistakes. That's how you grow.
Pain nourishes your courage. You have to
fail in order to practice being brave."
~Mary Tyler Moore

Nothing Of Value Can Be Removed

→ Rebecca Faye Grambort

"Therefore, we do not lose heart. Even though our outward man is perishing, yet the inward man is being renewed day by day. For our light affliction, which is but for a moment, is working for us a far more exceeding and eternal weight of glory, while we do not look at the things which are seen, but at the things which are not seen. For the things which are seen are temporary, but the things which are not seen are eternal."

~1 Corinthians 4:16-18 NKJV

When my husband was gravely ill in the hospital, I witnessed him quickly perishing in body and in mind. Although my flesh shook, my spirit remained steadfast, knowing that—although my husband's outward man suffered—his unseen inward man was being renewed.

I remember a time when he would gaze longingly at his wedding band that was pinned to the bulletin board in his hospital room. He silently motioned me to put it back on his hand where he so faithfully wore it for ten years. My heart broke for him as reality became crystal clear.

'You can't take anything with you' and *'Naked you come – naked you leave'* rung loud and clear inside of my head.

Yet, inside my spirit – a deep well of faith reminded me that Jesus was with him shepherding him in his valley and, because of this, I refused to lose heart. I knew there were things that were happening that were completely unseen to the naked eye. God's Word says that the goal of our faith is the salvation of our souls. (1 Peter 1:9)

I had to keep my thoughts fixed on this truth, believing my husband was taken on an intimate journey within. This life is temporary and Jesus has prepared a place for us that will be our eternal home one day – a place with no more tears or pain (Revelation 21:4). Jesus is also The Shepherd in our own valleys. Nothing of value can be permanently removed. Our loved ones' journeys home are momentary afflictions that achieve for them eternal glory. The pain left behind for us from those journeys are also temporary afflictions. They will also achieve eternal glory for us in God's appointed time.

Jesus, walk beside me, before me, and behind me. Hedge me in and Shepherd me as I walk through this valley. Amen.

Picture This - Envision in heaven everything of value entirely intact – safe in our eternal home in the presence and safety of Jesus. How can this help comfort you while you are grieving being temporarily removed from what you love?

Ask This - Close your eyes and quiet your spirit. Focus your heart and mind on the unseen; what treasures do you feel dropped into the possession of your eternal spirit? Write out your treasures here.

Pray This - Jesus, help me to keep my eyes fixed on You, knowing that nothing of value can be permanently removed! Amen.

Words of Comfort for Pain:
*"Your pain is the breaking of the shell
that encloses your understanding."*
~Khalil Gibran

Grief Is Just Love With Nowhere To Go

≫ Susan Brozek

"My tears have been my food day and night, while people say to me all day long, 'Where is your God?'"

~Psalm 42:3a NIV

"Grief is just love with nowhere to go." When I first heard this characterization of grief, it struck me profoundly. Especially as it pertains to missing a loved one who is no longer part of our lives, it expresses clearly the sentiment that all the love we have for that person is still within us, but now lacks an outlet. A void has been left that cannot be filled by anyone or anything else. It is a uniquely-shaped emptiness, customized for the person who has left us…whether through death, the end of a relationship, a geographical separation, or any number of other scenarios through which we can suffer the loss of a loved one.

This void left by grief begs the question: *'What do we now do with this love that, in essence, has nowhere to go?'*

I lost both of the key father figures in my life – my Dad and my Grandpa – within about two years' time. Both of their deaths were devastating to me. At the times of their passings, I had just begun my career as a Christian Psychotherapist and, therefore, many people close to me assumed that since I was a therapist, I should automatically know how to process through this level of pain and loss. Such was not the case! There is no "manual" for how to grieve. Yes, there are books about grief (you're holding one in your hands right now!), grief support groups, etc. There are even the commonly known "5 Stages of Grief" that have been endorsed by many clinicians in my field, identified by Dr. Elisabeth Kübler-Ross' Model: Shock/Denial, Anger, Bargaining, Depression, and Acceptance. (As you see through this book, there are additional sub-stages we're recognizing when you experience grief alongside God.) None of this seemed important to my broken heart. All I knew was that I had lost my Grandpa and my Dad, both of whom I deeply loved. During that season, my tears truly did become my food, as the Psalmist expresses.

When grief hits, let yourself feel your feelings; as much as they hurt, try to avoid stuffing them or distracting yourself from the pain. It will only come back up later if you do. Above all, let God's arms of comfort surround you and uphold you. Although I lost my two earthly father figures, I still knew that I had a Heavenly Father who would carry me through my season of mourning and great loss.

Today I pray – May those that need to feel God's arms of comfort wrapped around them be able to sense Your loving and secure grasp, Father God. Be the healing balm to their pain. Amen.

Picture This - Identify a season in your life when you could sense God's arms of comfort holding you and His loving presence healing your pain.

Ask This - Seek God on whether you have truly allowed yourself to feel your feelings, or if you chose to stuff some of them out of fear that the pain would overwhelm you.

Pray This - God, please help me to know that You care so deeply about our emotional pain; in fact, Your Word says that You personally comfort those who mourn. Help me to receive this in my heart and spirit. Amen.

Words of **Comfort** for Pain:

"Some days are just bad days, that's all. You have to experience sadness to know happiness, and I remind myself that not every day is going to be a good day, that's just the way it is!"
~Dita Von Teese

Mourning Into Joy

→ Traci Weldie

"Then maidens will dance and be glad, young men and old as well. I will turn their mourning into gladness; I will give them comfort and joy instead of sorrow."

~Jeremiah 31:13 NIV

Anna is grieving. And my heart breaks every time Anna falls into gut-wrenching sobs. The tears flow down her cheeks leaving salty white tracks on her dark brown skin and there is very little I can do to ease her pain. The grieving process is good and normal but Anna feels the pain so deeply, so badly, she simply cannot keep it in anymore. As I was braiding Anna's hair, watching cartoons and laughing, Anna's giggles suddenly stopped and the all-too familiar tears starting flowing once again.

"I miss my Ghana mommy so much it hurts," she sobbed, gasping for air in between her words of anguish.

There was nothing I could say, so I did all I could think of, I pulled Anna onto my lap and held her letting my tears mingle with hers over the great sorrow she was feeling. This pain of loss accompanied Anna when she stepped into our home as a new daughter and sister and this heartache often rendered Anna immobile. Even when her brothers and sisters were flitting away dancing to music on any given afternoon, Anna would sit and stare, unable to dance because the grief was suffocating her.

What an encouraging word God gave to Jeremiah to share with a people who were suffering. God allowed the Israelites to go through a process of exile, pain and anguish, not forsaken or alone, but with a promise that He will restore. Similarly, God allows us to walk on that dark road of pain for a while. On that road, though, God promises, "he will." When God says, "I will", it is definite, a promise you can count on, and in this verse, God says, "I will" more than once. God resolves to change the direction of our grieving. God gives us an about-face to turn our aching hearts into hearts filled with felicity and laughter, as we no longer have to stay on that road toward pain. God promises to grant us His unique, spirit-filled comfort. He alone provides the new direction, a detour that leads to peace when the grief wants to overtake us. With God, our sorrow turns to bliss; our aches turn into wonder.

As we grieve, the pain of loss is real and undeniable. But God leads us into a change of direction, putting us on a new road filled with comfort, joy…and even dancing.

It took a few years, but you should see Anna dance now!

Lord, thank You for being a God who says, "I will." Thank You for promising to turn our sorrow into joy and our mourning into gladness. Help me trust in Your word and embrace the path You have laid out for me as I walk through this grief. Amen.

Picture This - Identify a time when you felt God turning your mourning into gladness. Or imagine (write about) what your life will look like when God turns your mourning into gladness.

Ask This - What does knowing that God does the work of restoring your joy mean to you?

Pray This - Write a prayer to God thanking him for what He has done and what He will do.

Words of **Comfort** for Pain:

If no pain, then no love. If no darkness, no light.
If no risk, then no reward. It's all or nothing.
In this damn world, it's all or nothing."
~Glennon Doyle Melton

Be A Companion

Instead of,
"It's not your fault,"
Try,
"Tell me about it."

With Words Of Comfort

You may not understand their guilt.
But you can love them through it.

The Third Stage

GUILT *(noun) – according to your companions*
[gilt]

1. The gnawing, deep down inside your gut, that you could have done more to prevent something bad.
2. Slow death by suffocation; chokes the worth, life, and hope out of the living
3. Slavery to self-condemnation

*What does "**guilt**" mean to you:*

Love Is War

⇾ Ava Olivia Willett

"For our struggle is not against flesh and blood, but against the rulers, against the powers of this dark world, and against the spiritual forces of evil in the heavenly realms."

~Ephesians 6:12 NIV

Out of all of the family games we could have chosen, my newly blended family chose fighting. Whether it was my step sister starting a fight just to draw some attention out of my parents or my mum insisting my step-dad didn't understand her grief, there was always something to scream about. Day-after-day, this would go on. Fighting became pretty normal. I began to love working and being out of the house. I knew fighting wasn't the way a family should be, but I felt helpless, as if nothing I would do would change a thing.

I would try to interfere and tell them I didn't like the fighting – I was refereeing.

I would try to not come home to avoid them and the situation.

I would tell them I wanted to move to my old hometown.

Nothing worked.

I watched my mum wrestle with guilt. She cried and apologized every day. I never saw her happy. She didn't want to go out . . . or have others over. She isolated herself.

Finally, God said, 'Enough.'

Mum and my step-dad tried going to counseling and they stopped fighting for a while. Although both my mum and step-dad lost their previous marriages to the death of a spouse, they did not understand each other. They were both riddled with guilt at the failed attempt of putting the two families together. In return, the guilt ate them alive and aided them to the early signs of destruction to their new family. The enemy wanted so badly to tear the family apart. BUT GOD reminds us that the struggle is not against flesh and blood. The enemy loves broken families. Broken lives.

BUT GOD put on my mum's heart that we could communicate assertively, without yelling. Everyone's feelings matter. As a family, and with God, we learned to move past guilt and into real relationship with one another and with God.

Take a look at your situation. Choose to fight the good fight of faith in order to learn to love like Jesus.

Jesus, command Your angels to flock around me and protect me from the hand of the enemy. Help me to practice self-care and self-forgiveness in times of grief. Free me from the thoughts that hold me captive from living out my life for Your Glory. Amen.

Picture This - What do you hold in your hands that you need to place before the feet of Jesus? Self-loathing? Repressed anger? Guilt? What would your life look like without those things?

Ask This - What are some things you need to forgive yourself for in order to move on from your guilt?

Pray This - Lord, reveal what the enemy has been trying to destroy in my life and help me to choose my battles wisely for Your Glory only. Amen.

Words of Comfort for Guilt:
"We are all the pieces of what we remember.
We hold in ourselves the hopes and fears of those who love us.
As long as there is love and memory, there is no true loss."
~Cassandra Clare

Not My Guilt To Bear

> ⇒ Heather Taylor

"But I tell you, love your enemies and pray for those who persecuted you, that you may be of your Father in heaven. He causes his sun to rise on the evil and the good, and sends rain on the righteous and the unrighteous."

~*Matthew 5:44-45 NIV*

"Why? Why does she get to die and I am here left to suffer her sins?" These words came out of my mouth when I found out that a woman who I thought was my best friend for twenty years had died. Not the reaction you would expect, or even want to claim, but it was mine.

I was furious. I was downright "fit to be tied," as my Mother would say.

We hadn't talked in over a year. I had removed her from my life after many, many painful betrayals and I truly thought I was over it. I had forgiven her, but knew there wasn't a safe place in my life for her to be a part of. I was healing and rebuilding what she tried her best to destroy.

I was the bigger person.

I was moving on.

Turns out that wasn't exactly true. Her death didn't come as a shock; I knew she was dying. She had a long battle with breast cancer and, in the end, she lost. When the news came that she had passed away the only shock was how angry I was. I went through every emotion there was to go through, but anger was the one that stuck. I was mad that she died, mad that she died without me, mad that she left without trying to reach out and apologize to me, mad that she didn't have to suffer any longer . . . but I still did.

You see, in my mind, I had convinced myself that death was the ultimate punishment. It was easy to make myself believe that I had forgiven her, because she was dying. Once she actually died, I was faced with the fact that I hadn't dealt with any of my emotions.

I hadn't forgiven her; I just tried to forget her.

I still had the same pain that I had while she was alive – the same memories, the same betrayal. The only difference now was that I also had guilt on top of all that. Guilt was not something I wanted to deal with. She needed to feel guilty, not me. I was the victim. From the moment she betrayed me, all I ever wanted her to feel was guilt and here I was feeling just what I wanted her to feel.

This guilt was unwelcomed in my life but also a huge eye opener. I found myself running to God because I had nowhere else to go! She was dead, so I couldn't yell at her. So I ran to God and yelled at him! I cried, I begged, I listened and then I read Matthew 5:44-45.

I had to forgive her because he forgave her. I had to forgive her because he forgave me. I found myself praying for her and forgiving her and finally grieving her loss not her betrayal!

Jesus, help me to forgive myself and others, regardless of the circumstances of the need. In the end, You have forgiven all, so please give me the strength to do the same for those in my life and those no longer here. Amen.

Picture This - Envision the negative emotions that you feel so deeply that they are blocking you from the true source of your pain. Identify those layers of hurt so that you know what you are bringing to God.

Ask This - Are you ready to do the work with God, taking His hand, to go through layers of pain in order to grieve the source of your hurting and anger without guilt?

Pray This - Heavenly Father, I pray that You will lead me to the true source of my grief and truly begin healing, so that I can move forward.

Words of **Comfort** for Guilt:
"To love means loving the unlovable.
To forgive means pardoning the unpardonable."
~G.K. Chesterton

Breaking Guilt's Chains

➤ Amy Sikkema

"It is for freedom that Christ has set us free. Stand firm, then, and do not let yourself be burdened again by a yoke of slavery."
~Galatians 5:1 NIV

"Mom, why didn't you save dad from dying?" The words pierced my grieving heart like a dagger. The uninvited guilt gremlin settled in without invitation. There I was, hands firmly on the wheel, the innocent eyes of my two-year-old daughter and four-year-old son staring back at me in the rearview mirror.

Tears from my soul began to flow . . . uncontrolled, uninhibited.

This same guilt gremlin had plagued me before. Shortly after my husband's death, I wept many nights in agony and apologizing silently to my babies for not saving their daddy. Guilt swept over. It whispered in my ear: *'What else could you have done? Did you do everything you could? Should you have kept the platelet infusions going – continue to pray and hope for a miracle, even though the cancer had spread to his bone marrow? Was your faith not strong enough? Was his faith not strong enough?'*

I decided in that moment that those questions are lies brought on by the chains of guilt. I chose to let God break those chains of guilt. He tells me: I could not have saved my husband. It was not my job. He already saved him and each of us, by the ultimate sacrifice of His blood shed on the cross. It was my job to love my husband, and fight with him, but ultimately, I could not save him. That is not my guilt burden to carry.

Was our faith strong enough? Yes. After he took his final breath, he heard "Well done my good and faithful servant!" That is the truest measure of faith.

"Oh, my sweet boy, Mommy, daddy and many people who loved daddy very much did everything we could to help daddy feel better again, but daddy's body was very sick from cancer. God wanted daddy to feel better, too; so when daddy died, he went to heaven and now he doesn't have cancer. AND, we get to see him again someday!"

May we know, identify, and fight guilt with the truth and strength that our Heavenly Father gives to us each and every day. Amen.

Picture This - What chains of guilt are holding you back from being set free?

Ask This - How would your outlook on this aching guilt change if you let God speak through it and break the chains?

Pray This - Dear Lord, thank You for being the loving, merciful, all-knowing God that You are. When guilt comes, remind me of who I am and who I belong to. Help me to have full faith and confidence that You are in control. Help me let go of any control that continues to have a hold of me. Set me free, Lord, from the chains of guilt. Thank You for Your redeeming love. Amen.

Words of **Comfort** for Guilt:

"Sometimes we want to be left alone.
Sometimes we want to be included.
Most of the time, we want to be included
With the option of being left alone."

Bad Bananas

Karen Bruno

"And now, dear brothers and sisters, we want you to know what will happen to believers who have died so you will not grieve like people who have no hope."

~1 Thessalonians 4:13 NLT

In 1 Thessalonians 4:13 God is intimately addressing His children, those adopted through Christ Jesus, about the painful topic of death. He encourages them with the promise when He returns with a blasting trumpet and the voice of the archangel He will raise His children from the grave. There is incredible beauty, comfort and peace in this knowledge!

After singing Amazing Grace with his immediate family around my husband's grave, I felt a ray of hope. I looked beyond his grave to his father's grave and felt the same. These men loved Jesus and He will call them from the grave. I could comfort myself with nothing less or I would have no hope. We, the children of God, have this everlasting hope to comfort us at all times. He is returning, He will gather His children to Him and we will see our loved ones again.

During an awkward exchange in the banana section of the grocery store, I first felt guilt over having hope.

A woman I hardly knew, but on my Facebook friend list, drew guilt out in me when she said, "I've been following your family on Facebook and it's almost like you're doing too well."

I stared at the bananas. What I said in return was not as polite as I had hoped.

My retort went something like, "I thought about taking a picture of myself curled up in the fetal position on my bathroom floor, but the lighting wasn't right."

She, slightly offended, and I, feeling guilty, ended the conversation.

Should we not have hope during our trials? God tells us directly that we should not grieve as the world does. Why then should we feel guilt over showing our family and friends that we, through God's promise, will be okay? It is because the guilt we experience is not from God. He has clearly instructed us not to grieve in a way that shows hopelessness. We can be incredibly sad, devasted, and grieving coupled with the hope of resurrection. Having hope in the worst of times is what demonstrates to the world where our hope comes from. Hope doesn't diminish the grief of our circumstances; however it is what pulls us through.

Free me today, Lord, of any guilt that is not from You. Let me yearn to hear Your trumpet call knowing You will restore all that is broken and lost. Amen.

Picture This - How would the world be impacted if the children of God demonstrated hope in their trials?

Ask This - Can you seek God's Truth allowing you to guiltlessly adjust your definition of grief to include hope?

Pray This - Lord, thank You for not abandoning us in our times of grief. Thank You that we might have hope in times that feel hopeless to the world.

Words of Comfort for Guilt:

*"Defending the truth is not something one does
out of a sense of duty or to allay guilt complexes,
but is a reward in itself."*
~Simone de Beauvoir

God's Healing Touch

→ Lisa Danegelis

"There is therefore now no condemnation to those who are in Christ Jesus."

~Romans 8:1 NKJV

The puzzle pieces of my broken heart were not fitting back together. This mess of emotions . . . guilt, shame, confusion, relief, disdain, and love. Could they all be pieces from the same puzzle? My head was spinning and my soul ached as we drove away from the facility for emotionally and behaviorally challenged girls, leaving my bewildered, scared fifteen-year-old adopted daughter behind.

Would they have the balm to calm her erratic moods and rebellious spirit? I sure knew I didn't! Fifteen years of prayers, love, counseling and discipline proved that. My well was empty. My love tested to the extreme. My patience and compassion gone. The relief I felt as we drove away seemed like it would be a lasting stain on my maternal heart. In addition to the guilt, the inadequacy I felt at not being enough for my daughter only deepened the despair. What on earth was God thinking when He created motherhood? It seemed the jury was out, I was condemned!

My daughter handed me a handmade purple box during a future visit. It was simple, yet had a depth of beauty that only grew as I read the note inside. It was a note of passionate love flowing from her soul, a soul that was free from unforgiveness and bitterness. My daughter had a heart that God somehow started miraculously mending in this place where I felt I had abandoned her. I sobbed.

The purple box is one of my greatest treasures and a visual reminder of the tremendous healing God brought to our relationship over the next eight years. My daughter's tender heart melted my own, wiping away the stains of condemnation that seemed to be permanent.

If my daughter could so easily forgive, how much more can our Savior! Every morning, when we open our eyes, we have a clean slate on which to continue writing the story of our lives. What a gift! Unwrap that gift, free from the burdens of yesterday as you lay it at His feet. His mercies are new every morning, great is His faithfulness!

Thank You, merciful Lord, for freeing me from the burden of condemnation. May I see a clean slate before me every morning and embrace the new day in freedom. Amen.

Picture This - Imagine a physical gift that represents God's forgiveness – a trinket, a piece of jewelry, a book, or an article of clothing – something you see every day; take a moment to reflect on God's mercies every time you see this physical item.

Ask This - What are you condemning yourself for that you think is too great to have been covered by Jesus' sacrifice?

Pray This - God, I ask You to help me to forgive myself as you have forgiven me.

Words of **Comfort** for Guilt:

"When you make a mistake and the devil comes and tells you 'You're no good,' you don't have to take on the guilt and condemnation he wants to put on you. No! You can immediately confess your mistake to God, thank Him for forgiving you and cleansing you with the blood of Jesus, and move forward in the victory of His grace and forgiveness."

~Joyce Meyer

Who's To Blame?

⇒ Maria Notch

"For I know the plans I have for you, declares the Lord. Plans to prosper you & not to harm you. Plans to give you hope and a future."
~Jeremiah 29:11 NIV

'It's my fault. I'm supposed to protect my babies and carry them to term and I can't. I lost them. I MIS-carried them. There must be something wrong with me.'

Those were all the lies Satan told me and I believed in my grief. After all, it's a woman's job to carry the pregnancy to term, right? WRONG. It's the Lord's job, to give life and to take it away.

GUILTY. That was who Satan told me I was during that time. I felt guilty because my body couldn't carry these precious little ones to term. Guilty because I was angry at God. Guilty because I was jealous, even resentful of others. Guilty because, in my anger and hurting, it led me to sin.

It took me months, years even, of pursuing every single medical explanation and "problem" before I finally realized that, even if I did everything "right" and was in the best shape of my life, I wasn't guaranteed a baby. Life and conception were things that were out of my control. It wasn't my fault that I lost those babies.

In our fallen world, our bodies are broken. Since sin entered the world, God told woman that childbirth would be painful, and that includes the pain of losing a child. It's simply a part of our Earthly reality after the Fall. But the Lord plans our way, knows our steps, and works with and through our brokenness.

He knows when our bodies will thrive and when they will fail and He works for our good and for our future, despite our present. God freed me from my guilt, shame, and the thoughts that the miscarriages were my fault. He allowed me to see what He was bringing about through our losses. As our babies were birthed into Heaven, the Lord birthed a ministry in our lives and a new desire in our hearts.

In that freedom, I experienced God plant the desire to adopt, despite the broken pieces of my heart, and bring that little seed to life in the same nine months he was bringing a beautiful baby girl to life, who we now call our daughter!

Lord, take away the false guilt we take upon ourselves. Help us hold onto Your truth instead of believing the lies the enemy feeds us. Give us hope for our future and trust that You are working for our good. Amen.

Picture This - Imagine an innocent person who has been wrongly accused of a crime. Picture when the jury declares them to be "not guilty." Visualize the joy, the relief, the gratitude that washes over them as they realize they are free. Allow the Lord to speak those words and proclaim that freedom over your life.

Ask This - In what areas have you been taking on false guilt? How can you hand those areas over to God?

Pray This - Pray John 8:36 and believe it for yourself!

Words of Comfort for Guilt:
"Guilt is cancer. Guilt will confine you, torture you,
destroy you. It's a black wall. It's a thief."
~Dan Grohl

The Garment Of Guilt

» Rebecca Grambort

"Let's us draw near to God with a sincere heart and with the full assurance that faith brings, having our hearts sprinkled to cleanse us from a guilty conscience and having our bodies washed with pure water."

~Hebrews 10:22 NIV

I was a younger woman when I would find myself suddenly widowed and suddenly single. After a length of time, my deep desire for companionship caused me to seek out a new mate for myself and new father figure for my kids. Little did I know that I would be sucker-punched by the challenges blending a family would create and, in turn, added more heartache to our already heavy plates of grief. This riddled me with guilt and I blamed myself for the added pain that was inflicted on my innocent children. They, too, were subject to the consequences of my choices. Guilt and shame plagued me and I began harboring self-abasement towards myself.

One day while I was weeping in prayer, barely able to utter any words, I cried out - *'Daddy, It hurts!'*

In my spirit, I heard a loving reply . . . *'I know. Remove the garment of guilt.'*

His calm words settled my aching heart bringing peace in the midst of my pain. He completely understood me. I had to let go of the fact that what I did or felt would be misunderstood by others around me. I needed to find rest in being fully understood by Him alone. I also then realized that Jesus took my guilt at the cross and had forgiven me. It was I who refused to let myself off the hook. I had to forgive myself, because wearing that garment of guilt was leaving a door open in my heart for the enemy to relentlessly torment me day after day.

No one can go back and make a new beginning, but anyone can start from now and create a new ending. As we draw near to God, He will help us pen a new ending that no one could ever have written without His redeeming Grace. God transforms really ugly beginnings into beautiful, miraculous endings. Give yourself permission to start from now and take yourself off the hook. Jesus has removed your garment of guilt. He has new attire waiting for you; a robe of righteousness and a garment of praise (Isaiah 61). Let your life be free of guilt and free to praise!

Father, Thank You that You have released me from the guilt that I wore so heavily. Thank You for my new robes of righteousness! Amen.

Picture This - What might your life be like without carrying around a guilty conscience?

Ask This - What would be different in your life if you offered yourself forgiveness the way Jesus so freely forgives you?

Pray This - Father, I ask that I fully know that You took my guilt at the cross. I forgive myself and leave all of my past failings at Your feet.

Words of **Comfort** for Guilt:

"The worst guilt is to accept an unearned guilt."
~Ann Rand

Blessed Freedom

→» Lisa Danegelis

"Brethren, I do not count myself to have apprehended: but one thing I do, forgetting those things which are behind and reaching forth to those things which are ahead."

~Philippians 3:13 NKJV

There is an old story about an Arab ruler who offered convicted prisoners of war a choice. Captives were marched into the commander's tent for sentencing. Each prisoner was given the choice of the firing squad or entrance through a dark foreboding door at the back of the tent. Time after time, with a rare exception, the firing squad was chosen. One day, after another execution, the commander's aide asked, "What is behind the mysterious door? It's almost never chosen." The commander explained, "That's the door to freedom. By the time these condemned men appear before me for sentencing, most of them have already given up; they have accepted their damnation. I have only known a few courageous souls who have accepted my offer and walk through to freedom".

How many of us are held prisoner by the chains of shame and guilt and have no idea there is a door to freedom ready to fling open before us? What are the chains holding in us? Fear? Pride? Doubt? Maybe it is a lifetime's worth of those and more, and the shackles have you so bound you can't imagine breaking free. That is how those prisoners felt . . . helpless, and therefore doomed . . . unwilling to walk through the dark to freedom. Blessed freedom can be found in vulnerability before God.

Brene' Brown, a renowned research professor at the University of Houston, describes vulnerability this way: "Vulnerability is our most accurate measure of courage."

Consider courageously packing your bulky luggage and exposing the messy contents at the foot of the cross. A simple prayer of surrender and repentance is all that is needed. The Greek word for repentance is "Metanoeo". It means to "Think differently". You will walk away from that place of repentance with a whole new mindset, unburdened, now carrying a small treasured satchel loaded only with grace.

When reading the verse above, think of what a profound statement the Apostle Paul was making. Paul had brutally murdered Christians before his dramatic conversion. He had a lot of forgetting to do, didn't he? Also notice that, though he still had things to understand, he focused on forgetting the past as the one thing that mattered. Paul clearly understood that God's grace was only meant to carry us forward, one day at a time. Let us lay our pasts at the cross and rejoice in the new freedom each sunrise brings.

Most gracious God, how blessed I am that I can look at every morning as a fresh start! Help me keep my eyes on You as I run my race one beautiful day at a time. Amen.

Picture This - What are the options you see in front of you as you are in your grief? If the options were certain death and darkness, which would be more appealing?

Ask This - Why do you think it is hard for us to accept the possibility of forgiveness, freedom, and redemption?

Pray This - Write a prayer thanking God for free will and for always offering at least one door to freedom.

Words of Comfort for Guilt:
*"I began to realize that when people experience
the love of God, it casts out their fear and
frees them from guilt."*
~Joseph Prince

Maybe If....

⟫ Luanne Nelson

"Who will bring any charge against those whom God has chosen? It is God who justifies. Who then is the one who condemns? No one. Christ Jesus who died—more than that, who was raised to life—is at the right hand of God and is also interceding for us."

~Romans 8:33-34 NIV

He was an elegant man, an impeccable dresser with a biting wit and an endearing charm. A river ran deep inside of him, complete with a cavern of mystery deep in his heart. He frenzy-fed on adventure, heli-skiing in the Alps and daring himself to crack codes in the new frontier of computing. He cleaned his guns on our coffee table in the living room while our toddlers played, safely tucked behind the baby-gate in the next room. It has been said there is a fine line between genius and insanity.

We divorced. This beautiful, brilliant man remarried and had another child. We were friends to the end, frequently gabbing up a storm on the phone like two old hunting widows on a rainy day. I adored him and still do to this day. I can't wait to see him again so I can hug him and then punch him in the nose. I need to ask him what in God's world he was thinking.

Our children, who were nine, eleven and twelve years old, were spending the night with him, his wife and their toddler. They were sound asleep in the next room.

The call came one early summer morning. They had spent the night looking for him. His wife said he was upset and left the house. He took a gun.

They found him at the lakefront. Dead.

There is no wrong or right way to grieve. There is no specific timeline. Grief in response to suicide can be particularly intense and complicated. Feelings of guilt, shame and blame are very common.

We lit candles for his birthday and lit candles in the church. We had family meetings as necessary to ask, "How are you feeling?"

We brainstormed our feelings as a family eventually concluding, *'We're all damaged, but we're not ruined.'*

To this day, I wonder what signs I missed. Why didn't he talk to me about it? What about the children? If only he would have called . . . If this, if that . . . *Maybe if . . .*

It's jarring. The aftermath is treacherous. Don't be afraid to ask for help. Join a support group for survivors. Pray. Pray without ceasing. Be angry at God. He can take it. He will get you through the fallout with His healing grace.

This happened twenty-six years ago; I was in my late thirties. I've had time to heal. I do not know God's conversation with him in those final moments. It is God who justifies. We cannot judge – him – or anyone. What I will tell you with total confidence is this: Jesus Christ our Lord and Savior and Redeemer is at the right hand of God interceding for us.

Every one of us. We are, after all, his kids. He loves us. Love never fails. His love is perfect.

Dear Jesus Lord, have mercy. Amen.

Picture This - What are ways you can come to terms with the loss of a loved one by his or her own hand? Learn about depression? Seek counseling? Focus on the joyous memories of that person's time here on earth? List your own ideas for dealing with this struggle.

Ask This - Can you make a list of people who would be there to emotionally support you in grief if the unthinkable happened . . . a list of people who would be there for you spiritually if you felt broken?

Pray This - Dear Lord Jesus, please quiet my mind and my heart from asking the constant stream of questions: *Why, how, what could I have done?* Make me be still and know You are here with me. Keep me company and heal my heart. Amen.

Words of **Comfort** for Guilt:
"Guilt upon the conscience, like rust upon iron, both defiles and consumes it, gnawing and creeping into it."
~Robert South

Tower Of Strength

→ Traci Weldie

"Each time he said, "My grace is all you need. My power works best in weakness." So now I am glad to boast about my weaknesses, so that the power of Christ can work through me."

~2 Corinthians 9 NIV

When I entered the world of adoption, I had no idea how many new words, therapies, medicines, and acronyms I needed to learn. Eye Movement Desensitization and Reprocessing (EMDR), Trust-Based Relational Intervention (TBRI), Neurodevelopment healing, Neurofeedback training, essential oils, Latuda, Depakote, the list goes on and on. Each one of these medicines and therapies promises a "cure" for dealing with the symptoms of my special needs child.

As I was trying to figure out how to parent and love a child from a traumatic background, how to heal him, I fretted and cried over which therapy or medicine to try. Should I put electrodes on George's head or should I put him in a "time in"? Do I put bandages on every boo-boo or do I send him to intense therapy once a day to take him back to the deepest recesses of his memory? Do I find a horse for him to bond with or do I take everything out of his room when he rages? Do I take him off all his medications and douse him in essential oils before I send him off to school? I didn't know which direction to go, so I felt like a failure. Every time things would fall apart at home, I felt the overwhelming guilt of not putting on the right oil, or not putting enough bandages on the scrapes, or not doing enough neurofeedback.

Each time I got to a place of feeling guilt and shame, though, God responded gently with *'TRUST ME.'*

When I turned to His Word, a calm would wash over me as I put my trust in Him and not in the latest, greatest therapy.

Paul teaches us in 2 Corinthians that God's tenderness and goodness is all we need. When I was crying in my pillow, feeling the guilt of not being enough, God was actually able to move in my life to show me how His power works best in my weakness. When I was at the end, He showed me how I was making progress and how He placed George into my life intentionally for my benefit.

I gave a lot of lip service to being a Christian woman, but it wasn't' until I was made vulnerable, by admitting my limitations, that I understood the comfort and joy that comes in trusting God to be my tower of strength in my weakness.

Christ's power can then work through me . . . *that* is the key to my life! I know I can't "cure" my son. I know I can't "fix" George. He is made as he was meant to be made. What I do know is that God has called me to *love* George. It is God's grace that is pouring into my life that enables me to let go of guilt; to forgive, to show mercy, and to love.

Dear Father, help me to embrace my weakness and to see that when I am weak, You come in to provide me your all-sufficient grace. Amen.

Picture This - When I was little, I was taught that *grace* stood for "God's **Riches At** Christ's Expense." What does grace look like in your life?

Ask This - How can you begin to boast in your weaknesses?

Pray This - Dear Heavenly Father, to the One who has given me all I need, help me to see how Your power works best in my weakness. Help me to not see my weakness as a failure. Do not let guilt overtake my thought life. Rather, show me how Christ is working through me to demonstrate Your great grace towards us. Amen.

Words of **Comfort** for Guilt:

"For better or worse, we live in possible worlds as much as
actual ones. We are cursed by that characteristically human
guilt and regret about what might have been in the past.
But that may be the cost for our ability to
hope and plan for what might be in the future."
~Alison Gopnik

What Have I Done?

→ Victoria Dreckman

"Come now, let us settle the matter,' says the Lord. 'Though your sins are like scarlet, they shall be as white as snow; though they are red as crimson, they shall be like wool.'"

~Isaiah 1:18 NIV

Have you ever made a decision you later regretted? The kind that makes you feel so guilty you just want to crawl into a hole and hide from the shame? I have. Unfortunately, the guilt came after many years of making the same mistake over and over again.

I grew up in church my whole life, but never had a relationship with Jesus until I was in my thirties. I spent most of my time chasing after relationships and what I thought to be love, hoping that – in giving myself to men – I would, in turn, receive the love and affection I deeply desired . . . a desire never fulfilled by any of those pursuits. In fact, by needlessly giving myself away, I was left with a huge sense of grief.

I asked myself, *'what have I done?'*

The innocence and purity that was meant for only one person, now gone, was never to be recovered again, until I heard a woman at my church speak about the unfailing love of Jesus and His blood sacrifice on the cross.

If you've ever given blood, you've seen the bags that get filled. Hold up one of these bags. Can you see through the viscous blood? No, not at all! The blood not only covers up so no one can see into it or through it, but cleanses us completely.

Snow is white, pure, refreshing, and it quenches the earth. When we come to Jesus and repent of our sins, we become clean, purified, refreshed, and quenched with new life.

Father, as I release my guilt to You today, I thank You for also making me clean and whole. Amen.

Picture This - Identify a time when your feeling of guilt was more than you could bear; picture that guilt being wiped away.

Ask This - What are some biblical assurances for releasing your guilt to the Lord?

Pray This - Father, we come to You with sins and guilt greater than we can bear. Your Word says, though our sins are like scarlet, they are now as white as snow. Lift away that grief and guilt as we make a new commitment of obedience to You with a refreshed Spirit. Thank You that we are pure and clean by the blood of Jesus. Amen.

Words of **Comfort** for Guilt:

"Our huffing and puffing to impress God, our scrambling for brownie points, our thrashing about trying to fix ourselves while hiding our pettiness and wallowing in guilt are nauseating to God and are a flat-out denial of the gospel of grace."
~Brennan Manning

The Lasting Plan

→ Reji Laberje

"But God chose what is foolish in the world to shame the wise; God chose what is weak in the world to shame the strong; God chose what is low and despised in the world, even things that are not, to bring to nothing things that are, so that no human being might boast in the presence of God. And because of him you are in Christ Jesus, who became to us wisdom from God, righteousness and sanctification and redemption...."

~1 Corinthians 1 27-30 ESV

I had poured nearly twenty years into building MY business MY way. I did all of the things you are supposed to do (according to the world) to be successful, profitable, and fulfilled; instead I was exhausted, spent, and used. In my last year of my business, I felt like a prostitute, sold over and over to clients who needed what I could give, even though my heart was not in it. My maternal instincts added to my drain as I was often caring for my team like my children. I would give them the favorite projects, much the way a mom gives her kids the best cookies and eats the burnt ones. I continued doing it all, because—along the way—I had picked up others, that same team, who were relying on me. While I hadn't taken a paycheck in years, I ensured that my employees never missed one, even depleting my own family's personal savings.

Choosing to let the business go, even at a time when I had nothing left in me, physically, emotionally, mentally, or spiritually, felt like I was choosing . . . *to let all of them down*. It was also telling my whole family that I was giving up on making good on our years-long investments of time, energy, and money. The investments were in a constant state of paying off after the next project, then the next, then the next, and infinitely so on.

I failed and felt horrible for it.

What I didn't know at the time was that God is not a short-term tactician, but a long-term strategist. You have to trust that there is a lasting plan, and not a temporary fix, to the purpose God has in store for each of us. In the midst of my loss, my wallowing in paralyzing guilt, really, over failing in a lifelong dream, God was busy building it. He was using my low point, and all of the lessons I learned in landing there, to put together HIS business HIS way, served by the skills HE gave me.

I finally turned to Him to lead me in how I should use my gifts and, the moment I did so, He said, in essence, *'Here you go. I've been waiting for this moment to give you your purpose,'* and He dropped a Kingdom-focused livelihood in my lap without any of my own exhaustive efforts.

I never imagined that God would resurrect my business from the ashes, as a new venture – one that serves Him and that is successful and fulfilling. But, He is God; I am not; and that's just what He did.

Dear God, thank You for being You; that—even when we are in the ugliest, most painful emotions, such as guilt and shame—You will use our grief for good. I ask that you continue to sanctify, not just us, but our purposes, as well. Amen.

Picture This - Imagine your current situation and God-given gifts repurposed to serve Him. What could this look like in your life?

Ask This - What guilts in your life are you holding onto that God has given you permission to release?

Pray This - Ask God what negative emotions in your life He can use to create a positive for His Kingdom. Ask for His guidance in leaning into those emotions and living through them while HE does the work of laying out HIS plan for YOUR life.

Words of **Comfort** for Guilt:

How blunt are all the arrows of thy quiver in
comparison with those of guilt.
~Robert Blair

Be A Companion

Instead of,
"Why are you so angry at
everyone, everything,
me, or others,"
Try,
"I'll help you work it out."

With Words Of Comfort

You may not understand their anger.
But you can love them through it.

The Fourth Stage

A N G E R *(noun) – according to your companions*
[ang-ger]

1. The internal fire that burns
2. A short madness

What does *"anger"* mean to you:

I'm Mad, But I Don't Feel Any Better

→ Maria Notch

*"I have heard many things like these: miserable comforters are you all!
Will your long-winded speeches never end? What ails you that you keep
on arguing?"*

~Job 16:2-3 NIV

People simply don't know what they don't know and, unless someone has lost what you have lost and walked in your shoes, they truly do not know what you're experiencing. Becoming mad at others' inability to relate, understand or show compassion, as Job did, is a natural reaction. But does anger serve anyone well?

In my own journey of miscarriage after miscarriage, I found well-intentioned people, like Job's friends, offering what they thought to be helpful: defending God, rationalizing the situation, or finding someone or something to blame. People would even shame me for grieving and say things like "Well at least you didn't carry to term and then lose the baby." or "Shouldn't you move on already?"

What people don't understand is that there is no moving on after losing someone you love. There is only moving forward . . . without them. There's a big difference. One infers that you leave their memory and the love you had for them behind, without recognizing the value. That suggestion only seeks to serve the one giving the advice who is tired of seeing you hurting. Moving forward empowers the one who has lost someone to continue living, continue breathing, continue grieving, and continue loving.

The most common cliché I heard was "Everything happens for a reason." What I wanted to ask was, 'Really? What's the reason God's taken four babies from me?'

See, I don't believe that everything happens for a reason - and it's definitely not scriptural. What I do believe is that God promises to "use all things for the good of those who love Him" and yes; that includes miscarriages.

What those well-meaning people didn't realize was that none of those things they'd say were helpful; rather, they were hurtful. You see, God doesn't need defending. God's people need comforting.

Although oftentimes righteous, my anger didn't help me feel any better. It only added a second layer of negative emotion to the sadness I was already feeling. Anger doesn't hurt the person it's directed at, it hurts the one who is angry.

Heavenly Father, you tell us that vengeance is Yours. Help us relinquish our anger so that we may love like you love and forgive as you forgive. Heal our hurting hearts and protect us from adding a layer of anger to our already difficult situation.

Picture This - Imagine being stuck in a traffic jam on your morning commute. Do you choose to yell at the car driver in front of you, who is also stopped in traffic? This will do nothing to speed up the situation, rather, it will only make you angrier. Imagine the other choices you could make in order to keep anger from consuming you.

Ask This - What's currently making you angry? How can you make an empowered choice to relinquish what is out of your control and leave the rest to the Lord?

Pray This - Lord, please show me what it means to be "slow to anger" as it says in James 1:18-20. Amen.

Words of Comfort for Anger:
*"I sat with my anger long
enough, until she told me her
real name was "grief.""*

Trading Anger For Joy

» Amy Sikkema

"Create in me a pure heart, O God, and renew a steadfast spirit within me. Do not cast me from your presence or take your Holy Spirit from me. Restore to me the joy of your salvation and grant me a willing spirit, to sustain me. Then I will teach transgressors your way, so that sinners will turn back to you. Deliver me from guilt of bloodshed, Oh God, you who are God my Savior, and my tongue will sing of your righteousness. Open my lips, Lord, and my mouth will declare your praise. You do not delight in sacrifice or I would bring it; you do not take pleasure in burnt offerings. My sacrifice, O God, is a broken spirit; a broken and contrite heart you, God, will not despise."

~Psalm 51:10-17 NIV

There are times that anger grabs at my hand and my heart. I fight it off and have never let it become a companion of mine – praying, praising, and thanking my way through it. When it came to anger holding my grief, it really was no different . . . except when it came to my kids.

I understood that my husband's life fulfilment was completed here on earth. I was thankful that our love was a good one, a crazy kind of love. I prayed that God would sustain me and carry me through the darkest nights. What made me angry? That my kids didn't have their dad to hold them during the day and tuck them in at night. They no longer had the best man to teach them how to hunt, fish, restore old tractors, and show them the ropes of firefighting. My daughter no longer had her daddy to make memories with. Not only shouldering my grief, but also the grief of our three kids – that made me angry.

I asked the "whys" and, *'Was this really a part of Your plan? To take my children's dad?'*

This anger caused me (and still causes me) to take a step back, daily. It's the gut punching reminder that these kids are fatherless that stirs my anger and tries so very hard to harden my heart. As I battle this anger, I have found myself in this scripture and singing the praise from Psalm 51. God knows my heart; he hears my plea. And, take heart, because he knows yours too. There is nothing too big, no question too hard for God to shoulder. He is the Father to the fatherless.

It's easy for one's heart to become hard against life and God's will when devastation in our lives occurs. We can battle that hardness by asking God to simply change it. He can change the way we see our struggle, open our eyes, and take our broken spirit into his hands.

May God's goodness and love sweep over any anger and replace it with joy and strength that only comes from Him! Amen.

Picture This - What coping mechanisms are you using to deal with your anger?

Ask This - What are three specific things you can thank God for, today? What are three praises you have for Him?

Pray This - Dear Lord, thank You for being a God who hears our cries and knows our every thought. Thank You for the power that the Holy Spirit places within us to renew our broken spirits. I humbly ask that You create in me a clean heart, Lord. In my anger and fear, do not cast me from Your presence, but make known Your goodness. Help me to always sing your praise and continue to restore unto me the joy of your salvation. For You alone are worthy of all our praise. Amen.

Words of **Comfort** for Anger:
"Where there is anger,
There is always pain underneath."
~Eckhart Tolle

Why Not?

» Luanne Nelson

"Do not take revenge, my dear friends, but leave room for God's wrath, for it is written: 'It is Mine to avenge; I will repay.' says the Lord."
~Romans 12:19 NIV

Jesus got angry; He toppled tables in the synagogue. People were buying and selling in His holy place. He was angry when He was scolded for healing someone on the Sabbath. Job, in the Old Testament, was angry at God because of the things that were happening to him. God heard and answered him.

Anger is not a bad thing. However; it turns sour and deadly when it moves in and takes possession of our hearts in the form of bitter resentments and wrath. It can get so poisonous it will kill us.

So, what do we do with anger? We learn to forgive. We do not repay wrong with wrong, or abuse with abuse; on the contrary, retaliate with blessing, for a blessing is the inheritance to which you yourselves have been called. (1 Peter 3:9 NEB)

Sound hard? It is.

Give it to God to sort through and fix. Let go and let Him handle what you cannot. Cast your cares on the Lord and He will sustain you. (Psalm 55:22 NIV)

Be merciful, just as your Father is merciful. Forgive, and you will be forgiven. Forgive us our trespasses as we forgive those who trespass against us. Even when we don't want to. Especially when we don't want to.

"Forgive them Father, they don't know what they are doing."

Jesus had every reason on earth to be bitter at the people who were torturing Him and killing Him; He was completely innocent. We aren't. He forgave. We have to, too. We have to put away childish ways. We have to grow up. Forgive. Our entire salvation depends on our forgiveness of others – forgiveness in the middle of the hot fires of our own pride.

"Vengeance is mine," says the Lord. Lord Jesus, can you make it quick and let me watch?

(I love how we can talk to God like a friend. He gets it! On a more serious note . . .)

Lord, please give me a sense of humor and holy perspective. Silence me from saying anything vile about my avengers. Refine me. Please shine through me so my enemies will see I belong to you. I am Yours. Amen.

Picture This - What would our lives look like if we stopped "stuffing away" our feelings of anger, pretending everything is alright, and instead truly forgave with the power of God?

Ask This - Do you believe God can restore you despite your negative feelings caused by tremendous loss?

Pray This - Dear Lord Jesus, please help me work through this anger I am feeling! Keep me from breaking myself or anyone else while I get through it in Your care. Amen.

Words of Comfort for Anger:
"Anger doesn't solve anything.
It builds nothing, but
can destroy everything."

The Watchman

⇒ Ava Olivia Willett

"I will stand at my watch and station myself on the ramparts; I will look to see what he will say to me, and what answer I am to give to this complaint."

~Habakkuk 2:1 NIV

I grabbed onto a strand of Christmas lights that hung creatively around the corners of the walls and yanked it as hard as I could. They came spiraling down, crashing onto the floor around me. I grabbed the computer chair and flung it at the desk. Watching papers go flying at its disruption, I decided it wasn't good enough. I kicked the table down and the hinges shook beneath the violence. I grabbed the corkboard that had our pictures and love letters pinned to it and whipped it out the door.

The room was in ruins. My life was in ruins.

I had destroyed my former boyfriend's room, after our relationship fell to the hands of destruction. Right after the storm, I dropped to my knees and looked up to God. I felt as though this uncontrollable anger crept its way up in my heart. The loss of our relationship was devastating to me. In this loss, I felt anger I had never experienced before in my life.

I then thought about the prophet in the book of Habakkuk and how he would not only physically stand watch over his city, but also consciously keep his mind keen and ready for God's next careful instruction and direction to the questions he brought before the Lord. Through the story in Habakkuk, I put myself in the same shoes as the prophet; I would physically keep watch over my house and property, in case of any wrongdoing, and keep watch over what God was instructing me to do from here. God speaks to us, not only in His word, but also in our internal consciousness.

Stand still and keep watch on your high tower! Amidst the anger you may be feeling at whatever loss you're facing, God is still at work and ready to provide you with your next instruction. The Lord will forgive you for your impulsive actions and give you the tools needed to fix whatever was broken.

Jesus, Your Word says that, just as iron shapes iron, so does on person sharpen another (Proverbs 27:17). Equip me with the strength to be still in these turbulent times, so that I can be at peace with myself and the people around me. You never slumber. Be beside me, Jesus. I'm watching for Your next instruction. Amen.

Picture This - Where can you picture yourself a few months down the road by not being quick to anger in your grief?

Ask This - Think of a time in your life when you willingly jumped into anger and recollect how your body felt. Ask yourself what parts of your body you can calm in your current anger, in order to process the situation with a still and gentle spirit?

Pray This - Lord, teach me how to control my anger and recognize when I begin to act out of control. Amen.

Words of Comfort for Anger:
"Holding onto anger is like grasping a hot coal with
the intent of throwing it at someone else;
you are the one who gets burned."
~Buddha

I'll Do It For You

Heather Taylor

"Do not repay evil with evil or insult with insult. On the contrary, repay evil with blessing, because to this you were called so that you may inherit a blessing."

~1 Peter 3:9 NIV

'Ask God to lead you; allow Him to tell you who you need to forgive.'

This was not going to be easy . . . as the words left the Instructor's mouth I knew I was in for a rough day! The first sign was the uncontrollable urge to hit her! Seriously! I was mad at her!

'I don't want to do this!' was all I could think. I want to run, hide, get as far away from this room as I can. Nine other women had already found their quiet spot to chat with God. Some of them were already silently weeping and some were just closing their eyes and – *listening?* – I guess. Not me; I was looking for an exit. I spent the last two years running from this day and today was not the day I was going to face it. At least that's what I thought. As usual God had other plans.

When I finally accepted my fate, I brought my head into my hands and I told God, "I don't want to do this Lord! I don't want to forgive him! He took my Grandbaby away from me. He lied to get custody of my daughter's girl. He killed our life with her! He is evil! He hurt all of us including her. Most of all her! I don't want to do this Lord, but if you want me to, then you have to give me the ability to forgive him because I hate him and I don't have the desire or the want to do it myself. But I do want to please you. So Lord, If you want me to forgive him then give me the ability to do it."

Just like that, my hatred for him left my body. I was able to say her name for the first time in two years without breaking down in uncontrollable tears. Don't get me wrong I was weeping uncontrollably, but it wasn't out of pain it was out of relief! God doesn't want us to live our lives with stored up hatred and unforgiven wounds. He wants to bless us but to be able to do that we have to surrender all that hidden pain, resentment, jealousy, anger and disappointment because that is what keeps us from receiving God's blessings. I had to forgive this man that had done the unthinkable to my family but it wasn't to bless him it was so God could heal me.

Lord, I ask You to break the bondage of anger today. Help my heart feel forgiveness for the people that I am angry with so that You can complete the work in me that You have started.

Picture This - Imagine God reaching inside of your physical being, pulling out your anger, and replacing it with love. How do you think this would feel? Write down those new emotions.

Ask This - What is keeping you from letting go of your anger? Are you worried about what others will think? Are you willing to trust God?

Pray This - God, help me to release whatever is holding me back from forgiveness and help me to trust You to know that forgiveness is what I should do, no matter how much I do not want to forgive. Amen.

Words of **Comfort** for Anger:

"Speak when you are angry and
You will make the best speech
You will ever regret."
~Laurence J. Peter

I Uphold You

→ Jessica Chase

"Rescue me, LORD, from evildoers; protect me from the violent... I know that the LORD secures justice for the poor and upholds the cause of the needy."

~Psalm 140: 1, 12 NIV

Do you go to God with your anger or do you try and hide it? Do you feel guilty for being angry at people? Situations? Yourself?

"Yes, yes, and yes," for me.

The only person I was ok being upset with was me and I had a lot to be mad about, I could never do anything right. I proceeded to punish myself with what I "should" have done. "Should" was my favorite weapon. On the inside, I was boiling over with self-hatred.

That level of anger cannot stay contained, and my destructive behaviors eventually reared their heads and required attention. As I dealt with my childhood abuse, the true root of my anger, I learned about complex trauma, its neurological impact, and its effect on relational development. I learned that children, growing up in environments where caregivers neglect or abuse is the normal routine, learn to assign the responsibility for the abuse, along with the associated anger, to themselves. Otherwise, if the caregiver is responsible, a psychologically unbearable paradigm is created. This assignment leads to self-hatred so profound that it is actually associated with autoimmune issues; the body literally attacking itself.

I started talking to God about my anger. I yelled, I cried, I questioned. He met me in my pain. Sometimes, during prayer, He would take me into my past and talk to me about what He was feeling and doing during the abuse.

He would whisper healing words to my heart, "You were not alone, I was there and I wept with you. See Me there, I am sitting with you surrounding you with My love. I am sorry this happened, this was not My plan. I am angry that this happened too."

One day God said, "Are you ready to forgive her?" He was pointing to me as a little girl. I felt so angry; she represented everything about me that I hated. Even so I knew it was time to release her and so began my journey in forgiving myself.

Lord, examine our hearts, reveal where and at whom our anger for our hurt is directed. Help us to let go so that our anger doesn't trip us up and give the enemy a foothold. We want to be free to love like you, come with your mercy and grace, lead us into wholeness. Amen.

Picture This - What does anger feel like in your body? Does your chest feel tight? Do you clench your fists, do your cheeks get red? What do you do when you feel angry? Do you cry, yell, throw things? Journal about it.

Ask This - Who do you feel angry at most often: yourself, your family, someone in your past, God? How do you resolve your anger? Do you stuff it down; do you talk about it with God?

Pray This - God, help me to remember that You gave Your Son to heal every hurt, overcome every pain, and bring us to a place where there is no blame to be handed out. Help me to know Your forgiveness, deep in my soul.

Words of **Comfort** for Anger:
"For every minute you remain angry,
You give up sixty seconds of peace of mind."
~Ralph Waldo Emerson

Trading Anger For Understanding

→ Amy Sikkema

"Create in me a pure heart, O God, and renew a steadfast spirit within me. Do not cast me from your presence or take your Holy Spirit from me. Restore to me the joy of your salvation and grant me a willing spirit, to sustain me. Then I will teach transgressors your way, so that sinners will turn back to you. Deliver me from guilt of bloodshed, Oh God, you who are my savior, and my tongue will sing of your righteousness. Open my lips, Lord, and my mouth will sing of your praise. You do not delight in sacrifice or I would bring it; you do not take pleasure in burnt offerings. My sacrifice, O God, is a broken spirit; a broken and contrite heart you, God, will not despise."

~Psalm 51:10-17 NIV

'Help me to understand, oh Lord. Help me understand. What have I done wrong?' I thought it was me.

After my husband's death, there were big areas of our life that took on complete abandonment. That made me feel angry. Promises went unkept, and empty words were said. Holidays and other events came and went; we were forgotten. I was angry, mostly for my kids. There were people in our lives who promised so much . . . and delivered so little.

I prayed for God to give me a pure heart with this; to renew a steadfast spirit. I was so entirely hurt that it felt impossible to feel nothing but anger, and—in many ways—an even deeper grief.

I had to hand this anger and grief, and the people I felt those things for, over to God.

Then, God placed these things on my heart: *'For you, what if I'm removing parts of your past to make way for something new? And what if this stage is just part of your grief? For those you feel have abandoned you, what if those others can't look at you because it's too real and too raw for them? Maybe seeing you and the children brings a sadness and grief that is too hard for them to handle. You are each on your own journeys. Maybe the way those journeys look has nothing to do with you.'*

That, dear friends, is spirit breaking. When the people you believe in—the ones you thought would be there for you through it all—are not. The ones you thought you could rely on, trust, and count on in your most vulnerable days, months, and even years walk away; it is heart breaking.

What do we do with this broken, angry spirit?

Sacrifice it. Lift it up. Pray for restoration, healing, and to even forgive what we feel like cannot be forgiven. Sing praises from your lips. Rejoice in all He has done and in His goodness. Pray for the old to be restored and for new friendships to blossom; for He gives and takes away.

And last, trust. Trust that He is renewing a steadfast spirit, and that His ways are good and higher than we can ever imagine . . . for *all* of His people.

May God's goodness and love sweep over any anger and replace it with joy and strength that only comes from Him! Amen.

Picture This - In what areas of your life have your felt complete abandonment causing deeper grief and angers? Imagine what the bigger picture of those feelings might be.

Ask This - When anger rears its ugly head, what are three specific things you can thank God for providing in your life?

Pray This - Dear Lord, thank You for being a God who hears our cries and knows our every thought. Thank You for the power that the Holy Spirit places within us to renew our broken spirit. I humbly ask that You create in me a clean heart, Lord. In my anger and fear, do not cast me from Your presence, but make known Your goodness. Help me to always sing your praise and continue to restore unto me the joy of Your salvation. For You alone are worthy of all our praise. Amen.

Words of Comfort for Anger:
*"To be angry is to revenge the
faults of others on ourselves."*
~Alexander Pope

Who Will Take Care Of Me

→ Karen Bruno

"And my God shall supply all your needs according to His glorious riches in Christ Jesus."

~Philippians 4:19 NIV

My anger would hit like icy sleet stabbing against an exposed face on a frigid winter's day. It rocked me to the core and chilled my faith. I had never been this angry with God. Why? Why had He allowed my husband, best-friend, high-school sweetheart, father of our four children, provider, protector, the rock of our home, to die? These questions are a mere sample of the ones I yelled at God during fits of rage and tears. I swung back and forth, swung emotionally, like a pendulum having no middle in which to find rest. Living day to day was exhausting, everything sent me over the edge of anger, pain, sadness, and unrest.

One such moment occurred in my dining room while trying to sort through paperwork. I had set up a long table and began to "do life" while sitting at my laptop. My computer wasn't functioning properly and I completely lost it.

I stood up out of my chair and screamed at God, "Seriously! You are supposed to be my husband, isn't that what Your word says? You took the one person who could fix my computer now You fix it!"

And then I waited liked a stubborn, defiant brat with my hands on my hips. Simultaneously, a verse drifted softly to mind finding its way through the gale force of anger. "And my God shall supply all your needs according to His glorious riches in Christ Jesus."

In a brief moment of emotional clarity, I was not enraged with God. With one tender thought, He brought me to a middle. My arms dropped to my side and I sat, content. Yes, my computer was now working! Humbled I began to work through the disaster that was my life. This time, with knowledge coupled with faithful understanding that—regardless of my reactions—He was going to take care of me. He alone would be the source of finding a middle again. He would always calm the storm. He would always be my God.

God, You alone can withstand the gale forces of my raw emotions during times of trial. You can provide for all my physical, emotional, and mental needs. Your riches are glorious and the supply, endless. I can turn to You with any issue, problem, or need knowing You will take care of me. Amen.

Picture This - How would I change the way I live if I believed God could and would supply all my needs?

Ask This - What stands in the way of believing His truth that your needs will be met?

Pray This - God, remove any obstacle of unbelief I have about Your ability to supply all that I need. Thank You for allowing me to vent my anger so that I may release it to You as I move through the stages of grief. Amen.

Words of Comfort for Anger:
"Discussion is an exchange of knowledge.
An argument is an exchange of ignorance."
~Robert Quillen

Storms of Change

→ Lisa Danegelis

"And there arose a great storm."

~Mark 4:37 KJV

Do you ever look at the door of grief and see yourself fiercely storming through rather than limping? Maybe you have experienced a loss that not only brings deep sorrow, but also arouses feelings of anger. Such feelings certainly are justified, especially when our lives have been ravaged by an injustice perpetrated by others. Heartache over grave injustices can be fuel for necessary change. Righteous anger ignites passion within that should not be silenced.

Such was the case when my brother suddenly died from an iatrogenic illness (an illness caused by the medical community). I had unwittingly been on the same path, taking the same class of wrongly prescribed pharmaceuticals, the ones that abruptly ended his life. The rage consumed me as I thought of the many years he had lost. Rage sounds so "unchristian," doesn't it? I had always repressed my anger. This meek tempered soul would squelch the flames with a deep breath and turn of the cheek. Not this time! I arose with an indignation and fearlessness that surprised me and became productive and healing. I created a YouTube channel and Facebook group to educate and support others while speaking out against the evils of these drugs. My anger became cathartic and an open door into ministry.

A storm is defined as, "A violent disturbance in the atmosphere."

Storms in the natural can cause change as they roar; uprooting and repositioning the landscape. Though sleeping through the storm in the above verse, Jesus often caused the storm during other times in His ministry. In paintings, Jesus is generally portrayed as gentle and passive. I believe He was anything but! I see Him as courageous, bold, and intense. Jesus often *was* the storm . . . a "violent disturbance" that plowed up fallow ground bringing lost souls to repentance and calling out injustices. I can see Him staring down the Pharisees and rebuking the naysayers with sweat on His brow!

God also blessed us with the emotion of anger. See it as such and do not allow condemnation to set in when feeling it. Embrace it, temper it, and direct it to bring change in your corner of the world.

All knowing Father, who causes and calms storms; help me to embrace my anger and use it for Your glory! Temper it with forgiveness and love and bring justice in Your perfect timing. Amen.

Picture This - What evils do you see in the world that deserve your righteous anger?

Ask This - How can you allow anger to work through your grief for positive results and changes?

Pray This - Ask God to guide you to stir and calm storms for good in His Kingdom, based on the positive and negative experiences of your life.

Words of Comfort for Anger:

*"Anger is an acid that can do more
harm to the vessel in which it is stored
than to anything on which it is poured."*
~Mark Twain

Anger – It's Gonna Happen

» Victoria Dreckman

"In your anger do not sin. Do not let the sun go down while you are still angry, and do not give the devil a foothold."

~Ephesians 4:26-27 NIV

My anger and resentment began to strangle me as I grieved the part I played in my broken marriage, which ended in divorce. We were arguing a custody issue . . . again. I called a dear friend expecting to unload my version of the story and obtain some much-needed sympathy. However, something entirely different happened. I finished unraveling in supersonic mode to a deafening silence on the other end of the phone.

She spoke, calmly and sweetly, "You need to love him."

What?! Did I hear her correctly? I immediately interjected, "You don't understand!"

In the same calm and sweet tone, she answered with the same words she had said before, "You need to love him." Silence. I pondered what she said.

She already had a revelation that Jesus expects us to love one another. Not just the people we want to love, but also the hard-to-love ones.

The kicker of it all was this: *'Did I really want to stay angry?'*

Remaining angry would give the enemy a foothold. If I did remain angry, what would that lead me into next? I've had enough Bible education to know that I certainly did not want to continue down that path. I thanked that God-fearing woman for speaking the truth in love to me, even if it hurt my feelings in that moment.

You are not going to get out of this life without ever being angry. It's gonna happen no matter what you do. You do have control over whether or not you remain angry and what you do with your anger. I challenge you to find a friend you can unload onto, speaks the truth in love, and helps you release that anger to the Lord. Don't give the enemy any foothold.

Father, we ask that in our anger and grief, the love of Jesus Christ overwhelm our heart and bring us His peace which passes all understanding. Amen.

Picture This - Recount a moment when you allowed your anger to spill over or linger. Reflect on that moment with peace.

Ask This - In what ways can you abort the "anger" foothold of the enemy?

Pray This - Find a scripture that speaks to your personal situation where anger is concerned and turn it into your prayer.

Words of Comfort for Anger:
"How much more grievous are the consequences
of anger than the causes of it?"
~Marcus Aurelius

No More Barking

→ Traci Weldie

"My dear brothers, take note of this: Everyone should be quick to listen, slow to speak and slow to become angry, for man's anger does not bring about the righteous life that God desires."

~James 1:19-20 NIV

I feel like I am in a pit, deep in the mire. I am angry. In fact, I am angry at God. So angry, in fact, that I shouted at God in my car, just to make sure He knew it!

Parenting a child with significant special needs was never what I planned or asked for, and, sometimes it is too much to bear. I struggle to love my son and then I feel like a failure for being a mom who is struggling to love her child.

I am being tested, pulled, pushed, stretched . . . all by God simply asking, "Do you trust Me?"

I humbly admit that I don't always trust God, because I don't always believe He loves me. How can God actually love me? I mess up all the time, I was so angry with Him for leading my family to this crazy life of adoption that I actually screamed at Him in my car . . . for like an hour.

If I can be very honest, little good is ever accomplished through my anger.

In fact, God's Word is clear that, as believers, we are called to be slow to yell, bark, roar, grumble, or fly off the handle. Those descriptions of anger hurt, because–often—my anger at God and, frankly, at my son, lead me to lash out at anyone and everyone. Instead, we are to be sudden and swift to tune in, listen, and accept. When I let the Spirit lead me, I take notice of my son, how he has been greatly hurt, how he never asked to go through the trauma and pain he has been through. Something changes inside me when I do not yell or stamp my feet or reply with harsh words in my anger, but instead just listen.

Man's anger is filled with animosity and resentment. Man's anger says, *'You don't deserve the pain you are in. You have a right to be angry.'*

Believer, when we instead choose to be quick to listen and slow to speak, God brings about the righteous life He desires in us; a life that brings glory to God! My journey with my son is not meant to tempt me to angry outbursts every day, but rather to teach me how to listen and love.

Dear Father, thank You for Your Word that so clearly teaches us about anger. We are often tempted to justify our anger when instead You call us to something very different. Today, may I be "quick to listen, slow to speak, and slow to become angry." Amen.

Picture This - How would my life look different if I were to be quick to listen and slow to anger?

Ask This - What do you think is the righteous life that God desires to bring out for you?

Pray This - Pray about your trust in God and thank Him for how much He loves you.

Words of Comfort for Anger:
"When anger arises,
think of the consequences."
~Confucius

The Same Boat

→ Rebecca Grambort

"Forgive them for they know not what they are doing."
~Luke 23-24 NIV

Years ago, after the tragic death of my husband, I remarried, in turn, blending families. To be honest, it was one of the most challenging and painful experiences I have ever coped with. Power struggles – favoritism and conflict plagued our home. I was angry and resentful at everyone, including myself.

Anger wasn't my issue, or my husband's – sinning in our anger was (Ephesian 4:26). I was desperate for answers. One time, at a Christian conference, we were asked to close our eyes and ask God who we needed to forgive.

Immediately, my husband and step-daughter came into my vision . . . I then heard these words; "Forgive them for they know not what they are doing – *and neither do you.*"

God lovingly rebuked me, revealing that I was in the same sinful and ignorant boat as they. Ignorant behavior was a symptom of our pain and lack of self-control. I had no right to hold a grudge towards them; I was equally at fault.

Look at Jesus; He knew that those who persecuted Him on the cross truly didn't understand the magnitude of what they were doing. They sinned in their ignorance!

God's gentleness in the midst of sin allowed forgiveness to come easier, even though I knew it didn't make the situation right. Things needed to change – and so did I. We were all in the same boat!

We all had suffered great loss. My husband and I had both lost a spouse, and our children each had lost a parent. We were all grieving and coping with change – struggling to find a way to feel normal and happy again.

We should have had each-others' backs, saying *'Hey, I understand – I get it! I'm sorry, are you okay?'*

Instead, we bit and devoured one another, comparing and competing for first prize in the grief game. We refused to see beyond our own pain. This rendered us powerless. We were selfish-sufferers, when unselfish suffering would hold the power to save us.

Jesus' example on the cross was one of unselfish suffering, despite the ignorance of those who caused His pain. We should practice the same.

Father, Forgive us all, for we know not what we are doing! Amen.

Picture This - Stages of grief rarely occur one-at-a-time, or in a particular order, such as this experience with anger, denial, and looking back all at once. Identify your own grief symptoms and which one you are allowing to control your actions and keep you from living life to the fullest.

Ask This - If we truly understood the magnitude of what we were doing, would we do it? What are some ways that you can steward your own behavior in a Godly manner?

Pray This - Help me to know that we are all in the same sinful boat in desperate need of Your saving! Amen.

Words of **Comfort** for Anger:

"The ignorant mind, with its infinite afflictions,
passions, and evils, is rooted in the three poisons.
Greed, anger, and delusion."
~Bodhidharma

Be A Companion

⌄⌄

Instead of,
"You didn't deserve this,"
Try,
"I know it isn't fair."

⌃⌃

With Words Of Comfort

You may not understand their bargaining.
But you can love them through it.

The Fifth Stage

B A R G A I N I N G *(noun) – according to your companions*
[**bahr**-g*uhn*-eng]

1. A vain attempt to strike a deal with God
2. Trading one pain for another
3. Haggling with God about something you want, but He knows is not best for you

What does **"bargaining"** *mean to you:*

God Wants Us To Be Obeyers

» Kimberly Joy Krueger

"Samuel said, 'Has the Lord as great a delight in burnt offerings and sacrifices as in obedience to the voice of the Lord? Behold, to obey is better than sacrifice, and to heed [is better] than the fat of rams.'"

~1 Samuel 15:22 AMP

Ha!

1 Samuel 15:22 is God's response to Saul's offering: to obey is better than sacrifice and to heed [God's Word] is better than [offerings]. God doesn't want us to be bargainers; He wants us to be obeyers. This is really hard to do when it comes to loss . . . ESPECIALLY loss you see coming. Oh, the things we will promise to God to stop a loss from happening! Even when loss is past tense, we still try to strike up a deal with God (that may even involve a wee bit of time travel) just to hold onto that thing or person we lost.

I remember saying to God, "If you knew the enemy was going to steal from me, why didn't you stop him? Why would you let me be blindsided like that? How could I pray against the enemy's attack when I never saw it coming?"

I didn't like the way God did it. I wanted God to do it MY way. In my scenario, I could be informed and equipped to prevent the loss. Kind of like Saul . . . I was figuring out a way to keep the treasure . . . even if it was only some of it!

I have been like Saul in my grief. As a mother to twelve kids, most of whom had sticky fingers in the candy aisle at least once, I can really relate to God in this story, too. He is saying what every mom inevitably says to her kids: "There's a reason I said you can't have it this time. I see the bigger picture. I know what is best for you. I need you to trust Me on this."

I have found that when I choose to stop bargaining and TRUST that my God has good reasons and ALWAYS has good intentions, I am once again a light-hearted daughter of God. Even if it is a heart broken in pieces.

Lord Jesus, please forgive our tendency to be like King Saul. We want what we want, but we also want to obey you. We want to be faithful, but we also want our hearts to stop hurting so bad. Please show us how to obey your Word and honor You, even in our times of sorrow. Amen.

Picture This - Describe a bargain you tried to strike with God. What was His response?

Ask This - What were you trying to hold onto by bargaining? What might God be asking you to do instead, as an act of obedience?

Pray This - Write a prayer releasing your tendency to bargain with God. Ask Him to give you a hunger and thirst for His righteousness instead. Ask God to give you the strength to obey His Word, even in your brokenness.

Words of Comfort for Bargaining

"Another form of bargaining, which many people do,
is to replay the final painful moments over and over in
(one's) head as if by doing so (he or she) could
eventually create a different outcome."
~Kate McGahan

Bargaining Plus Pleading Does Not Equal Expected Results
→ Victoria Dreckman

"'For the mountains may be removed and the hills may shake, But My lovingkindness will not be removed from you, Nor will My covenant of peace be shaken,' Says the Lord who has compassion on you. 'O you afflicted [city], storm-tossed, and not comforted, Listen carefully, I will set your [precious] stones in mortar, And lay your foundations with sapphires. And I will make your battlements of rubies, And your gates of [shining] beryl stones, And all your [barrier] [a]walls of precious stones. And all your [spiritual] sons will be disciples [of the Lord], And great will be the [b]well-being of your sons.'"

~Isaiah 54:10-13 AMP

When you hold your child in your arms for the very first time, a sense of overwhelming responsibility seeps into your soul. You instinctively want the best life has to offer. What happens when you do everything you know to be "the right way" and they still get off track? So off track that you grieve their lost behavior as if losing a piece of yourself.

I relentlessly tried to "train up" my oldest daughter, as the bible instructs. When she was younger, I'd read bible stories to her in addition to regularly attending church and Sunday school. Biblical values were steadfast rules in our house. Somehow, she managed to defy all the values I held dear to my heart.

I decided to have a heart-to-heart with God, "Lord, I don't understand. I'm doing everything Your word says to do! Why isn't it working?"

I'm so glad our God has a sense of humor. He imparted to my heart, "You were no peach at fifteen, either."

'Wait, what? Did I really just hear God, my Heavenly Father say that to me? Yes, He did!'
I was always breaking my parents' rules.
I stepped outside of everybody's boundaries.
I had non-God-honoring relationships with boys.
I defied authority.
'I guess I was one of Your difficult children.'
He also said this: "I know you are feeling afflicted and tossed around right now. Your world is shaking and trembling and you're not finding comfort in the moment. I am your comfort. I am giving you my lovingkindness and peace. Let me build your foundations. Let me build your walls. The beauty with which I am building will sparkle more brightly than any manmade jewel. And *all* your children will be disciples of the Lord and great will be their peace."

I'm still not a perfect child, but God has taken me so far from where I was to respect the boundaries God has given me. Obedience has importance in my life. I'm in the moment, listening to HIS step-by-step. And I know that His promises are "Yes," and "Amen," in His timing, not mine. And His promises are for my daughter as much as for me.

Father, when the storms of life become overwhelming, remind me that Your peace and loving kindness are not determined by my "goodness," but by Your grace and mercy. Amen.

Picture This - Who are the "difficult children" in your life?

Ask This - What are some ways you've bargained with God on behalf of others in your life, instead of trusting them to His promises?

Pray This - Lord, there is no amount of bargaining with You that could ever change Your love for us. Through Your Holy Spirit, continue to lead me with Your compassion and peace. Amen.

Words of Comfort for Bargaining

"Bargaining with God is pointless.
He already has a thousand followers that
will do what you bargained to do for free."
~Shannon L. Adler

Here's The Deal

→ Neesie Cieslak

"And she answered and said unto Him, Yes, Lord: Yet the dogs under the table eat the children's crumbs."

~*Mark 7:28 KJV*

The woman in Mark 7:28 wasn't a Jew – she was a gentile who knew Jesus was the answer to her need. So she asked! At first, Jesus' answer was "no," but this woman, in her suffering and pain, wasn't going to give in easily. She bargained with Jesus!

She said, "Yes, Lord: Yet," "But," and "Remember," in confidence of His character.

She reminded Him that even the crumbs are left for the dogs. *'Lord, I'll even take the crumbs of your blessings,'* was in essence what she is stating. *'Give me even a little bit. I know I'll be better for it; but you gotta do something for me, Lord.'*

I used to bargain like that as a child. I'd pray to God, not even knowing if He was real.

"Dear God, if you would just let him not come into my room tonight, I'll...."

"Dear God if he stops beating my mother, I'll...."

"Dear God, if they will give us something to eat, I'll...."

Bargain after bargain I'd bring to God.

God knows our frame. He's aware of the anguish that cloaks our soul when we're grieving and we cry out to Him with a bargain – a *'Lord, if you do this, then...'*

We wish and we bargain by crying out to God in our pain. Father God knows. There was bargaining happening in the heavens before you or I were even born. Satan was there bargaining with God over Job. The Lord has an infinitely greater understanding of our wagering than we ever will. The Lord gets us - if He would give His ear to the devil, how much more will He give His ear to you, His precious child, for whom he sent Jesus to die on the cross?

Father God, You know that we are feeble and only dust. You're aware of the confusion and wondering that comes with grief. Help us, Jesus, to keep coming to you. Your ear is attentive to our pleas. And You understand. Amen.

Picture This - Imagine sitting at Jesus' feet with your current bargain. How does this change the perspective on what you bring to God

Ask This - Read the story of the "Persistent Widow" and ask yourself how you're similar.

Pray This - Father, Abba, I know You desire good for me. Sometimes I'm not even sure how to pray in my grief. Please take my "bargaining" prayers and teach me to trust You, for You are a Good Father. Amen.

Words of Comfort for Bargaining

*"Human fairness does not
equal divine justice."*
~Pastor Ken Whitten

Better Than Normal

→ Reji Laberje

"Formerly, when you did not know God, you were slaves to those who by nature are not gods. But now that you know God—or rather are known by God—how is it that you are turning back to those weak and miserable forces? Do you wish to be enslaved by them all over again?"
~Galatians 4:8-9 NIV

After a particularly trying time for my husband and me, a time that included our separation agreement drawn up (but not yet enacted), we were in the midst of our healing through newfound relationships we each had in Christ and one another. The process was slow, though. Past pains, guilts, and distrusts held by each of us formed a slow, depressing haze over everything we thought, said, and did. We were nearly a year into our choice to stay married and we still weren't back to normal.

One day, during the simple task of folding and putting away clothing in our bedroom, my husband, frustrated with our rebuilding process, exclaimed, "I just thought things would be back to normal by now!"

Without thinking the words at all, I snapped back, "I don't want normal! Our normal sucked. I want better than normal."

It was a breakthrough moment for each of us. We realized that, while we had Christ as part of our lives, the thinking, saying, and doing routines we were living had not changed at all with this addition. We were trying to hold onto our old selves and old expectations with Christ serving only as scotch tape, a weak adhesive at the joint of our marriage. He was never meant to be so small a hinge and we were never meant to be old people in a new life. We were meant to be new people, better than normal, and never back to the way we used to be.

Bargaining with God to keep bits of our past (though we didn't know that's what was happening at the time) when God offers us a new future is the definition of fruitless. In Him, we have a fruit*ful* life. We must surrender to it, giving up all of our old selves, in order to embrace our new lives in Him.

After our laundry day outburst, "better than normal" became an anthem for my husband and me. We haven't tried to go back to our past, rather, we constantly build a better future, and joy has returned, or – more accurately – *come* to our marriage and lives.

God, thank You that You offer more to us than the weak and miserable forces of this life. I pray that You constantly remind me that life with You is "better than normal." Amen.

Picture This - Envision a future with Christ as, not just a player in your story, but the leading role. What has changed?

Ask This - What from your past once gave you satisfaction but pales in comparison to a joy given by God in your life, today?

Pray This - Pray Jeremiah 29:11 back to God, giving gratitude for his promise of a full life.

Words of Comfort for Bargaining

"You can't always get what you want,
but if you try sometimes, you just might find
you get what you need."
~Rolling Stones

Small Potatoes

» Traci Weldie

"I'll never forget the trouble, the utter lostness, the taste of ashes, the poison I've swallowed. I remember it all – oh, how will I remember – the feeling of hitting the bottom. But there's one thing I remember and remember, I keep a grip on hope. God's loyal love couldn't have run out, his merciful love couldn't have dried up. They're created new every morning. How great your faithfulness! I'm sticking with God (I say it over and over), He's all I've got left."

~Lamentations 3:19-24 NIV

After hearing the news that I had a chronic illness, I shared the news on social media. Probably a huge mistake because, within minutes, my page and inbox were filled with suggestions on how to combat this disease. Try this special drink. Go sugar free. Fast. Of course, get rid of gluten. Eat more fish. No more dairy. Drink at least a glass of milk a day. And my knee-jerk reaction was to listen – and I purchased a whole pantry full of gluten free food, bought supplement drinks, filled my medicine cabinet with holistic pills filled with plant oils.

I thought, *'If only I change my diet, I'll beat this disease.'*

I also convinced myself that somehow, I must not be made more spiritual through this. God is trying to teach me a lesson. *'If I just become MORE devoted to God, he'll miraculously heal me.'*

Unfortunately for me, genetics play a huge part in my disease and it's just something I have. My response is to figure out how to bring glory to God in this and stop the "what ifs." The desire to bargain our way out of the inevitable is a human quality, but it's just an attempt to hit a temporary pause button on what is to come. Sometimes, God just asks us to be ok "hitting the bottom," and then remembering how His loyal love simply will not run out. He is not going to leave us there and it does not take any bargaining chip on our part.

My body is going to waste away – that is inevitable. God *could* cure me. Breakthrough treatments *could* develop, but—until then—I cling to one thing: hope. That hope is not in the cure, but in the ONE who loves me with abandon, the ONE who offers glorious mercies every morning. I can't negotiate my way into a different outcome, but I can stick with God.

Dear God, thank You that Your love is an endless supply of life-giving love. Thank You that Your mercies are created new each and every morning. Thank You for literally being all I've got left some days. Amen.

Picture This - Describe what you have been tempted to use as a bargaining chip with God.

Ask This - Share at least three times in your past when God has been faithful to you.

Pray This - Ask God to reveal how He is working inside of you during this trial.

Words of Comfort for Bargaining

"Don't bargain with God.
You'll always cheat yourself."

Burn Your Plow

>> Ava Olivia Willett

"Timothy, guard what has been entrusted to your care. Turn away from godless chatter and the opposing ideas of what is falsely called knowledge, which some have professed and in so doing have departed from the faith. Grace be with you all."

~1 Timothy 6:20-21 NIV

I used to think God was selfish. I knew I was selfish; all humans are born into selfishness. But one day my first boyfriend and best friend, who I was in love with, confessed to me that he was no longer a Christian. He told me he was walking away from faith and didn't ever believe in the stories and miracles of God. I was in love with someone who was selfish.

I asked God, "Why? Why is this happening to him? And even if he makes this decision, can I still be his girlfriend? I love you both, so why can't I keep you both?"

God warns His people of investing their hearts and lives into earthly pleasures. He warns us that sowing into relationships that do not glorify God, sowing into earthly pleasures and sin, will only reap an empty and unfulfilling life for us. It also stores no treasures in Heaven.

I thought about the story of Elisha in 1 Kings 19. Elisha lived a simple and easy life, plowing a field with his oxen and only making just enough money to get by without ever gaining more wealth to strive for a better and richer life. It was the same in his walk with God- he would do just enough to stay complacent in his faith. Then one day Elisha is called to do an act of faith and burn the plow his oxen are attached to and leave the city in search of a better job that would bless him.

In my grief of trying to determine whether or not it was worth hanging on for dear life to my now unequally yoked relationship, I bargained with God. I remember insisting I'd do more things for Him in the church if he let me hang on to this one thing in my life that didn't quite line up with His perfect will.

Fortunately, I was obedient and "burned my plow," ending the relationship.

As I stood in the flames, completely devastated and left empty handed before the Lord, He told me, "Well done."

Jesus, the things of this earth are temporary. Our lives are just merely a blink of the eye. Heaven is eternal, and You promise me that if I invest my labor and heart within Your treasures, I will have eternal life in Your everlasting Glory. Amen.

Picture This - What benefits (consider making a list!) are there for you personally when you let go of something God is inviting you to lay at the foot of the throne?

Ask This - Recall a time in your life when you fully trusted God and stepped away from your own design of life.

Pray This - Lord, set me free from my own decisions that plague my life. Encourage me to let go and let You take control of my life. Amen.

Words of Comfort for Bargaining
"God's not going to negotiate His holiness in order to accommodate us."
~RC Sproul

Be A Companion

Instead of,
"You need to stop crying all the
time and start living again,"
Try,
"It's okay to be sad right now."

With Words Of Comfort

*You may not understand their depression.
But you can love them through it.*

The Sixth Stage

DEPRESSION *(noun) – according to your companions*
[dih-**presh**-*uh*n]

1. Anger turned inward
2. The inability to construct a future
3. A shameful sadness

*What does "**depression**" mean to you:*

Cleansing Fire

» Lisa Danegelis

"I have chosen thee in the furnace of affliction."

~Isaiah 48:10 KJV

What do you do when the dawn breaks into darkness yet again? The bright morning light only illuminated the dark night of my soul. I stood in front of the bathroom mirror forcing an unfamiliar smile, it had been so long that my facial muscles ached. My therapist asked me the last time I had felt any happiness. I had to think back months to connect to a singular fleeting moment. I was years into a chemically induced depression caused by wrongfully prescribed drugs. I would not have believed such a suffocating darkness existed had I not been experiencing it. I wanted to die. I begged God to take me daily. Yet, in the above verse, God says He chooses us for such fiery trials . . . not that he chooses the fiery trials.

Webster's definition of "chosen" is: *One who is the object of choice or of divine favor: an elect person.*

God began to show me that I, indeed, was chosen and thrown into the fire of affliction for a divine purpose. As I slowly heal from the toxic effects of the drugs and the resulting depression, God is flinging open doors for ministry to lost broken souls that would have never opened without me having laid face-down for years on the hot desert floor. He has given me these precious jewels:

-Your desert belongs to everyone who will drink from the oasis there.

-Your darkness belongs to everyone who will be illuminated by your light.

-Your pain will be the bandage for other's wounds.

-Your tears will water other's souls.

-Your emptiness belongs to those who will be filled.

-Your death to self belongs to those who need life.

-Your cries will fill the mouths of others with laughter.

Earlier in Isaiah 48, God rebukes the children of Israel for their backsliding and rebellion, later saying He will "defer His anger". He then explains to them they have been tested by fire for their good and His glory. God uses processes to purify in the narratives of our lives.

Father, This fiery furnace is hot! Help me to embrace the flames knowing I am a chosen one in Your divine plan. May I see past the flames and look into Your eyes of love. Give me a vision for my future helping me to see the beauty the refining fire will bring. Amen.

Picture This - Imagine your own pains as precious jewels to help others. Picture these as actual jewels and bring to mind the people you would like to adorn with them.

Ask This - What desert, darkness, pain, tears, emptiness, death, or cries in your life could be turned around for purpose in God's Kingdom?

Pray This - Ask God to move your daily focus from your fiery furnace to what you are forging through it so that you may connect with joy in your life.

Words of Comfort for Depression
"Grief is real, but so is healing."
~Better Not Bitter Widower

Delivered By His Promise

⇻ Annabelle Ahlers

"I will not die but live, and will proclaim what the Lord has done."
~Psalm 118:17 NIV

I would describe depression in one word: drowning. I have drowned before . . . for days, weeks, months. I would feel this weight come over me, this intense feeling of nothing. I remember, in particular, a few miserable weeks of deep nothingness. I went from being on fire, excited for Jesus, to questioning whether I even believed. I just could not understand how, almost overnight, I lost all passion for God. I thought that I would never feel happiness or extravagant joy for the Lord ever again, that all my passion was dried up, and that this was the end. That was a bitter lie; I found the truth in the scripture and it became my promise.

What kept me from losing all hope in believing that I would return to a vibrant life, was the promise that the Lord gave me. Psalm 118:17 was the Lord showing me the other end of my episode. He showed me what He saw when He looked at me – a victor, one who overcame. I took that promise and held onto it. I stopped feeling guilty or ashamed for my emotions and, instead, focused my energy on picturing myself on the other side. The Lord did not instantly take me out of my depression, He carried me through it by this promise.

With deep feelings of hopelessness, it seems absurd to declare that there is good to come, yet that is exactly what there is. The devil wants you silent and mute to drown in your pain. The Lord wants you out there declaring the good news before it has arrived in your life. In depression, it feels like the end of everything good. The Lord wants you to know that there is more to come. You will live and not die and declare what the Lord has done, and it will be a great story.

Thank You, Lord, that You sustain us through anything and that we can trust in You. You are a Good Father. Amen.

Picture This - What do you look, sound, and feel like on the other side of your depression episode?

Ask This - When you are starting to feel pulled into depression, what are some scriptures that can ground you?

Pray This - Jesus, thank You for giving us clarity and soundness of mind. Thank You, that You and Your Word are my anchor and that You sustain me in my weakest moments. Lord, give me the vision of how You see me. Help me believe in what I cannot see. Comfort me in my hopelessness and speak to me with words of life. I trust that You are good and that You are God. Whatever may come, I will cling to the truth of Your Word. Amen.

Words of Comfort for Depression

"Concern should drive us into action, not depression."

~Karen Horney

Trapped

⇒ Luanne Nelson

"All at once he followed her like an ox going to the slaughter, like a deer stepping into a noose till an arrow pierces his liver, like a bird darting into a snare, knowing little it will cost him his life. Now then, my sons, listen to me, pay attention to what I say. Do not let your heart turn to her ways or stray into her paths. Many are the victims she has brought down; her slain are a mighty throng. Her house is a highway to the grave, leading down to the chambers of death."

~Proverbs 7:22-27 NIV

There were just too many people in my life dying and I hadn't had enough living yet to know how to get through the grief without breaking. So, I drank the pain away. Not at first. At first, I was prescribed a little Xanax to keep me from crying myself to sleep, and that worked great. Then, a few months later, my doc stopped prescribing it. I thought, "That's alright, I'll just have a glass of wine instead." The day came, a few years later, when I was drinking more than a bottle of chardonnay a day and couldn't stop. I sipped my wine from Baccarat crystal glasses convincing myself I didn't have a problem.

This, of course, is not a healthy way to grieve. As a matter of fact, it halts the grieving process. The grief was still there, I was just anesthetizing myself so I didn't have to feel it. I truly can count on one hand the number of times I've been inebriated in my life. I simply wanted that nice little pain-killing buzz going on so I didn't have to deal with the pain. We all try to avoid pain after all, don't we?

Which thinking he goes to the pasture willingly to his own destruction? Who goes cheerfully, not knowing they will be chastised? (Proverbs 7:22)

I didn't know alcohol is a depressant. I cried often. I felt sorry for myself. I did things I would never have done sober, cried some more and felt trapped. It has been said a person's will is not destroyed in an instant; rather, it is taken little by little, almost imperceptibly. We imagine we are strong as ever, not knowing we are being drained little by little until there is nothing left.

So, my dear friend, ride out the pain. Let it buck you right off of its' back. Land on the ground broken. It's alright. Eugene O'Neill said it beautifully, "Man is born broken. He lives by mending. The grace of God is glue."

Dear Jesus Lord God, please glue us back together. Keep us on Your straightaway path. We know You'll get us through this. You never fail us. Thank you for Your tender mercies. Amen.

Picture This - The walls are pressing in and it seems like there's no way out. Have you ever wondered where God is? Realize there is a life and death difference between sadness and depression. Suicidal thoughts warrant a call to your doc. Right now.

Ask This - How am I coping with the tragedy of loss? Am I eating too much, drinking my sorrow away, delaying the inevitable by numbing the pain instead?

Pray This - Dear Jesus Lord, help me to recognize the difference between sadness and depression. Take this cup of pain from me; replace it with the joy of your everlasting Glory. Amen.

Words of Comfort for Depression

"Depression is rage spread thin."
~George Santayana

That Inner Battle

⤏ Amy Sikkema

"Do not be anxious about anything, but in every situation, by prayer and petition, with thanksgiving, present your requests to God. And the peace of God, which transcends all understanding, will guard your hearts and your minds in Christ Jesus. Finally, brothers and sisters, whatever is true, whatever is noble, whatever is right, whatever is pure, whatever is lovely, whatever is admirable- if anything is excellent and praiseworthy- think about such things. Whatever you have learned or received from me or seen in me- put into practice. And the God of peace will be with you."

~Philippians 4:6-9 NIV

It steals our joy; causing pain and suffering. It's a thief and a liar. It's sneaks untrue thoughts in our minds and physically weakens our hearts. Its name: Depression. When we are walking through the valley, it is easy to be swept away in the negative, in the complaining, and in the fear. Depression is a veil that blinds us in every way. It puts fear at the forefront. Fear is a spirit so far from what God wants for us in this life.

Depression and anxiety try to attack in the late evening hours of the day, when my babies are tucked in bed, and when the stillness reminds me so deeply that I am still a widow. These sinister thoughts tell me I am completely alone and can't possibly do this another day. They tell me that I made all the wrong choices today and that I'm messing up God's plan. They tell me I am not strong enough to withstand this storm; surely, I will drown. They tell me I do not have what it takes to fulfill what God has revealed to me. I should just give up and take the easy way out.

And then, dear friend, I open my scripture and am reminded of this: Pray with a grateful heart and bring my requests to God. He reminds me and assures me of the truth, that I am never alone, and I can do all things through Him who gives me strength (Philippians 4:13). He reminds me that He is working all things for our good because we love God and we are called according to His purpose (Romans 8:28). He tells me I can withstand any storm because He is my rock and my salvation, my fortress where I will not be shaken (Psalm 62:6). He reminds me to never give up for we will reap a harvest (Galatians 6:9). He reminds me that I can experience the peace that passes all understanding.

Today I pray that if any of you are battling this monster, that the veil would be pulled back and that the Holy Spirit will give you rest. Amen.

Picture This - Identify a time in your life when you fought the "inner battle."

Ask This - What truths, as a child of God, do you cling onto to help you fight the devil's schemes of depression and anxiety?

Pray This - Dear Lord, thank You for Your goodness and sovereignty in our lives. Thank You for the truth that You speak into our hearts and for making me Your child. Help me to remember that, when the dark times come, I am Yours and You are mine. Help me to remember that my help comes from You and that You are a safe place and my refuge. Amen.

Words of Comfort for Depression

"The opposite of depression is
not happiness, but vitality."
~Andrew Solomon

Feel However You're Feeling

>> Maria Notch

"Come near to God and he will come near to you...Grieve, mourn and wail. Change your laughter to mourning and your joy to gloom."

~James 4:8-9 NIV

Depression is what happens when you're so deep in the darkness, you cannot see the light. In essence, it's the absence of light in the soul. Depression is how a person feels when Hope cannot be found. For me, this stage of my grief seemed to drag on and on and on as we suffered three concurrent miscarriages in eighteen months and a journey through three years of barrenness after that.

During my darkest days, I remember feeling, not only depressed, but guilty as well, because I was unable to be present as the fun and joyful mommy to our son as I wanted to be. As women, isn't that what we often do? Add a second layer of negative emotion to an already tough emotion! As if being sad isn't enough, we feel ashamed for not being joyful about the blessings we have. In addition to being lonely, we add feeling guilty for not recognizing the Lord is near. When we add guilt or shame on top of our sadness, it's the work of the enemy trying to overwhelm us.

I finally realized that it was okay to feel the way I was feeling. The Lord could handle my sadness, darkness, and grief. But I could not handle feeling that way along with guilt. I gave myself permission to be depressed and grieve. With a great capacity to love, comes a great capacity to feel pain. My pain stemmed from how deeply I loved each of my babies from the moment I found out I was carrying them.

Feelings aren't right or wrong. They are just feelings - emotions - sensations that wash over us. They do not define us and we get to decide how we are going to respond to them. I decided to be okay with however I was feeling and chose to recognize where it was coming from, to be able to respond in a healthy way.

James gave us permission to grieve and wail and mourn. Jesus himself grieved and wept at the loss of His friend Lazarus. Why would we be any different?

Lord, there are days that, like You, we weep and mourn. Help us accept that it's ok to feel depressed. Give us the strength to bear the darkness, pain, and loneliness a bit longer. Grace us with Your presence amidst the darkness and doubt. Amen.

Picture This - When in your life have you been in a physically dark space? Perhaps you toured a cave or visited a place where the sun seldom shines. Compare that to a time when you've been on a warm beach on a sunny day. If you're feeling discouraged, or like you'll never see the sunshine again, know that even the smallest glimmer of light can give you hope!

Ask This - Where is somewhere I can go or something that I can do that will bring light to my day today.

Pray This - Read 2 Peter 1:19 and ask the Lord to be Your "shining light in a dark place."

Words of Comfort for Depression

"Depression is when you have lots
of love, but no one's taking."
~Douglas Coupland

Don't Waste It

» Traci Weldie

"I love the Lord, for he heard my voice; he heard my cry for mercy. Because he turned his ear to me, I will call on him as long as I live."

~Psalm 116:1-2 NIV

Depression is beating me down. There are days I want to throw in the towel because life is just too much. It's me admitting that I am doing a lousy job of parenting my child with special needs. I can no longer stand on the playground, chatting it up with other moms, when—deep down inside—I know how tired and low I truly am.

Yet, in the midst of dark days, God has been sending me little messages. First, they came from the radio. Another from a Bible study. Finally, a clear message from our nightly family devotionals.

"DON'T GIVE UP."

In my desperation, I have cried out to God and He has heard me! This is where I have to start – knowing God hears me.

Then, he sent another message. "Don't waste this! I am up to something you can't see yet."

'But, I don't want this. I want to see what you are doing.'

"Just wait upon me. I have heard you. I have turned my ear to you. You can call on me. Just wait."

'Wait? Who wants to wait?'

If I fail to wait on the Lord, I will miss out on what He is doing with my life. If I fail to wait, I will never see the tapestry He has been weaving. If I fail to wait, I will stop changing . . . which means I will fail to look more like Jesus.

I must not waste the opportunity to grow more intimate with my Lord. During each of the moments I am laid out on the floor crying, I have never felt more intimate with Him. I must not waste the opportunity to be sanctified. I must walk through dark days to learn what it means to hold on to Jesus during the dark days. I must not waste the opportunity to become more like Jesus. God listened when I called for compassion and has lovingly reminded me that He's got this.

Dear Lord, thank You for hearing my cry. Thank You for turning Your ear to me and telling me I can call on You for all my days. Thank You for allowing me to go through tough times in order to see how truly life-changing Your love is. Help me to not waste this moment, but to bring You glory through my life. Amen.

Picture This - What experience has God allowed in your life that you need to start using?

Ask This - Describe the times you see God hearing your cries, seeing your pain, protecting you.

Pray This - God, teach me what it means to be sanctified through this process of pain and grief. I ask that You help me to not waste this experience but to envision the tapestry that you are weaving through my pain and grief.

Words of Comfort for Depression

*"In depression, in part because
of the shame attached to it,
it's harder to be honest."*
~Andy Dunn

He Is Enough

>> Lisa Danegelis

"Be still and know that I am God."

~Psalm 46:10 NKJV

"I feel like I have nothing left to fight with, I want to die."

"How can I live in daily agony, I can't keep doing this!'

"Where is God, why is He allowing this?"

This is a glimpse into the desperation I deal with daily as the online administrator of a group of very ill, traumatized souls. The suffering is extreme as we fight to stay alive, having been emotionally, mentally, and physically assaulted by wrongfully prescribed medications. I need to add "spiritually" to that list as well. I cannot imagine a more daunting test of faith than surviving years in this living hell. Dark depression is only one of the many debilitating symptoms.

The normal words of encouragement remained stuck in my throat one day when responding to a particularly desperate soul. As at times before, I felt my immediate words may be the only thing that would keep them breathing. A prayer seemed redundant. A Bible verse seemed inadequate. Commiserating seemed pointless. Offering cyber space hugs and high fives seemed trivial.

So I offered Him.

I wrote: "When nothing brings comfort, and every breath brings pain, when we can't see past our tears and we are sure we will not survive the rest of the day . . . think of Him . . . bloody and bruised on the cross. His flesh shredded and every one of His breaths was extreme agony. His soul was in hell, taking on every hideous sin of every human being who ever existed. He also felt the deep angst of His Father's love and presence removed. He did it for us! We can suffer one more day for Him. We don't need to understand it, we can beg for it to be removed, we can hate every minute of it, but please, please, don't ever say, "He's not worth it". We owe Him every shred of our being . . . He is enough."

And so we keep pressing on, following the group motto I felt compelled to use: #onemoreday4jesus.

Earlier in Psalm 46, David references the conditions God is asking believers to be still in: Mountains shaking and being cast into the sea, waters roaring and nations raging. We can add any number of things to the list, including the dark cloak of depression. God is sovereign; be still before Him. He is our refuge and strength, and, as verse 5 declares, He "will help us just at the break of dawn."

My frailty resonates with You, Jesus. Your earthly experience connects us deeply. Help me to sit in silence with You knowing You understand my human emotions. I picture You holding my hand and reassuring me that the path ahead will straighten and that You will not leave me desolate. Amen.

Picture This - Bring to mind the sight of Christ on the cross for every awful thing in this world. Hold on to that image as you work through your greatest trials.

Ask This - What platitudes have been fed to you by well-meaning souls offering comfort? Replace those words with the vision of Jesus you created.

Pray This - Write a prayer leaving all of your hurts at the foot of the cross with Jesus so that He may take them away in death and resurrect a new, healed life for you.

Words of Comfort for Depression

"Getting better from depression
demands a lifelong commitment."
~Susan Polis Schultz

Praise You In This Storm

⇀ Rebecca Grambort

"I lift up my eyes unto the hills - where does my help come from? My help comes from the Lord, the Maker of heaven and earth. He will not let your foot slip - he who watches over you will not slumber; indeed, he who watches over Israel will neither slumber nor sleep."

~Psalm 121:1-4 NKJV

'I will praise you in this storm, and I will lift my hands, for You are who You are, no matter where I am. And every tear I've cried, You hold in Your hand, You never left my side. Although my heart is torn, I will praise You in this storm. [1]'

I had never listened to Christian music before. I was flipping through radio stations, not in my home area and not knowing the stations. I landed on a station and God interrupted a very dark and painful day with this song. The music, new to me, warded off the fresh storm in my heart. I'd been traveling to the hospital to be by my husband's side, as he was experiencing life threatening complications from a routine surgery gone awry. Heaven must have commanded an army of angels to my case, because in that moment I felt the overwhelming Love of God camp out in the corners of my soul. Yes! I will praise you in this storm, my heart responded.

The song continued . . . *"I lift my eyes unto the hills, where does my help come from?"*

When I got to my husband's room, different clergy staff were at the hospital and I was visited by a Rabbi who shared the same words back to me. I didn't even know it was a scripture until He read it aloud for comfort at my husband's bedside. It was the day we were told we needed to say our last goodbyes. It was a clear sign that God was truly with me. I knew I had to keep looking up. He was the only One capable of sustaining me for the brutal storm I was about to endure. Excruciating pain relentlessly surged throughout my body tormenting me day and night, and I had lost the ability to sleep. In this scripture, God revealed to me that He did not need this valuable resource I so desperately craved. Each night, I would lift my eyes unto the hills - eyes-wide-shut. It was then that I sensed angels sitting at my bedside, tending to me. Some were even collecting and counting my tears. All of Heaven nursed me back to health during that lengthy season of grief, and later restored me to full health.

God does not slumber nor sleep. In fact, He is at complete rest even while He is at work. Even before we begin looking to the hills; He is already watching over us 24/7/365. He carefully pre-arranges a solution to prevent us from slipping. Keep looking to the hills . . . He does not slumber nor sleep!

Father, I will praise You in my storm and keep looking to You! Amen.

---

[1] Casting Crowns, "Praise You In This Storm"

Picture This - Imagine our God who never sleeps. How can this bring you comfort when you are restless and in need of recharging your own strength?

Ask This - In what ways can you envision Gods twenty-four-hour guard so that you can begin to close your eyes while you look unto the hills?

Pray This - Write a prayer about looking to the hills and how it gives you comfort that your God never slumbers or sleeps.

Words of Comfort for Depression

"The pupil dilates in darkness and, in the end,
finds light, just as the soul dilates in misfortune
and, in the end, finds God."
~Victor Hugo

The Many Faces Of Grief

⇻ Susan Brozek

"Why, my soul, are you downcast? Why so disturbed within me?"
                                                    ~Psalm 42:35a NIV

Depression tends to be the condition most associated with grief and loss. It is a key part of the process of grieving and mourning. People tend to think that grief should look a certain way on the face of a mourning person. When it comes down to it, though, there is no right or wrong way to grieve, and it doesn't necessarily always involve prolonged depression (though it certainly and oftentimes can). We put ourselves in a precarious position when we judge the grief processes of others. Everyone needs to process their grief and pain in their own way and it is important to let a person work through grief and loss without a tidy formula for what we think it "should" look like! For example, some people process it through journaling their feelings, writing a letter to the deceased or absent loved one, looking through old photographs, or spending time reminiscing with other family members. All of this is well and good. Others prefer none of the above and may choose to just pay weekly visits to the gravesite, while still others may never choose to go to the gravesite at all.

Those who lose a loved one can even feel relieved for various reasons, but these people are often afraid to admit to feeling that emotion due to fear of being shamed. It's okay to feel relief. Of course you love and miss the person you've lost, but it's not uncommon to feel that a burden has been alleviated-especially if that someone is lost before he or she is gone-when losing a loved one after a prolonged state of mental decline.

They may choose to isolate themselves, assuming that others won't understand. Other people may use creative outlets to express their pain and grief in drawing, painting, and the like. Some may train for a sporting event such as a marathon, and participate in it in honor of the deceased loved one. In Biblical times, grief was frequently processed via something the Jewish people call "sitting shiva", which is a tradition that still carries on to this day. Family members spend seven days together, often at the house of the deceased loved one, sitting on low stools and sharing meals and stories. Also typical in that era and culture was the "rending of garments"; those left to mourn would frequently tear their garments in half while crying out in emotional pain for the loved one who had passed.

We need to take into account the whole range of human behavior when considering pain and grief…and be cautious to not harshly judge the way someone is processing his or her particular loss, even though it might be a way that doesn't seem to make sense to us.

Today I pray – May Your grieving ones receive Your help today, Lord, in dealing with all of their emotions, including feeling depression and sadness, as they grieve their losses. Help them to take comfort in the fact that You understand and have experienced all of these same feelings Yourself! Amen.

Picture This - When you think of someone who is grieving, how do you see them?

Ask This - Ponder the many faces of and expressions of grief, including being downcast or depressed. Allow the Lord to minister to you if you may have unknowingly judged someone negatively for how they expressed their grief and mourning.

Pray This - Write a prayer that reminds you that God is big enough to handle every expression and emotion contained within the process of grieving the loss of a loved one.

Words of Comfort for Depression
*"I fell in love with Jesus because He
loved me when I couldn't love myself."*

My Mind Is Made Up

→ Neesie Cieslak

"You will keep him in perfect peace, whose mind is stayed on You, because he trusts in You. Trust in the Lord forever: for in YAH, the LORD is everlasting strength."

~Isaiah 26:3-4 NKJV

She's gone. Her number is still in my phone but I can't call her. My mother, at sixty-one-years-old, died suddenly of an aneurysm. Gone. All I could think about was one last conversation, which was done via text message, and it wasn't one with many warm feelings. We had lost my grandmother not long before and I had put my inheritance into missionary work. I believed it was my grandmother's wishes, but my mother wasn't sure and, this conversation, especially over text, wasn't going to go well. I told my mother that I wouldn't have this discussion this way and, "I love you, goodnight."

That was our last conversation . . . in conflict.

After my mother's passing, I slipped into a pit of despair and depression unlike anything I've experienced before. Darkness. Utter darkness. For over two weeks I could do nothing but lie in bed. My prayers were "Jesus" and that was enough for Him. Eventually the cloud began to shift and I could get my mind set more on His goodness and mercy. His peace began to fill my room and I was able to lift my head again. Jesus lifted my head and laid it on His beautiful lap. He soothed me in my depression. He brought me rest with His own "I love you, goodnight."

You may not be able to get up or lift your head because of your loss. Jesus is here to help you. He is not rushing us through our grief; He joins us in it if we allow. You can call His name and His perfect peace will begin to present itself. The Lord promises to respond to our trusting in Him. Moment by moment, day by day, we can turn and keep our minds on Him, releasing Jehovah's (YAH's) everlasting strength.

Father, I call to You now. I am setting my mind and heart on You. I trust You. Send Your perfect peace and lift my head. In Jesus' name, Amen.

Picture This - Picture Jesus lifting your head and placing it on His lap.

Ask This - What do you need from God in your depression?

Pray This - Jesus, help. I need _____, and I trust you to keep me. Amen.

Words of Comfort for Depression

*"Don't hide your scars. Wear
them as proof that God heals."*

Be A Companion

Instead of,
"You just need to
accept your situation,"
Try,
"I'm here for you
When you're ready."

With Words Of Comfort

You may not understand why they look back.
But you can love them through it.

The Seventh Stage

LOOKING BACK *(noun)*
           – according to your companions
[Luh-**keeng** Bak]

1. Reflecting
2. Living in nostalgia instead of the present
3. The bittersweet process of revisiting and remembering

*What does "**looking back**" mean to you:*

Eyes Forward

⇾ Victoria Dreckman

"Why do you keep looking backward to your past and have second thoughts about following me? When you turn back you are useless to God's kingdom realm."

~Luke 9:62 NIV

Sometimes we can be our own worst enemy, our harshest critic, and most damning judge. When you made the decision to follow Christ, did life get easier or harder? Initially, my life got easier. My devotion time was sweet and fulfilling. My prayers were pure and powerful. Praise and worship left me exhilarated and inspired. However, I met challenges that really tested my faith.

I looked back and realized that I allowed myself to fall away from faith, because I wasn't seeing the results I wanted, specifically in my marriage. I would read my devotions, but not take them to heart. I had stopped listening to the teachings at our women's fellowship meetings at church. Especially when it came to those hard truths, I chose the flesh over the spirit. It was a true Israelite moment. I walked away from the things that kept me in God's favor: obedience, faithfulness to His word, time in His presence. How did I get here? I knew better.

In my grief, my mind was barraged with, "don't shrink back," "run your race," and "work out your salvation." All I could see was that the starting line was just as far as the finish line. But Jesus' words in Luke 9:62, "useless to God's kingdom realm," convicted me. I didn't want to be labeled useless . . . ever!

I'm sure Jesus' disciples experienced this type of turmoil. Otherwise, I don't think He would have bothered to make this statement so plainly. Jesus knew we would have times of doubt, and insecurity would rear its ugly head. Looking back to the past doesn't allow us to focus on our present or enable us to catch His vision for the future.

Let me assure you, our Heavenly Father has deemed a very important purpose and plan for each and every one of His children. Keep your focus upward to the cross, and looking forward to the kingdom to come.

Heavenly Father, we know that You designed us for a greater purpose than we are able to comprehend. When we grieve over the past, and the decision to follow Jesus becomes challenging because of the obstacles and fears we face, help us to dive into Your Word more deeply. Lift us up by Your Holy Spirit and drench us in Your loving kindness. We ask that Your grace and mercy overflow into our lives as we pursue our assignments in the body of Christ and reaching forward to Your kingdom. Amen.

Picture This - Identify a time in your life when looking back seemed easier than the challenges ahead of you.

Ask This - What verse in the bible will be your "go to" verse to keep your eyes on King Jesus?

Pray This - Use that verse to write your prayer request.

Words of Comfort for Looking Back

"Remembrance and reflection how allied.
What thin partitions divides sense from thought."
~Alexander Pope

What Are You Looking For?

→ Neesie Cieslak

"Do not remember the former things, nor consider the things of old. Behold, I will do a new thing, now it shall spring forth, shall You not know it? I will even make a road in the wilderness and rivers in the desert."

~Isaiah 43:18-19 NIV

How does a person not remember? It seems almost impossible, yet it is what God said to His people in Isaiah 43. Don't remember . . . don't even make your past a consideration. This scripture stings me like a mad hornet! For years I allowed the abuses and losses of my childhood to define me and make me special. It was my identity. It came to my attention that my reasoning for holding on and continually reminding those around of the horror and trauma that makes the story of my life, was unhealthy. My remembering and regurgitation of the hurts, wrongs, and neglect was indeed keeping me stuck.

The Lord says, *'it's of old, look, I will do something fresh and new.'*

What keeps you from moving forward? What causes you to continually look back when there's a loss in your life? There comes a point where we must make a marked decision to behold the new thing the Father desires to do for our lives. Instead of our loss and wounds remaining the great mark of our life, anticipating the new.

The Lord will begin to reveal to us the vision and plan He has. He'll set us on a path and say, *'this is the way, walk in it'* and He'll supply the river of His Holy Spirit to refresh you along the journey.

Lord God I need Your strength to move on when it's time to move on. Help me to anticipate the newness of life that will flow from Your hands in blessings beyond my imagination. Thank You, Father. In Jesus' name. Amen.

Picture This - Envision yourself on a freshly paved road with bubbling rivers on each side, Jesus is saying, *'This is the way. Walk in it.'*

Ask This - Find two or three verses speaking of paths or rivers of God, let them refresh you.

Pray This - Jesus, thank You for the new fresh things You are doing in my life. Show me the new plans You have for me. Amen.

Words of Comfort for Looking Back

"Nostalgia is a file that removes the
rough edges from the good old days."
~Doug Larson

Calm My Soul

⇒ Ava Olivia Willett

"Remember how the Lord your God led you all the way in the wilderness these forty years, to humble and test you in order to know what was in your heart, whether or not you would keep his commands. He humbled you, causing you to hunger and then feeding you with manna, which neither you nor your ancestors had known, to teach you that man does not live on bread alone but on every word that comes from the mouth of the Lord. Your clothes did not wear out and your feet did not swell during these forty years. Know then in your heart that as a man disciplines his son, so the Lord your God disciplines you."

~Deuteronomy 8:2-5 NIV

In January 2014 my mom broke the news to me that we were moving. It was over 200 miles away from the home we lived in for seven years – the longest I'd ever lived in a house my whole life. As the free-spirit I am, I was awed at the idea of this adventure that awaited me this coming summer. New friends, new school, a new backyard- what more could a little girl wish for?

It wasn't as easy as I expected it to be. We had to sell our house. All fun and games were over as I remember walking into my childhood home for what would be the very last time. I didn't know for certain that it would be my last time walking in there, but something in my heart shifted and I had a sense of understanding.

Ever since my dad passed away, life was difficult and also wonderful at the same time, which seems ironic. We could be going through a time with no money or food, so we would eat these huge boxes of saltines that would fill us up. My mum would make us laugh. She would sometimes throw things at the wall, wanting to give up and, other times, when we would be up in the night, making grilled cheese, glad to have one another. Now, mum was going to be married – I wouldn't be able to crawl into bed with her when sad or scared at night. I just felt it deep within my soul – this was goodbye to this life I was living before. Nothing would be the same after I left. There were many wilderness seasons in my life that seemed harsh and bitter in the moment, but looking back at the bad times in life encouraged me to see how God still provided supper (even if it was just saltines) and good memories. I used to hang on to my past, afraid that growing older would erase these bittersweet memories from my mind. But as I matured in my faith and moved forward in my grief, I realized that even if I'd taken a hundred steps or only two, the point is that I still have to turn my head to look back at the past, for I don't live there anymore. I also grew and learned from my mistakes, and from examples in the lives of the people around me.

So when I returned home in May, before the move, I realized that what had changed wasn't the blooming flowers on the trees on that familiar street; I realized what had changed was not my home – but me. I began to recognize the scent of my own house, for I was not there long enough anymore to become desensitized to its scent. As I sat there on the dusty floorboards of a house that would no longer be mine, my soul was calm.

Jesus, as I look back at the past, I am reminded not to question why the former days may seem better than the days I am currently living (Ecclesiastes 7:10). Each day I am making more progress in my grief with the love and support from You and other loved ones around me. Amen.

Picture This - What lesson(s) from your past have shaped you into who you are becoming today?

Ask This - In which days did God provide a light in the darkness for your grief?

Pray This - Lord, amidst my previous sufferings, You always provided rest, laughter, and a full tummy. I am thankful that I can look at the past and see You by my side through it all. Amen.

Words of Comfort for Looking Back

*"Looking back on everything with a perspective
That only time and distance can give, there's only
One thing I still wish I could say to you in person . . .
Thank you for loving me."*
~Ranata Susuki

I See Thy Faithfulness

→ Amy Sikkema

"For everything that was written in the past was written to teach us, so that through the endurance taught in the Scriptures and the encouragement they provide we might have hope."

~Romans 15:4 NIV

When I think of teaching endurance, there are so many amazing examples of extraordinary people who endured trials of all kind and yet continued forward. Moses comes to my mind. He was asked to leave his land and lead an entire people out of Egypt. He had to fully and wholly trust that God was who He said He was. He came to the water when the Egyptians were right on their heels and didn't flinch. He did as God asked. He set down his staff at the shore of the water and, through the staff, separated the waters. The Israelites walked right through the parting.

Moses did not question God. He didn't say, *'What if?'* or *'How will we all make it through?'* He just did as God said with bold faithfulness and God answered.

It takes endurance to suffer through pain and trust that God is making beauty from the ashes. When we look back and remember how faithful God is to us, we can only choose to be faithful to Him and grateful in whatever He calls us to. For me, it was years of infertility, waiting on our family to grow; the diagnosis of my husband's brain cancer, and the unfathomable fear that comes with a terminal disease; and now a solo mother raising three beautiful children in the care of the Lord. He has brought me through each and every trial of life and shown His goodness through it; each time revealing more and more of who He is and who I am in HIM!

May we be able to look back and see the handiworks and faithfulness of God and his goodness and let it propel us into the future He has prepared for us! Amen.

Picture This - At what time in your life can you look back on, and see, God's faithfulness guide you through?

Ask This - In what situations has God revealed to you a different side of who He is?

Pray This - Dear Lord, thank You for always guiding me. May Your word always be a light unto my path and a lamp unto my feet. When I am discouraged or feeling weary, help me to look back upon the times when You revealed who You are in a way I wasn't expecting. Thank You for your faithfulness through all of my life. Until my last day, help me to remember Your plan for me is good because You are good. Amen.

Words of Comfort for Looking Back

"Whatever you do, never run
back to what broke you. "
~Frank Ocean

No Wisdom In Why

» Rebecca Grambort

"Do not say why were the former days better than these, for it is not wise to ask such questions."

~Ecclesiastes 7:10 NIV

When my husband passed away and I was left to single parent our daughters, looking back would become a stronghold in my life; I was longing for my former days. I was still grieving when I formed a new family and comparing my "first family" to my new situation was a major hindrance in moving forward. I kept wondering why I couldn't have what I had before. A blended family was so much more complicated, painful, and challenging than the traditional family I was originally blessed with. Asking why kept me stuck, unable to go on in my earthly life. At the end of the day, I wanted so desperately to move forward into the land of the living, but I kept waking up in a graveyard of memories.

I knew I had to let go of my whys and, later, concluded that—even if God would offer an explanation—I may not be capable of comprehending His answer. Perhaps that's why He seldom offers us a reply. His ways are not our ways (Isaiah 55:8).

There is no wisdom in asking why.

Accepting your today and giving yourself permission to step into tomorrow will bring healing. The road has been marked with suffering yet there is joy that awaits you in the goodness of the land of the living. Move your mind, will, and emotions towards the Solution and keep looking to the Prize – Jesus – who also did not ask why. He simply prayed, "not My will but Your will" and accepted His today. He did not look back. He was fully present and kept His eye on the prize and goal, enduring the cross to save His people. He came so that you could have life and have it to the full (John 10:10) . . . so, dear one . . . live!

Jesus, my Shepherd, I ask that You walk with me along this journey. When I look back, may I only see You encouraging me to keep looking forward.

Picture This - Losing a loved one is like an amputation – like losing a part of yourself. Picture now that, as a believer, you get to use the arm of Jesus moving forward. Your weakness is His supernatural strength. What strength for the journey will you have moving forward because of Jesus?

Ask This - In what ways do you think it is unhealthy to compare your former days to your present days? How can you change your focus from looking back to hoping forward toward the future.

Pray This - Help me to remember that my blessings are not contained in the past, they are contained in who God says He is and who He says I am.

Words of Comfort for Looking Back

*"I'll look back on this and
smile, because it was life and
I decided to live it."*

New Birth

» Lisa Danegelis

"Therefore, the Lord will wait that He may be gracious to you…...blessed are all those that wait for Him."

~Isaiah 30:18 NKJV

As I scraped away the earth from the dead stem of a beloved perennial, I saw the new birth of another forcing its way up through the same pocket of soil. Gardens are resplendent with the lessons of life and death.

I remember how my husband and I felt when we discovered we were not able to have children of our own after many years of waiting. The heartache seemed to rob my soul of all joy. All I had ever wanted was to be a mom of a half dozen kids. Yes, I had decided that six children would give me the "Brady Bunch" life I had adored when watching the 1970s show. Yet, here I was in my late twenties, barren . . . feeling dead inside.

God was writing this chapter of my life in a book I now didn't even recognize. The grief was consuming. Over the next year and a simple turn of the page, the narrative in my life changed and a new exciting chapter unfolded. It began with a phone call. Four months later a nine-hour-old baby boy was in our arms capturing our hearts. In God's time, He blessed us with four more perfect children. Our adoption agency, bewildered themselves, said they had never given more than three children to any family. Oh, the extravagance of our God! We truly were "blessed because we waited", as His Word said!

As with my treasured perennial, new life – more abundant life, grew right above the death in my womb and blossomed in my heart. As you wait on the Lord, stop focusing on what is missing and broken. Wait with patience, which in the Greek means, "sound and constant." The Lord waits *that He may* be gracious to us. What a promise! The blessing is in the waiting! His deep wisdom and love cannot fail as you wait for His gracious provision. The next chapter in the book of your life may be beyond your wildest dreams!

Heavenly Father, You know waiting is difficult for me. I ask that You give me the grace to be patient and full of faith as I wait before You. I know that You cannot fail me, and that You will bless me as I honor You during this time. Amen.

Picture This - What seeds are you planting in your life, now, that – in waiting – you can count on God to grow?

Ask This - What gifts in your life came to you in a way you didn't expect? List them here.

Pray This - Meditate on James 5:7-8.

Words of Comfort for Looking Back

"Rose-colored glasses are never made in bifocals.
Nobody wants to read the small print in dreams. "
~Ann Landers

Triumph Over Lies

→ Annabelle Ahlers

"My heart rejoices in the Lord; in the Lord my horn is lifted high. My mouth boasts over my enemies, for I delight in your deliverance."

~1 Samuel 2:1 NIV

The power of the Lord's perspective is astounding. Knowing that Jesus has already delivered us from our enemies as a result of the cross and, in the end, we will reign forever with the Lord, is life changing! In this age, we do not always experience that feeling of triumph, especially dealing with the pains of our pasts.

In my own life, having to revisit the past was a painful occasion that occurred a lot. As I was unable to confront my past, it had a way of confronting me. Most notably, all the times I felt that I had failed would appear before me . . . failed myself, others, family, God . . . the list was long. As someone who viewed herself as a failure, it was laughable to think that I could win at anything – yet alone at life! Triumph and victory, I decided, were just not for me.

I am not a failure. The truth of who I was, am, and am going to be, is that I am a child of God and a co-heir with Christ. In order to view my past accurately, I had to start to view myself as the Lord sees me. When I looked up to God as His beloved child, I was then able to look back with His eyes.

What happened was unimaginable. I began to see the past with a new, eternal lens. No longer was I full of shame, but I was beloved by God. I also realized that I did not just think I was a failure, I secretly thought, that God was, too. Somewhere along the way, I let my circumstances tell me who my God was. In this blame-shifting mindset, I did not realize my terrible narrative was not terrible at all.

As I can now see myself as a champion in Christ over everything that comes my way, I am able to go back and see my story for what it is: a beautiful love story with Jesus. Where I fell, he caught me. When I failed, he never did. When people let me down, he was there to uphold me. My story is not something I am ashamed of anymore, nor do I want to run away from it. Now, I am able to confront it with the revelation of who I am in Christ.

Thank You, Jesus, for who I am in You – a victor. You have delivered me from the pains of the past and the ones to come. In whatever circumstance I find myself, I can confidently rejoice over my enemies as a child of God. Amen.

Picture This - What are your current or past "enemies?" (tribulations, strongholds, stumbling blocks)

Ask This - How do you see yourself? How does God see you? Search it out.

Pray This - Lord, show me who I am in You. I want to know the truth of my circumstances – even if they are painful. No longer will I tell myself lies about You or my past; instead, I will hold fast to the truth of who You are and who You will always be – a Good Father. Amen.

Words of Comfort for Looking Back
*"The hardest part of moving forward
is not looking back."*

Be A Companion

Instead of,
"I've been there. I get it,"
Try,
"I'm here with you.
I'm listening."

With Words Of Comfort

You may not understand their loneliness.
But you can love them through it.

The Eighth Stage

LONELINESS *(noun) – according to your companions*
[lohn-lee-nes]

1. Awareness of a hole resulting from missing or needing someone
2. The achy emptiness that reminds you of a great loss
3. Overwhelming discontentment with being alone

*What does "**loneliness**" mean to you:*

I Am With You

Jessica Chase

"Turn to me and be gracious to me for I am lonely and afflicted. Relieve the troubles of my heart and free me from my anguish."

~Psalm 25:15-17 NIV

Where do you feel most alone? By yourself, or in a crowd, after everyone leaves, in the noise, or in the silence?

Loneliness is strange, it isn't really about the number of people around as much as it is about being seen and known. Made in the image of our triune God, the deepest longing of our heart is authentic connection.

For years I didn't want anyone to 'see' me, much less 'know' me. I believed that if anyone saw me or knew me they would run away. I didn't like me, and I didn't think others would either. Growing up in an unsafe home, survival is based on being able to read people and proactively respond, so I am an expert in being able to anticipate what people want and doing it before being asked. Although this helps in a survival situation, when applied universally to all relationships we are reduced to shape shifting circus performers.

I took my first step out of loneliness when I said yes to Jesus' invitation into family. I was so relieved when I learned that the foundation of our relationship is His GRACE, not by works (Ephesians 2:8)! As I studied the Word, I learned that we are invited into God's family where children can have confidence that they are beloved, that their Abba God is good. Over time the truth of adoption into God's family dropped deep in my soul alleviating my loneliness (Romans 8:15, Galatians 4:6).

Through prayer, old ways of thinking and doing are gone. God teaches us to look to Him to shape our identities, and trust that the overflow of right relationship with Him is the foundation of rightly loving self and others. Little by little I have learned to trust what God says about me and lean on my relationship with him, growing more and more comfortable being seen and known.

Lord Jesus come, wrap your arms around us when we feel lonely. Relieve our troubles and free us from our anguish that we may love You, ourselves, and others well. Help us to recognize the truth about who our Heavenly Father is, our place in the Kingdom family, and of who You are as our Brother, Bridegroom and King. Amen.

Picture This - When do you feel the loneliest? When and with whom do you feel the most accepted?

Ask This - Do you really want others to see and know you? What do you think keeps you from letting others in? What would it take for you to be more available to be known?

Pray This - Write a prayer asking God into your relationship so that He can become your companion and you can lean on Him in your loneliness.

Words of Comfort for Loneliness

"We sometimes think we want to disappear,
but all we really want is to be found."

God Sees

→ Karen Bruno

"She gave this name to the Lord who spoke to her: 'You are the God who sees me,' for she said, 'I have now seen the One who sees me.'"

~*Genesis 16:13 NIV*

Alone in the wilderness, Haggar gave the name, El Roi, to the Lord who spoke to her. "You are the God who sees me," for she said, "I have now seen the One who sees me."

She felt abandoned, abused, and lost until she encountered the God who sees. Nowhere else in scripture is God referenced to as El Roi, the God who sees. He saved this introduction for a desperate, single mother experiencing a great trial. We, too, can know Him as the God who sees us. He sees all of a trial, all of the people in it, all their actions, and all of ours. Nothing is kept from God.

Throughout my life, God has shown Himself as my banner, healer, provider, almighty. In my season of grief as a lonely, heart-broken widow, He was revealed as El Roi, the God who sees me. The attribute of being omniscient is both powerful and comforting. God was the only one who saw what really happened the night of my husband's suicide. He alone sees the dark places of grief we all experience. We can approach Him, with our unexplainable pain, and do not need to set the stage and explain the sources of our hurt. He sees it all, knows it all, and can carry us through it all.

Using counselling, especially in times of trauma, is very important. If you go through enough counseling, you discover the exhaustion of it. It's exhaustion that stems from recreating for the counselor the setting, the people, and their characters, thoughts, and emotions . . . the whole web of what occurred is relived so the counselor can envision what occurred. You're retelling your whole story. When approaching El Roi in counseling, he already knows every person and every occurrence. He knows the motivations of all involved and thus the counseling with Him is less burdensome. He lightens that piece of the burden. You can enter into His relief and crawl up into someone's lap like a parent who knows how badly you're hurt. In the counsel of God, we are spared the explaining because He can bring us rest through His all-knowing presence. Like Hagar in a vast desert of loneliness, we can be brought comfort and direction from the God who sees me. Plus, the other component is that God's Counsel comes from absolute truth. There is no more perfect a Counselor.

Today God, I call You El Roi, the God who sees me. Thank You for Your all-knowing presence in my life. I can stand fully before You, naked in my actions, thoughts, and ways without shame. Let me take comfort in knowing You have seen every pain, loss, abuse and trial in my life. Amen.

Picture This - Live with the assurance God sees everything. Any harm, abuse, loss or pain is seen by Him. We are never alone and He is always aware.

Ask This - What areas in my life do I still think God cannot see?

Pray This - Lord I want Your all-seeing presence to bring me comfort and healing.

Words of Comfort for Loneliness
"Loneliness and the feeling of being
Unwanted is the most terrible poverty."
~Mother Teresa

God Is My Companion

→ Amy Sikkema

"Do not conform to the pattern of this world, but be transformed by the renewing of your mind. Then you will be able to test and approve what God's will is- his good, pleasing and perfect will."

~Romans 12:3 NIV

Loneliness is the bottom of a widow's darkest hole. This hole is given to every person who has experienced loss. It's raw and real. Everything else about grief is thrown into this dark hole. Loneliness is death's companion. With this companion I am alone in parenting. I am alone in paying my bills. I am alone in making the best choices for my family as we move forward. And, the big one for many young widows: I am physically alone. I have no one to hold my hand. I have no one to comfort me when the tears fall. I have no one to partner with when the kids are overwhelming my patience. I have no one to be a "couple" with and now feel like the third wheel with loneliness as my companion.

When loneliness grabs hold, it can bring along deceiving company from patterns of this world – the type of company that can look sweet and promising to grief. It brings crutches like alcohol or drugs to numb, social media or work, any type of business- all serve as a distraction. Food is used to satisfy. We are shown an untimely new relationship to "fix" it all. All of these things are just empty boxes to hold all the emotions where they can be hidden away.

In my darkest hour of loneliness, I have prayed that God would instead reveal to me who He is as my companion. He has revealed to me that, in His companionship, He can satisfy that craving to be numb. He has great plans for me and I can't get distracted. He satisfies all of my needs. There is no need to hide anything from Him; he already knows. It is His love that is rebuilding and it is His handiwork putting all the pieces back together.

Dear friend, if you are feeling lonely, I pray that God reveals Himself and fills that deepest void in you that only He can. Amen.

Picture This - What might God be trying to reveal Himself to be through your loneliness?

Ask This - Are there any crutches, distractions, or patterns in your life that need to be evaluated? If so, what are they and what small step can you make today to change them?

Pray This - Dear Lord, thank You for the gift of who You are to me in my loneliness. Thank You for satisfying my every need. Help me to turn to Your word and focus on how You are growing me in this season. Help me to only drink from the well whose supply comes from You; the well of living water. Amen.

Words of Comfort for Loneliness
"Loneliness breaks the spirit."

The Company We Keep

» Karen Bruno

"When Job's three friends, Eliphaz the Temanite, Bildad the Shuhite and Zophar the Naamathite, heard about all the troubles that had come upon him, they set out from their homes and met together by agreement to go and sympathize with him and comfort him. When they saw him from a distance, they could hardly recognize him; they began to weep aloud, and they tore their robes and sprinkled dust on their heads. Then they sat on the ground with him for seven days and seven nights. No one said a word to him, because they saw how great his suffering was."

~Genesis 16:13 ESV

Job's friends came on their own accord, no one had sent for them. They traveled not for their own comfort,` but to comfort their friend. Allowing people to enter into our pain and grief is difficult on many levels. However, we must be mindful of God's design for us to be in fellowship with one another, to develop and experience true friendship. A friend loves at all times, even at our worst.

My friend, Renee, lives so remotely as a missionary that it took her three days of traveling to arrive in the US. She came after the funeral was over, after my family had returned to their out of state homes and after the intensity of major decision making had ceased. She came to comfort us. She sat in our grief for ten days.

Often, we isolate ourselves because we don't want to share our pain with others. The pain is so great; why would we expose others to it? I was relieved of this thought from a dear friend. After calling on him for the third time to fix the garbage disposal, my neighbor, Scott, wisely said "When you allow us to help you, it helps us grieve too." Those words freed me to ask for help, support and broke down walls of loneliness.

Grief can isolate and bring bouts of loneliness. God's design is for us to experience and receive comfort from not only Him but through our relationships with others. Allowing people to come and be present in our suffering is a healing gift for everyone.

Lord, keep me from loneliness by bringing supportive, healthy people into my life to sit with me during this trial. Amen.

Picture This - What would your life be like if you could allow others to sit in the rawness of your suffering and be comforted by their presence?

Ask This - What is stopping me from allowing close friends to enter into the painful part of my life?

Pray This - Lord, thank You for the gift of friendship. I ask, Lord, that You provide me with strength to allow those people into the painful parts of my life to support and comfort me. Amen.

Words of Comfort for Loneliness

*"Loneliness expresses the pain of being alone
and solitude expresses the glory of being alone."*
~Paul Tillich

Riches In The Dark

» Lisa Danegelis

"Moses drew near the thick darkness where God was."

~Exodus 20:21 NKJV

"It's me, God, where are You? What are You doing? I'm scared." I was so very lonely. My church family had dissolved, the pastor I had cherished was disillusioned, my work friends had dissipated, and others seemed to scatter. My heart was empty and aching. This loneliness amidst escalating anxiety, depression, and insomnia was consuming. Life had thrown me blow after blow and I felt like I was down for the count.

The God who had been convenient, a genie-in-a-bottle, and a quick-fix had orchestrated a wilderness experience that would drive me to my knees before Him alone. And do you know where He was? In the dark abyss . . . with me. This descent into loneliness and bewilderment would be the rock bottom He would use to rebuild my life – a life with Him in the center.

There we sat together in silence as He held my tattered heart in His hand. I knew He had to be enough. He was no longer an acquaintance; He was my next breath. He was no longer an option; He became my all. God and I have been walking this wilderness path hand in hand for years now, which in time, became scattered with flickers of light in the form of new friends. These precious ones have embraced me in the dark night of my soul, becoming even more dear than those left behind.

Darkness is rich and abundant with growth. Life sprouts in the shadows of the womb, and seeds are nurtured in dark soil. Even the richest foods such as: coffee, chocolate, and red wine express God's love for the mystery of darkness. Moses knew his God; the God who only shines brighter in the darkest night.

The words of King George VI on his deathbed resound with wisdom: "I said to the man at the gate, "Give me a light that I may walk safely into the unknown. Go out into the darkness and put your hand into the hand of God. It shall be to you better than the light and safer than the known."

Praise You mighty God, for light and dark! Give me the wisdom to look for You in all circumstances. Please give me the courage Moses had to draw near to You when darkness surrounds, knowing You will meet me with loving arms. Amen.

Picture This - Have you ever used one of those charcoal face masks? They go on black and thick but, when wiped away, leave behind skin that is soft, clean, and clear. What can the darkness soften and clarify in your life?

Ask This - What action can you take today to feel peace in the darkness?

Pray This - Invite God into the dark times of your life. Write your prayer here.

Words of Comfort for Loneliness
"Loneliness is not the absence of affection,
But the absence of direction."
~Mike Murdock

With Hands Raised, I Will Worship

» Traci Weldie

"As long as Moses held up his hands, the Israelites were winning, but whenever he lowered his hands, the Amalekites were winning. When Moses' hands grew tired, they took a stone and put it under him and he sat on it. Aaron and Hur held his hands up – one on one side, one on the other – so that his hands remained steady till sunset."

~Exodus 17:11-12 NIV

I used to run half marathons, coach volleyball and throw a baseball in the backyard for hours. Last year, I was diagnosed with Rheumatoid Arthritis (RA) and it has severely affected my life in twelve months' time. I went from an extremely physically active woman to a woman in constant pain and depression over the loss of what I used to be able to do.

When I was diagnosed with RA, I retreated. I did not want to burden anyone with my expanding grief of losing the physical ability to function. My desire was to isolate myself intentionally, thinking no one would understand what I was going through. I had lost any sense of normalcy in my life and now I was losing the physical ability to even raise my arms.

I have often read the story of Moses leading the Israelites through the wilderness all the while being attacked by several wicked tribes. I love in Exodus 17 the story of God's chosen people facing an attack by the Amalekites and as Moses stood atop a hill overlooking the battlefield, the Israelites were winning as long as Moses' hands were raised. When Moses grew tired, he had two friends there literally holding his hands up in order to ensure victory.

Most days, I cannot lift my arms anymore. My heart's cry each day is to stand in the humbled posture of a woman admitting I need God. *'I've got nothing here. God, it's up to you to hold me up.'*

Even if only figuratively, I stand with my arms raised, the only way to start my day . . . and get through it for that matter. But notice that Moses got tired. He couldn't continue to lift his hands. What Moses needed were two friends who held Moses up when he could not do it anymore. Two friends who understood the need for Moses to stand in that humbled position, two friends who did not even say anything, they just held up his arms for him. I need those two friends and cannot afford to intentionally isolate myself. I trust God will provide, I just need to be willing to put myself out there.

Lord, thank You for creating us to be in community with others. I thank You that You have not left us alone in our sufferings and trials, but instead give us family and friends that hold our arms up until we win the battle. Amen.

Picture This - Identify and describe two people in your life who are holding you up even in your trial.

Ask This - What is the significance of the posture of raising your arms to heaven, especially in the midst of suffering?

Pray This - Read the scripture listed in the devotional above and earnestly seek God today.

Words of Comfort for Loneliness

"You're only lonely if you don't like the person you're alone with."
~Wayne Dyer

Out Of The Mud And Mire

→ Heather Taylor

"I waited patiently for the Lord until he turned to me and heard my cry. He lifted me out of the slimy pit, out of the mud and mire, he set my feet on a rock and gave me a firm place to stand."

~Psalm 40:1-2 NIV

Dark loneliness is the very definition of depression for me. Even if you are in a room surrounded by everyone who ever loved you, you still feel completely alone.

There was a time when I thought that loneliness was going to consume me. I had lost all joy in my life and had to drag myself out of bed every day. I didn't have the energy to shower, so most days I would simply do without. My world consisted of one continuous fight to find a reason to stay alive for another day. For me, that reason was my two children. They needed a mom and although I hated myself, I loved them way too much to leave them alone.

One afternoon, after a very loud, very long fight with my husband, I went into my laundry room to do something I seldom did anymore: LAUNDRY!

I began to cry, and once the tears started they didn't stop. I found myself laying on the floor with the piles of unwashed clothes surrounding me and doing something else I hadn't done in a very long time, praying.

I begged God to save me from myself. I needed a Savior, I needed a light to fill the darkness and love to fill my loneliness. I needed a miracle!

Somewhere through the crying and praying and more crying I fell asleep.

When I awoke I knew that God had lifted me out of my pit, and placed me on solid ground. I had to break to be healed, I had to ask to be heard. God hears our cries even when we think we are all alone. He wants nothing more than to save you from the mud and the mire.

All you have to do is ask.

I've been where you are and I was set free. Please ask God to raise you out of that pit of darkness. He can stop your pain.

Lord, I pray that You will take the loneliness that I am feeling and replace it with comfort and security while I rest. Help me to look up to You and to Your presence so that I know I am never truly alone.

Picture This - Picture God fixing your biggest mess while you rest in His comfort and security.

Ask This - Are you willing to surrender the pain of your loneliness and let Him comfort you before you fall into your own messy pit and find yourself in the dark?

Pray This - You have seen my prayer: "Lord, I pray that You will take the loneliness that I am feeling and replace it with comfort and security while I rest. Help me to look up to You and to Your presence so that I know I am never truly alone. Amen." Pray this as your own or write another prayer for what you desire God to bring in place of your loneliness.

Words of Comfort for Loneliness
"The loneliest moment in someone's life is when
they are watching their whole world fall apart
and all they can do is stare blankly."
~F. Scott Fitzgerald, "The Great Gatsby"

Comforter, Counselor, Advocate

» Luanne Nelson

"But the Advocate, the Holy Spirit, whom the Father will send in my name, will teach you all things and remind you of everything I have said to you."
~John 14:26 NIV

I have a brother named Joseph and a sister named Elizabeth I've never met. They died before I was born.

As a young teenager, I found the death certificates while snooping through papers in my parent's unlocked safe. I was not supposed to know. The discovery explained much to me. Like, why my Mother baked so many birthday cakes when it wasn't anyone's birthday. Like, why my Mother was so overwhelmingly protective of us, my surviving siblings and me.

I think we all have secret rituals that keep us tied together with the ones we've lost. It's a way to keep them alive somehow.

Mother is an expert in the art of graceful losing. She's lost children, her husband, and—most recently—large parts of her memory. She is ninety years old and remembers every detail about how to bake her delicious lemon chiffon pie. She does not, however, remember anything we've talked about two minutes earlier.

Many years ago, I was mean to her. Time passed. I grew up. Embarrassed and sorrowful, I apologized. She immediately completely forgave me. We've talked nearly every day since then for the last twenty years. This is the person she knows, now. I truly believe the dementia is a blessing. She has lost so much and doesn't even realize she's lost it. She asks me if I've seen Dad lately and I tell her he's waiting for her in Heaven. She seems to be happy about that. I will keep calling her, knowing the day will come when she will not remember me. I'll call her anyway. She is not lonely. She is very loved. Her heart knows this. Her Spirit lives this.

"Now it is God who makes both us and you stand firm in Christ. He anointed us, set his seal of ownership on us, and put his Spirit in our hearts as a deposit, guaranteeing what is to come." 2 Corinthians 1:21.

Father, today I ask You to shine a light in the dark. Help me to receive Your joy even during the darkest of nights.

Picture This - Picture yourself in a situation where you do not know anyone, you do not speak the language and you can't remember how you even got there. Can you feel God's arms around you keeping you safe?

Ask This - What does the loss of memory as a blessing look like? What ways can I bless the person who is fading away? What can I do to respect the loss of memory as a part of the journey in Jesus Christ?

Pray This - Dear Jesus Lord, please never let me forget all things work for the good for those who love You and who have been called according to Your purpose (Romans 8:28). Amen.

Words of Comfort for Loneliness

"Loneliness does not come from having no people around, but from being unable to communicate the things that seem important to oneself, or from holding certain views which others find inadmissable."

~C.G. Jung

You're Never Alone

→ Maria Notch

"He will allure her to the desert and speak tenderly to her."

~Hosea 2:14 NIV

The desert is a dry and desolate place, one to which most people might not easily be allured. The squelching heat and blowing sand fend off those other than the most resilient and the sheer vastness of the landscape isolates anyone who dare stay awhile. Yet the Lord allures us to the desert to speak tenderly to our hearts. The desert is where He knows we will be humbled and vulnerable. The desert is where He leads us, so that we remember we need Him and the saving food and drink He is for us.

For me, the desert stretched for nearly five years. The dryness and drought came from three concurrent miscarriages, years of secondary infertility, multiple surgeries, and extreme loneliness. In the desert is where I learned just how close the Lord was to the brokenhearted, and that—despite the fact that others couldn't relate to my situation—the Lord was the only One I needed.

I'm a people person and a verbal processor, so the Lord really needed to take me into the desert and get me alone with Him, so that I would turn to Him . . . and Him alone. He accomplished that by allowing me to endure pain that most mothers don't have to endure (thank God!) and burdening me with a load to which very few people I knew could relate. It was amidst that pain, isolation, and loneliness that I realized God the Father lost His Son, too. He also gave us women the example of the Virgin Mary, who lost her Son, so that we'd have a Biblical example to follow.

It is in those desert times that the Lord wants to speak tenderly to our aching hearts. He wants us to long for HIM as the nourishment that sustains us and the salve that heals our wounds. He wants us to intimately know His voice and His tender touch.

Lord Jesus, we thank You for the desert times in our lives. We thank You for modeling to us what it means to faithfully endure the desert and still cling to the Father's truth. We rest in the truth that You are with us, even in the desert. Settle our hearts so that we may be open to Your tender word and healing touch.

Picture This - Imagine the Lord physically isolating areas of your heart, so that He can speak tenderly to them? What parts of your spirit has He set aside for this conversation into your life?

Ask This - Are you allowing God to nourish and heal those areas He has identified, or are you shutting Him out?

Pray This - Read through the Old Testament story of the Israelites in the desert and notice how God provided food for them every morning and evening. He was present to them every day they were in the desert and is near to you as well. Spend time in prayer over the verses you discover in your Old Testament study time.

Words of Comfort for Loneliness

"Only God can truly satisfy our loneliness."

Weapons In The Word

→ Rebecca Grambort

"No temptation has overtaken you except what is common to mankind. And God is faithful; He will not let you be tempted beyond what you can bear. But when you are tempted, He will also provide a way out so that you can endure it."

~1 Corinthians 10:13 NIV

After the sudden and unexpected death of my spouse, I was blindsided. Plagued with what I refer to as empty-bed-syndrome, loneliness encompassed my days as young single widow.

WARNING! REAL TALK:

Sex in my marriage was a blessing and, now widowed, it was considered a sin! To be honest, I was struggling and I was mad! It wasn't just about sex, though. I believe that the hormonal factor was just one of the many symptoms of my loneliness and excruciating grief. I didn't understand, at that time, that Jesus could be my intimate companion in an entirely different and Holy way. My focus was askew. Like Eve, I was focused more on what I couldn't have than what I so abundantly did have and it led me into temptation and sin.

I became pregnant and had a shotgun marriage that quickly failed. Now, I was not only a single mom to two young daughters, but also an infant son. My lack of self-restraint added more grief and heartache for me to deal with. I had put myself in a good hard corner – thankfully I might add (and not just because of the blessing of my son)! This is exactly where I needed to be in order to hit rock bottom and land safely on The Rock – the only One who could save me. That is where I surrendered my will to Jesus and took responsibility to bring my flesh under control as I leaned on Him for strength through His Spirit and through His Word.

God is faithful to always provide us the way out with weapons in The Word for any problem that we encounter big or small. 1 Corinthians 10:13 is the strategy and solution for any temptation that we face. He is the only One who can make our impossible situation possible, and put out any fire that has been started by our sinful flesh, with the powerful Holy Water of The Word!

Lord, Your Word says that I cannot be tempted more than I can bear and that You will always provide a way out. Please reveal to me the way out! Amen.

Picture This - What rewards do you think you might reap by resisting temptation and choosing to take the way out that God is faithful to provide?

Ask This - What other *weapons in the word* can you find and use as strategies to wage war against the enemy of your soul in your present storm? Write them here.

Pray This - God, help me to use these weapons in the word and trust these weapons are trustworthy to defeat whatever the enemy brings my way!

Words of Comfort for Loneliness

"The most daring thing is to create stable communities
In which the terrible disease of loneliness can be cured."
~Kurt Vonnegut

A Deeper Place In God

Lisa Danegelis

"And you will seek Me and find Me when you search for Me with all your heart. I will be found by you says the Lord, and I will bring you back from your captivity."

~Jeremiah 29:14 NKJV

Did God ever go missing in your life? What do you do when He hides? He said He would never leave us or forsake us; so where is He when He seems to have disappeared?

I read once that a holy hide-and-seek game is found throughout the scriptures. The effort to live out our faith is at the heart of the challenge. It will take conviction, fortitude, trust, and patience, but in the end, God is no different than an earthly father who cannot wait for his child to find him! There is a celebration with hugs and laughter; there is victory!

The ravages of wrongly prescribed psychiatric drugs had anesthetized my soul. I became disassociated and deeply depressed. The peace, the thrill when worshipping, and the simple awareness of Him completely vanished . . . for years. There is a story of three women kneeling in prayer, each at a different place of faith in their journey. God knew what each needed. He hugged and comforted the first, simply smiled at the second, and completely ignored the third as He walked past. After years of suffering with a silent God, I felt like a fourth woman needed to be added to that story!

I wrote in my journal the first year, *"There must be a place with God I have not accessed yet, beyond believing, way beyond what I have experienced before. Favorite Bible verses don't resonate. My tattered and treasured devotional seems blank. Moving worship songs don't move me. I've heard it said that joy and peace are always available, but what about when they're not? What do you do then? You do what Job did, you do what I am doing, you hang on anyway, not looking for a feeling, a word, or a thought. You hold on with sheer determination knowing, yes, knowing it all has to be true. Because really, if it's not, what on earth are we doing this for?"*

I am still the "fourth woman" in the story, now years later. But she is changed. Oh how she has changed! She sees God everywhere and in everything! God became visible to me in the darkness. And soon I believe, I will be that first woman! I won't only be getting a smile, but leaping victoriously into His arms!

God uses the darkest night of the soul to play hide-and-seek. Desperation to find Him will drive you to look in the dark corners rich with mystery. When you search with all of your heart, you will not only find Him, but you will come to know Him, and the freedom only He can give.

Father of mystery, may I never stop looking for You! Use the desperate situations in my life to draw me closer. I know You are waiting just around the corner, and at just the right moment I will jump into Your arms of love and find the deeper freedom available in knowing you intimately. Amen.

Picture This - List the places in your life where you forget to look for God? Where and why?

Ask This - Which of the four women of prayer do you most relate to and why: the comforted woman, acknowledged woman, ignored woman, or searching woman?

Pray This - Ask God how to seek Him in the darkest corners of your pain.

Words of Comfort for Loneliness
"Loneliness has been described as a chronic disease with no redeeming features."
~John Cacioppo

Alone In My Sin

→ Reji Laberje

"For Jerusalem sinned so horribly; therefore, she is tossed away like dirty rags. All who honored her despise her now, for they have seen her stripped naked and humiliated. She groans and hides her face. She indulged herself in immorality and refused to face the fact that punishment was sure to come. Now she lies in the gutter with no one left to lift her out. 'O Lord,' she cries, 'see my plight. The enemy has triumphed.'"

~Lamentations 1:8-9 TLB

When I reflect on my life, my biggest pains have been caused by . . . me. I spent more of my life as an Atheist than as a believer and the faithlessness to which I proscribed was accompanied by a moral-less life. Maybe it was a "more-or-less" life, since the days after it have shown me how much I really wasn't living at all. I digress.

When you're the one who caused your own anguish and, through it, the anguish of others, you feel very alone. It's awkward and difficult to relate to others in your grief, not because people say all the wrong things to the grieving, but because—when you caused your own pain— they don't say anything at all to you. They offer sideways glances and behind-the-back whispers. What's more is that you don't even feel like you deserve their words of comfort. You are judged because others feel like your sins carry a weight that is greater than that of their own sins.

Satan himself fell from the "mere" sin of pride. In the eyes of God, sin is sin and grief is grief. He feels the same about a liar as He does about a murderer; He wants to heal both of the pain caused by a sinful life and He wants to heal them as much as He does the people who are harmed by the sins of others. They are all His children. God leaves no room for a gray area in His Kingdom and, whether your pain was caused by others . . . or by yourself . . . He will hear your cries. They will not fall on deaf ears. He hears every cry through the lens of Jesus, who took the judgment and punishment for all of our sins. You never have to be alone in your grief, even when that grief was caused by your own actions.

From a valley I dug on my own, it was God to whom I could turn; in His mercy, He picked me up and said, 'What took you so long? I have plans for you.' He has since used me for good and surrounded me with believers who keep me from feeling alone.

God, thank You for being a God who pulls us out of the gutters we put ourselves in. Thank you for hearing our cries, even when our pain comes from our own sinful choices. Thank you for sending Your Son to cover every human and every sin. I am humbled at Your gift of grace. Amen.

Picture This - What does life look like when you have forgiven yourself?

Ask This - Make a list of those you can go to with your troubles. Where does God fall on that list? Is He on it at all?

Pray This - Read Luke 23:39-43 aloud, reminding yourself that God is there for every pain and Jesus is the friend of every sinner.

Words of Comfort for Loneliness

"Being alone is being away from others because
You choose to be. Being lonely is when there
Is no one there for you."

He Is There

⟶ Susan Brozek

"….but the Spirit Himself makes intercession for us with groanings which cannot be uttered."

~Romans 8:26b NIV

I wonder as I write this how many people reading this book have experienced the feeling of being completely and utterly alone. I'd like to think very, very few. But in reality, loneliness is part of the common human experience and condition, and it's different than just being alone. Alone is a neutral descriptor, but loneliness is a perceived emotional experience. Common times you may feel loneliness might be the first time you move away on your own as an adult to a new geographic location, or make lifestyle changes that remove you from your friend circles.

You can even be lonely in the context of a relationship because you feel misunderstood. Our God knows us intimately; he never misunderstands us, is far from us, or leaves his children stranded. While we may know that God is always with us, the longing for interaction with another human being can be powerful, as well as very painful, when we feel such a connection is not available to us at a time when we most need it. As we progress through the process of grieving, we can experience moments when we feel entirely alone in our mourning. We may think to ourselves that no one else on earth could possibly feel as heartbroken, crushed, hopeless . . . or alone.

It's during those moments of loneliness when the Spirit of God Himself intervenes and comes to our aid. God's Word says that He intercedes "with groanings which cannot be uttered". Think about it: the Holy Spirit Himself, groaning on our behalf to Elohim, the Creator of the Universe!

In looking at the Greek word for "groanings" in this passage from Romans, the Greek Interlinear Concordance reveals that "stenazo" (the word for "groanings") has a rich range of meaning. "Stenazo" means to sigh, to groan, to wail, to shed tears, to weep silently, to give formal expression to grief by singing a dirge, to weep audibly, to cry as a child, to lament, and to express grief by inarticulate or semi-articulate sounds.

It amazes me that the Holy Spirit employs all of these diverse methods as He intercedes for us to our Heavenly Father! He pleads our case through sounds, not even necessarily through words in this particular passage of Scripture! That fills my heart with a brand-new glimpse of understanding in terms of just how much He loves us, and how we truly are never alone. Even in our darkest hours when we think our pain can't get any more intense, we can know that His Spirit is praying for us, even through mere sounds. He longs for us to truly comprehend that He will never leave us nor forsake us, much less in our time of need. This is a promise we can count on when we feel that there is no human being there for us. But . . . HE. IS. THERE.

Today I pray – Help all of those who are lonely to know in their heart of hearts that You have promised them that You would never leave nor forsake them, Lord. Enable them to strongly sense Your presence today! Amen.

Picture This - What do you see (or hear) when you think about the Holy Spirit interceding for you in the ways described above?

Ask This - Has there ever been a time when you doubted God's promise that He never leaves you nor forsakes you? What were (or are) the surrounding circumstances in your life when you doubted?

Pray This - Holy Spirit, I am so moved that You pray for me on my behalf with groanings and sounds. Draw me ever closer to You as I walk through this journey of grief. I need You. Amen.

Words of Comfort for Loneliness

"All relationships have only one law.
Never make the one you love feel alone,
Especially when you are there with them."

Be A Companion

With Words Of Comfort

Instead of,
"You'll get through this
Before you know it,"
Try,
"I want to be here for
you. Take your time."

You may not understand their transition.
But you can love them through it.

The Ninth Stage

TRANSITION *(noun) – according to your companions*
[tran-**zish**-*uh*n]

1. A passage from one place of being to another
2. The place between not anymore and not yet
3. The prelude to transformation

*What does **"transition"** mean to you:*

Where Else Can I Go?

⇻ Karen Bruno

"As a result of this many of His disciples withdrew and were not walking with Him anymore. So Jesus said to the twelve, "You do not want to go away also, do you?" Simon Peter answered Him, "Lord to whom shall we go? You have words of eternal life."

~John 6:66-68 NIV

I read my Bible every day. My grandmother, the sweet woman to whom I attribute praying me to salvation, taught me that discipline.

She simply stated "If you want to be with God, be in His Word."

I wanted to be with God, so I followed in her footsteps- that is until the day my husband died. That day I did not read the Bible, and I didn't read it the next or the next. Weeks went by; I glared at my Bible resting on the side table where I would sit in a soft chair to read it every day. Dust collected on the suede Bible cover. I did not want to be with God.

The group of disciples, beyond the twelve chosen, described in John chapter 6 were faced with a truth they would not accept and thus walked away. They turned back to their old ways, back to a religious hopelessness. Peter knew Jesus was speaking truth about eternal life and proclaimed there was nowhere else to turn to live in truth.

The disciples in this verse had turned away because life is hard, truth is hard and following Jesus is hard. My life was hard, the truth of my life was hard, and following Jesus was hard. I had set my Bible down and walked away.

In my youth, I had walked down the dark, empty path of new age religion.

I had chosen a dangerous and careless lifestyle, as if I didn't care whether or not I lived.

I did drugs, too . . . like, a ton of drugs.

Each of these paths led to a life of emptiness until I had nowhere else to go.

When faced with the truth and eternal words of God versus the life choices and paths of the world, the realization that you can't have both paths becomes clear. One must be chosen and you get to pick it. All the other paths I had tried in my youth were just stumbling through life. I knew truth; I drank it in every day. I knew I had to turn back to Jesus.

Finally, the day came when I sat in my chair and looked at my dusty Bible.

The day after that, I unzipped the cover and blew off the dust.

The next day, I opened the pages . . . and was home again.

Lord, help me to accept the difficult truth of my trial. Do not let me turn away from You and wander aimlessly in untruth. Guide my journey of grief on Your path and not my own. Amen.

Picture This - Envision a world of people living authentically in truth.

Ask This - If you turn away from God what will take His place?

Pray This - Lord, Your arms are always open for our return and Your patience, when we wander, is endless. Thank You that I may choose to live fully in Your truth and follow You every day.

Words of Comfort for Transition

"Your life is a story of transition.
You are always leaving one chapter behind
while moving onto the next."

The Process Of Life

» Victoria Dreckman

"Jesus replied, 'You don't understand yet the meaning of what I'm doing, but soon it will be clear to you.'"

~John 13:7 TPT

One of the hardest things to do is watch your child grieve and struggle with a situation. I'm not speaking of the kind of grieving when someone passes, but the kind they experience when they don't understand the "whys" of life.

Three months before our family moved from St. Louis to Milwaukee, the reality of this huge change set in . . . hard. The sign was in the yard, we had an open house every weekend, and the school year was coming to a close. My son, in particular, was having a difficult time. He became angry and obstinate at the thought of leaving his newly established friendships. This whole time, I had been praying for a way to help him understand, but nothing was coming to me.

One afternoon, he came downstairs as I was packing boxes in the kitchen. "Mom, I think I know why we have to move now."

I was intrigued by his statement, "What reason is that?"

He proceeded to tell me the story from his devotional. To be honest, I didn't really know if he read it anymore since it was a couple years old. He shared, "There was this bible verse that said, 'Jesus replied, 'You don't understand yet the meaning of what I'm doing, but soon it will be clear to you.'" He then added, "I guess Jesus is telling me that, even though I don't understand and I am upset now, soon I will find out the reason we have to move."

My jaw dropped to the floor! My ten-year-old had an amazing encounter with the Word of God.

Sometimes, there are transition periods in our lives that don't make any sense to us at the time. It is absolutely alright to grieve through the transition process.

The words of Jesus still ring true to us today: "Soon it will be clear to you."

It is our trust in an Almighty Omniscient Loving God that will see us through the unknown times and usher us into His perfect will.

Let's pray for His perfect will to come to pass in the midst of your transition.

Heavenly Father, we thank You that even through our transitions in life, You are faithful and loving. We thank You for Your provision and Your timing that are always perfect. Help us to seek, not our will, but always, Your will be done, on earth just as it is in heaven. In Jesus' Name. Amen.

Picture This - Recall a transition period that was particularly challenging. How could you grow from such a time?

Ask This - What did you learn about yourself during this transition?

Pray This - Thank You, Lord, for teaching and guiding me through the transitions in life. Amen.

Words of Comfort for Transition
"It is when we are in transition
That we are most completely alive."
~William Bridges

184

Between The Rock And The Hard Place

>> Kimberly Joy Krueger

"Now Deborah, a prophetess, the wife of Lapidot, was judging Israel at that time. She used to sit under the palm tree of Deborah between Ramah and Bethel in the hill country of Ephraim; and the sons of Israel came up to her for judgment."

~Judges 4:4-5 NASB

Transition is simply the place in between "no longer" and "not yet." It's not a fun place to be; you've said goodbye to one place (or person or thing) and are waiting for the new, but don't yet have it. No one I have ever talked to has said they liked transition. Not in the final stages of birthing a baby (the most painful part of labor before we hold our new baby) and certainly not after losing someone or something we love. Let's face it. The place in between kind of sucks.

Deborah sat in a place in between—on purpose. She chose to sit between Ramah, which means "a hill" and Bethel, which means "the House of God." Maybe neither option appealed to her. This makes me think of a grieving person who feels like their great loss has put them between a rock and a hard place. The rock; their pain. The hard place; the house of God. Yes, God's house, Word and people can be a hard place when you have an open wound from a loss. Reminders of your loss (pain) and anything churchy (even God, Himself) are equally dreaded by a person who is grieving. You don't want to think about the pain, but you don't want to be around a bunch of rejoicing Christians. Like Deborah, you may be sitting in an in between place right now. I have been there.

I am comforted knowing that Deborah's whole "in between" scene sat atop the Mount of Ephraim. It was all there: the hill, the House of God, the rock, the hard place. The comfort comes from knowing the meaning of the word Ephraim: "double ash-heap – I shall be doubly fruitful".

Friend, between your rock and hard place, atop your double ash heap, is the very place God wants you to declare His promise: I shall be doubly fruitful.

I don't know what that fruit will look like in your life, but I believe you will see it if you hold on tight to Jesus' Hand through the "in between." After all, Isaiah 61 declares that He came to "provide for those who grieve in Zion – to bestow on them a crown of beauty instead of ashes, the oil of joy instead of mourning, and a garment of praise instead of a spirit of despair."

He came to make this Heavenly trade with you. He came so that you wouldn't have to stay, "in between."

Kind Lord, I take Your hand today as I navigate this in between place. I believe You when you say you will provide for me, comfort me, crown me and give me joy. Help me not to shrink back from the pain or from Your Presence. Help me to believe that one day, I will instead of an ash heap, I will be doubly fruitful. Amen.

Picture This - If you are in between right now, what do you think is up ahead? What might doubly fruitful look like for you?

Ask This - What would need to happen for you to feel as though you are no longer in between, that you have crossed over to a new place?

Pray This - Write a prayer asking God to do what it takes to make you ready for that new place He has for you. Ask Him to show you a glimpse of what He wants to give you in place of your double ash heap.

Words of Comfort for Transition
"You are allowed to be a masterpiece and
a work-in-progress, simultaneously."
~Sophia Bush

Checking Out

>> Luanne Nelson

"As Jesus was walking beside the Sea of Galilee, he saw two brothers, Simon called Peter and his brother Andrew. They were casting a net into the lake, for they were fishermen. 'Come, follow me,' Jesus said, 'and I will send you out to fish for people.' At once they left their nets and followed him."

~Matthew 4:18-20 NIV

He was bigger than life to me. He taught me how to ride a bike and how to drive a car. He taught me patience, kindness and how to forgive. Then, he taught me how to die. Dad had stage four lung cancer and would be gone in a few months. I had to get in my car right away and drive as fast as I could to see him. Living six hundred miles away, I buckled a stuffed animal named Annie Bunny into the passenger seat and drove east. Annie was along for the ride as a gift to Dad to keep him company when I couldn't be there. She, to this day, twenty-seven years later, is propped on a chair in my bedroom reminding me about Dad's lessons in grace.

When I got there, Dad knew he was "checking out." He used those words. Here was this man, my beloved Dad, with one foot here and the other foot in heaven. He divided up his earthly goods. Dad gave me his favorite chair. But, I also treasured his non-material gifts – a love of jazz. He said his goodbyes. He even wrote his own eulogy remembering to include apologies to loved ones he'd felt he'd hurt along the way. He knew, as painful as it was to be in his situation, it was a necessary place to be. None of us gets out of here alive anyway and it simply was his turn to go. He knew there was no time for the bitterness of bile; instead, he embraced the sweetness of grace.

Grieving in the aftermath of the tremendous loss of him, I remembered he taught me how to listen for Jesus' Voice, how to put down my personal nets and follow Him. He showed me, "This is how we get to His Holy Place." We lay down every single thing and follow Him.

I know, deep down inside, Dad is with Jesus. And I know, deep down inside, everything is alright.

I think I'll go listen to some Duke Ellington and Miles Davis now.

Thank You, Dear Jesus, Lord God Almighty, for replacing our earthly nets with Your sacred and holy nets. Thank You for giving me such a good Dad. Please make sure he has fun up there with You and Your saints. He was one of the good ones, which You already know. Amen.

Picture This - Imagine that Father God has you firmly in the palm of His hand, no matter how shaken to the core you are.

Ask This - Can you describe a time when you received news that seemed completely unbearable? What did you do, how did you respond?

Pray This - Dear Jesus Lord, please guide the way through craggy passages of grieving. Every step hurts; every mile stretches us to the limit. Your grace is soothing salve. We need Your help through this. Amen.

Words of Comfort for Transition

"Transition is the natural process of
disorientation and reorientation that marks
the turning points in the path of growth."
~William Bridges

Faith Heals

→ Linét Lewerenz

"Jesus said to the woman, 'Your faith has saved you; go in peace….' But Jesus said, 'Someone touched me; I know that power has gone out from me.' Then the woman, seeing that she could not go unnoticed, came trembling and fell at his feet. In the presence of all the people, she told why she had touched him and how she had been instantly healed."

~Luke 7:50, 8:46-47 NIV

I have a friend who is on a path of healing. She has been divorced for over a year now. In America, at least one in two marriages end in divorce. That loss manifests itself in many disguises: hurt, loneliness, depression, and several other negative emotions. Many women also move into poverty. A loss of income gives them this added challenge during an already difficult time. My friend's income would not be sufficient to meet her immediate needs.

Instead of giving up, she turned to her faith to sustain her. The women of her community prayed for her, reached out to her, and surrounded her with God's love. While their prayers continued, she was forced to seek out work. It was not the work she would normally seek, but her need for funds were immediate and she had to take the "menial" job. Those of us close to her recognized that she was always a woman with a pleasing air of dignity. She possessed pride in being a financially secure wife. Her fresh loss caused her dignity to diminish and this simple labor job was equally difficult. Surely God had better plans for her than such easy work.

When she told her friends of her news, though, their support and joy surprised her. They saw this work as a means to meet her needs and they were happy. It was their prayerful support and sincere joy that allowed her to cast aside false pride and accept her new position in life. Not only has she been happy at her job since, but she has met another divorced woman in her work and is able to help this person find a path to healing, as well, through a relationship with Jesus. Her message rings true, her healing continues, and her purpose in Christ is forming. She is a woman of faith.

Today I pray: Thank You, Jesus, for Your healing touch. Thank You for giving dignity and purpose to those with faith. Thank you, Lord Jesus, for Your everlasting love. Amen.

Picture This - How could you reach other people in need, while continuing on your own personal journey? Establish a help circle? Have a simple conversation? Attend a support group? Brainstorm an idea.

Ask This - How could you begin to engage your religious community to fulfill a purpose of healing one another through faith?

Pray This - God, I ask that You equip me with the ability to bring the Word of the Lord to those in need of Your healing presence.

Words of Comfort for Transition

*"A permanent state of transition
is man's most noble condition."*
~Juan Ramon Jimenez

Almost Time To Push . . . But Not Yet!

⇾ Maria Notch

"For everything there is a season, and a time to every purpose under the heaven: A time to be born, a time to die; a time to plant, and a time to pluck up that which is planted: A time to kill, and a time to heal; a time to break down, and a time to build up; A time to weep, and a time to laugh; a time to mourn and a time to dance; a time to cast away stones, and a time to gather stones together; a time to embrace, and a time to refrain from embracing; A time to get, and a time to lose; A time to keep silence, and a time to speak; A time to love, and a time to hate; a time of war, and a time of peace….He hath made everything beautiful in His time."

~Ecclesiastes 3:1-8, 10 NIV

During childbirth, the transition period between pregnancy and birth is known as the most intense time. Fear commonly overwhelms laboring mothers during this time and nausea and intense contractions make them doubt that it's even possible to make it through to delivery. It's also a sign that the woman is coming down the homestretch!

The most intense time in my grief was one year post a corrective surgery when I was the healthiest in my life and we not only didn't have a baby, we hadn't conceived either. During this time, two of the closest women to me called to inform me that they were expecting. This was rock bottom. My body was working and cycling like clockwork. My husband passed all his tests with flying colors. So WHY was it not happening for us?

This was the point in our journey where I literally cried out to God in my pain, questioning if He knew what He was doing, and doubted that our baby would ever come. I sobbed, wailed even, because in my anger and grief and jealousy and sadness, I gave way to despair, just like a laboring mother in transition.

About two months after my doubt, we turned a corner and began "pushing" through. What we didn't know was that time of transition was literally preparing our hearts for the desire to adopt . . . to take hold and be birthed in our lives. Those exact months were the months our birth mom conceived and found out she was expecting. Those were the months that I now look back on in my joy and thank God for, because—without the extreme sadness—we wouldn't experience the same appreciation for this incredible joy!

For everything, there is a season. Lord, please help us be present in the season You have us in right now. Allow us to enter in more fully to the joy or sadness we are experiencing in it, knowing that You are with us and are faithful to Your promise to work all things for our good. Remind us when we are in transition that this intense time may signal that we are in the homestretch. Increase our faith in times of despair and give us the strength to push through. Amen.

Picture This - Picture a woman, screaming through her labor pains and, moments later, crying tears of joy as she holds her newborn baby. Seasons change, sometime slower than others, but change they do. What has your most painful season been like? What about your most joyful season?

Ask This - What "stage of labor" do you think the Lord has you in? If you're in the toughest time of transition, have hope and push through!

Pray This - Pray for the perseverance to continue through the tough seasons to the arrival of new life.

Words of Comfort for Transition

"There will come a time when you believe
everything is finished. That will be the beginning."
~Louis L'Amour

The In-Between

→ Traci Weldie

"So, we're not giving up. How could we! Even though on the outside it often looks like things are falling apart on us, on the inside, where God is making new life, not a day goes by without his unfolding grace. These hard times are small potatoes compared to the coming good times, the lavish celebration prepared for us. There is far more here than meets the eye. The things we see now are here today, gone tomorrow. But the things we can't see now, will last forever."

~2 Corinthians 4:16-18 MSG

Transitions are a place of in between; the past is in the rear-view mirror, but I am not quite sure where I am going. My diagnosis has completely changed my life. I look in that rear view mirror and I see a physically active woman, strong and capable. Where I sit now, I am in daily pain, I have little energy and I battle depression constantly. I just do not know where I am headed.

As I was talking with my husband yesterday about how difficult it is to live each day in pain, he looked at me and started crying, "Don't you give up!"

God is clearly calling me to be in a place of peace during this in-between, not the woman I was, and not yet arrived at who I will be. What my eyes tend to focus on is the outward wasting away, the things falling apart around me. But, God is calling us to gaze upon the work being done on the inside.

When I think about what God has done on the inside, while the outside has been perishing; empathy where I once failed to care about others, patience where I once was rude, quiet where there once was constant chatter, dependence where there once was proud self-sufficiency. In this in-between, I lean into the new life that God is creating in me.

I have to admit it is difficult for me to understand the eternal. My mind can only truly understand the finite, and when I read that this life is just small potatoes compared to the lavish celebration prepared for us, I admit I struggle with truly grasping that truth. That is where faith must come in, faith that choses to believe these words are true. Scripture tells us that the unseen things are what will last forever; not my half-marathon medals or the plaques from teams coached. No, what will last forever is the new life that God is creating in me.

Dear Father, help me to see beyond what meets the eye and to truly see how You are transforming me into Your Son's likeness. Amen.

Picture This - Describe how you might feel like your life is falling apart and imagine God cheering to you, "Don't you give up!"

Ask This - Where have you seen God making life new for you?

Pray This - Dear Lord, pour out Your wisdom into my life so I can know the trial I am going through is small potatoes compared to the celebration to come.

Words of Comfort for Transition

"We are all hypocrites in transition. I am now who I want to be, but I am on the journey there, and Thankfully I am not whom I used to be."
~Erwin McManus

Transition Into Transformation

» Neesie Cieslak

"For you shall go out with joy and be led out (forth), with peace. Instead of a thorn shall come up a cypress tree, and instead of the brier shall come up the myrtle tree; and it shall be to the LORD for a name. For an everlasting sign that shall not be cut off."

~Isaiah 55:12a, 13 NKJV

What a fantastic promise from Father God. He sees the beginning from the end. I'm so glad he does. Upon graduating from high school, I was homeless. The foster family that took me in when I was fourteen, had provided me a lot of "conditional" love. If I cared for their children, I was "cared for" in return . . . in the way that they could care. In weeks when I couldn't be their "nanny," I couldn't stay there. I so wanted someone to say, "I love you," (even if they didn't mean it) that I accepted this definition of family. When I graduated, I wasn't going to be able to be a babysitter, anymore. I was told, "graduate and you're out." I had no job and nowhere to go. The reality that I was just a servant to them sunk in. I had nowhere to go. The military was going to give me food, a bed, shelter . . . and they'll even pay me a bit. Alright. Sign me up.

I went to Basic Training angry, lonely, hurting deep within. This one decision though, was used by God to begin my transition from a broken, wounded little girl and transform me into a woman. From day one of that boot camp, the purpose of our sergeants was to transition us from a civilian mindset by transforming us into soldiers of the U.S. military. I had no time to wallow in self-pity regarding my lost childhood. The transitioning and transforming was a 24/7 process in boot camp. One of the things I saw was that I could do things well in the military. I was one of my sergeant's favorite. I could just be who I was and it was enough. That military experience was the first picture I had of what God's love would become to me. You didn't leave someone behind. You didn't drop anyone on the track. You encouraged them. You stuck together. That whole time we were there, we were family. It was deep commitment to one another.

Upon completion, I truly was a different young lady – physically, mentally, emotionally, and even spiritually. Although I wasn't even a follower of Jesus at that time of my life, that portion of my journey prepared me for the walk I would have with the God just a few short months after returning "home." God planned the transition of my soul and transformed the ashes of an abused, frightened, cast-down trapped girl into a vessel fit for His purposes, and His glory. And then He gave me the smallest taste of what being in His family would look like. Then came the call. One day, a pastor asked at the end of service: "If you want to be a part of a family that never stops loving you, now is the time for you to become a part of the family of God."

Father, thank You for the transition and transformation You've done in my life. I'm only safe in Your capable hands as You transform my broken pieces and replace them with beauty and wholeness. Amen.

Picture This - Hone into a transitioning spot in your life. Are you able to look back and see where God was giving you small glimpses of what life would look like with Him?

Ask This - Are you allowing the Lord to transform you during transition resulting from loss or grief?

Pray This - Father, I release myself to You as I transition into a brighter, more joyful, and peaceful place in my journey.

Words of Comfort for Transition
"Once your mindset changes, everything on the outside will change along with it."
~Steve Maraboli

Old Clothes

⇢ Ava Olivia Willett

"Do not be afraid, little flock, for your Father has been pleased to give you the kingdom. Sell your possessions and give to the poor. Provide purses for yourselves that will not wear out, a treasure in heaven that will never fail, where no thief comes near and no moth destroys. For where your treasure is, there your heart will be also."

~ Luke 12:32-34 NIV

I remember the day I asked my mum if I could go through daddy's clothes with her, and maybe we could find something in one of the pockets, or maybe the collar of a shirt would smell like him a little bit. We'd only gone through his clothes one other time before that after dad had passed away. Now we were living in a new house and I realized that mum's closet seemed a lot . . . emptier. That day, she sat me down and explained that she had given dad's clothes away. He didn't need them anymore and neither did we.

I realized that mum was transitioning in her grief. She was realizing she didn't have to hold onto everything anymore. He was in Heaven with our Lord now, she'd explain to me. All the things of this earth will eventually fade away.

My mum began to invest all of her time into a prophetic-heavy and charismatic church called Destiny. There, I got rooted into a youth group and worked my way up to being a leader and example for the students there. I watched my mum sow into a life that would please God and a life that would store up treasures in Heaven. I watched her carefully and admired her shifting from a life full of sorrow and pain to a life full of hope and aspiration. I learned that life on Earth was temporary and grief comes in different stages. Although still grieving, my family and I transitioned into a life that would praise the Lord who gives, and the Lord who takes away (Job 1:21).

Grief is sometimes like clothing; it can be worn in so many ways and looks different on every person. As we clothe ourselves in grief, we should realize that it is only temporary, just as our clothes on our bodies are also temporary. Our sweet, loving, compassionate God reminds us of His promise to bless us in heaven when it is our time to walk away from this earth.

Jesus, although I am currently clothed in a certain shade of grief, these clothes will soon be worn out, and You will clothe me in Your everlasting love and peace. My grief does not define me. I strive to be more and more like You. I am transitioning out of these old clothes, for You have made me brand new! Amen.

Picture This - What items, grudges, or emotions are you ready to let go of, in order to transition into a new and fresh start?

Ask This - By overcoming reminders of the past, how will your grief be affected or changed for the better?

Pray This - Lord, I trust in You. Nothing the earth has to offer will ever surpass the Love You offer us. I wholeheartedly accept this precious Gift! Amen.

Words of Comfort for Transition

*"Times of transition are opportunities to purge, rethink
Priorities, and be intentional about new habits. We can
Make our new normal any way we want."*
~Kristin Armstrong

Be A Companion

Instead of,
"You'll get through this
Before you know it,"
Try,
"I want to be here for
you. Take your time."

With Words Of Comfort

You may not be able to help in their rebuilding.
But you can love them through it.

The Tenth Stage

REBUILDING *(noun) – according to your companions*
[ree-**bild**-eeng]

1. To restrengthen, reinforce, reshape, or reorganize
2. The opportunity to give yourself completely to God to be rebuilt

*What does **"rebuilding"** mean to you:*

There Is Purpose In The Pain

⇛ Jessica Chase

"You intended it to harm me but the Lord intended it for good, to accomplish what is being done, the saving of many lives."

~Genesis 50:21 NIV

What is the first thing you remember when you think of your childhood? An event? A song? A place?

When I think back to my early years, I find two companions: profound pain and divine presence – pain stemming from abuse, betrayal, and abandonment and an ever-present companion I would later come to know as Holy Spirit.

Wanting to minimize and escape pain is natural. Maybe you even begged God like I did to give you a way out of the pain and if He delayed, maybe you did what I did, try and make your own way out.

More than once, apparent situational salvation led me to a more dangerous and unsafe circumstance than the one I originally faced. I found myself in a cycle of betrayal and pain.

My hope was Holy Spirit's whisper of encouragement after each re-injury, "This is not the end of the story, purpose arises from pain".

As I began to read the Bible I learned that God has a long history of bringing purpose from pain and rebuilding broken lives. In fact, I didn't have to go further than the first book to find my story, in the life of Joseph. Joseph, like me, had been betrayed by those he served and trusted, but – wow, did God ever rebuild His life! From a shepherd to second to the King of Egypt.

Over the years, God has given me many opportunities to share His goodness and faithfulness with women who have been exploited, abused, and who feel forgotten, betrayed, abandoned, and alone. I can see that the pain I suffered and the journey to healing that I yield to is accomplishing a purpose, to bring Jesus and His hope to wounded hearts.

I know that I will have a full and abundant life (John 10:10) and I will help lead other women into their best lives as I continue to gain freedom and see restoration in every area of my life.

Oh Lord, thank You that whatever the effects of sin are, You are greater. Come, teach us how to surrender our past hurts, the wrong done to us, and the wrong we have committed, so that You, in Your infinite power, can transform evil and its effects to life more abundant. Amen.

Picture This - When you think about times of loss or pain, how do you experience that? Do you see something, hear something, feel something or smell something?

Ask This - Ask Jesus to enter into these painful memories, ask him to explore these through the lens of his healing power and goodness. Journal what you experienced. What did Jesus say and do?

Pray This - Ask God to transform your most painful moments, into a platform for growth or a way to share with others the comfort you received or the lessons you have learned.

Words of Comfort for Rebuilding
"Courage is not having the strength to go on,
it's going on when you don't have the strength."

New Beginnings With Old Roots

→ Ava Olivia Willett

"'You expected much, but see, it turned out to be little. What you brought home, I blew away. Why?' declares the LORD Almighty. 'Because of my house, which remains a ruin, while each of you is busy with your own house.'"

~ Haggai 1:9 NIV

The churches in my new hometown were vicious. That's something I never got a clear warning on as we moved away from our previous home church. Not even half a year upon moving up north, my step father's home church shunned him and our newly blended family. Their opinions on the new marriage were sour; my parents were moving "too fast for God."

We were churchless.

My parents tried to comfort me several times, saying that wasn't the case. We were just "church hopping." Either way, I didn't get invested into another youth group, so I went the rest of my high school life without a church family. This broke me.

Upon moving back to southern Wisconsin as an adult, I immediately applied at my former church as a youth pastor. I became a leader to teach the youth on my own. This became a stage of rebuilding in my grief. It's a precious privilege to be the person the youth can look up to and from whom they can learn about Jesus. It's my new beginning with old roots.

Just as I'm now rebuilding what was lost by serving the Lord through youth ministry, let your current stage of grief invite you to pick up the broom in God's house and begin cleaning.

When you get off the path of your purpose in life, you start to feel like things are too broken. You don't know where to start. You have all sorts of broken sticks of this house that fell down. You feel like you don't know how to start. Don't procrastinate because you don't know how. God will provide.

Invest your time and energy into the Kingdom and worry not about how dirty your own life seems at the moment. God will provide you with the proper material needed as you explore His house, as referenced in the book of Haggai. We can use the story of Haggai in our lives by observing how the people of Judah were becoming complacent with the fact that the empire was just invaded. God gave Haggai a message to tell them this: Stop procrastinating, set your priorities straight, and rebuild the temple.

Jesus, it reads in Psalm 84:10 "Better is one day in your courts than thousands elsewhere; I would rather be a doorkeeper in the house of my God than dwell in the tents of the wicked." Seal this on my heart as I invest my labor and thoughts into benefitting the Kingdom. We all fit a specific role in the body of Christ. Show me where I fit the puzzle. Amen.

Picture This - Can you think of a time when you were procrastinating an assignment from God due to a loss in your life? Your destiny does not have to have a deadline. What would happen if you picked up that assignment today?

Ask This - Since God can use your grief as a stepping-stone to rebuild, what new beginnings can you work on to make progress in your personal life (such as working out, eating better, or reading more scripture)?

Pray This - Lord, breathe Your life into my lungs and motivate me to begin working on Your Kingdom in my personal life. Amen.

Words of Comfort for Rebuilding

"Rock bottom became the solid foundation on which I rebuilt my life."
~J.K. Rowling

He Can Level Your Mountains!

→ Karen Bruno

"I will go before you and will level the mountains"

~Isaiah 45:2a NRSV

As a young mother, I hung a beautiful piece of scrolled art work with Isaiah 45:2a in my son's bedroom. I felt compelled to read it, pray it, and speak it into my children's lives. I wanted to instill in them an unshakeable belief that regardless of the twists and turns they encountered on the route of their lives God alone would go before them. He can and will level any obstacle in their way.

Several weeks after my husband died, I walked into my son's room, drug myself into his room is more accurate. I had to change his bedding. It had been so long since I had laundered sheets their state was plain gross. As I stripped his sheets, I was faced with the truth in Isaiah 45:2a still hanging on the wall "I will go before you and will level the mountains"

There are moments during loss and grief when everything feels like a mountain . . . laundry, mail, visitors . . . all mountains. A vast expanse of impassable mountain ranges that engulf every direction we try to traverse. It can be overwhelming and the mountain range can deplete us of the motivation needed to press on. This is true if we only focus on the mountains. The more time we fixate on the mountains, the larger they grow in the landscape of our lives. God wants us to focus on Him. He is infinitely larger than all our mountains. His desire is for us to see how great He is, thus keeping the mountains in perspective. Anything we cannot traverse ourselves He will level completely.

God, I trust You to go before me. Any impassible mountain range I face you will level. You will guide the route of my life; every twist and every turn. I do not need to fear or manage the mountains in my life without You. I can forge forward trusting You will always make a way. Amen.

Picture This - Identify the mountain or impasses in your life.

Ask This - What behaviors or thoughts do I have that stand in the way of allowing God to level my mountains?

Pray This - I pray You draw my focus off the mountains and onto You, Lord, believing You will level them.

Words of Comfort for Rebuilding

*"It is the neglect of timely repair
that makes rebuilding necessary."*
~Richard Whately

God's Abundant Mercy

» Lisa Danegelis

*"Have I not commanded you? Be strong and of good courage; do not be afraid,
nor be dismayed, for the Lord your God is with you wherever you go."*
~Joshua 1:9 NKJV

I dreaded opening the mail every day. The stack of bills was growing as fast as our apprehension. We had taken a leap of faith and opened a restaurant over two years earlier and it had failed. Our dreams were shattered and our bank account was running on empty. We had drained our savings and remortgaged our home. We were disillusioned. Our other business, a catering company, had been successful for years; we were making a name for ourselves in the culinary community. A restaurant had seemed like a natural next step. Yet, here we were on the verge of bankruptcy. A Christian attorney all but told us to declare it. God made it clear that wasn't His plan.

He had a miracle awaiting us as we courageously moved forward in faith.

We were determined to pay off our overwhelming debt and refused to claim bankruptcy which—I have to admit—was very tempting! God honored our faithfulness and diligence by miraculously depositing funds in our checking account! Seriously! I tried and tried to balance our books and there was always an unexplainable surplus. Within a two-year period we paid off our staggering debt and were also able to pay for our fourth and fifth adoptions! To this day, I have no explanation other than the extravagant miracle-working power of our God. Paying that final bill was such a victory! God truly was with us drying our tears, holding our hand, and helping us rebuild our catering company, which is now more successful than ever!

In Joshua 1:9, Joshua was being given a directive by God. Moses, who had been the fearless leader of the Israelites had died and new leadership was needed. This powerful verse asks Joshua to push aside fear and step into courage. Courage means: "Strength in the face of pain or grief". God is not just suggesting Joshua and his tribe be courageous here, He commands it. Joshua honors it. God blessed it.

Rebuilding after loss can seem overwhelming; but when placed in the Father's hand, the perfect plan for our lives can go on uninterrupted. As He did with my family, the Master Builder will pick you up, dust you off, turn you around, and set your feet on new solid ground.

*Mighty God, grace me with the strength and courage to continue on as
I rebuild the broken places in my life. I know You will be right by my
side helping me carry the load and blessing my every step. Amen.*

Picture This - What are the physical things in your life that require mending beyond your personal capacity.

Ask This - Recollect a time in your life when your physical needs were met unexpectedly.

Pray This - Read Matthew 6:25-34 and thank God for His provision in your life.

Words of Comfort for Rebuilding

"There is a little bit of pain in every transition,
but we can't let that stop us from making it. If we
did, we'd never make any progress at all."
~Phil Schiller=

Trust Him

>> Luanne Nelson

Give thanks to the Lord, for he is good; his love endures forever.
Let Israel say: "His love endures forever."
Let the house of Aaron say: "His love endures forever."
Let those who fear the Lord say: "His love endures forever."
When hard pressed, I cried to the Lord; he brought me into a spacious place.
The Lord is with me; I will not be afraid. What can mere mortals do to me?
The Lord is with me; he is my helper. I look in triumph on my enemies.
It is better to take refuge in the Lord than to trust in humans.
It is better to take refuge in the Lord than to trust in princes
All the nations surrounded me, but in the name of the Lord I cut them down.

They surrounded me on every side, but in the name of the Lord I cut them down.
They swarmed around me like bees, but they were consumed as quickly as burning thorns; in the name of the Lord I cut them down.
I was pushed back and about to fall, but the Lord helped me.
The Lord is my strength and my defense; he has become my salvation.
Shouts of joy and victory resound in the tents of the righteous: "The Lord's right hand has done mighty things! The Lord's right hand is lifted high; the Lord's right hand has done mighty things!"
I will not die but live, and will proclaim what the Lord has done.
The Lord has chastened me severely, but he has not given me over to death.

~Psalm 118:1-18 NIV

This is the beginning of final psalm in the collection of psalms sung during the celebration of the Passover. We are in need of the Passover, of healing, of life in a world that brings nothing but bondage and empty promises. Throughout this Psalm, God is thanked because of His perfect goodness and his unending mercies.

We can trust that our holy God is continually by our side. He doesn't just give us strength, He is our strength! He is our salvation! We can have unshakable confidence and trust in Him!

No matter how sad, frightened, lonely, fed up, angry or desperate we may feel, all we have to do is TRUST in HIM for strength and deliverance.

He delivered me from every moment of pain and suffering in my life, no matter the situation. I know he's right here. He's here with us right now. I have no doubt whatsoever. I don't need to be reminded anymore. It doesn't mean I won't be human, because I am. But, as a human, I am His Creation and I know He's got this.

Only God can set us free, and only God can truly assuage our fears and anxiety. This Psalm reminds us that placing our trust in anything but God does not bring forth salvation from fear and death. The Lord is our source of salvation and victory. We are safe rebuilding our lives with Him as our foundation, our center, our everything.

As the last song after the Passover, this would have been the last song that Jesus sang with his disciples before going out into the Garden of Gethsemane. Because salvation is our greatest need, God's loving kindness should be our continual song of praise (Psalm 118:1-4) He has not given us over to death (Psalm 118:18), He has granted us eternal life through Him!

Dear Lord, Jesus God Almighty, thank You for setting us free! As we go forward rebuilding our new lives, please give to us every brick of mercy and wisdom we need. Amen.

Picture This - Can you imagine an entire world of people singing, *'Give thanks to the Lord, for he is good; his love endures forever.'* It will happen someday on earth as it is in heaven! *(Matthew 6:10)*

Ask This - What has to happen to us to realize the need to reconsider our entire perspective, to reshape our goals, to rebuild our lives?

Pray This - Dear Lord Jesus, please be my Holy Builder in this life You've given me to live. "For it is written: "Be holy, because I am Holy." 1 Peter 1:16. Please help me to live a life of holiness from now on. I love You; I trust You. Amen.

Words of Comfort for Rebuilding
"Only in the shattering can rebuilding occur."
~Barbara Marciniak

Moving Forward And Up

Neesie Cieslak

"And he said unto me, Son of man, can these bones live? And I answered, O Lord God, thou knowest. Again he said unto me, Prophesy upon these bones, and say unto them, O ye dry bones, hear the word of the LORD. Thus saith the Lord God unto these bones; Behold, I will cause breath to enter into you, and ye shall live"

~Ezekiel 37:3-5 KJV

I've always admired when someone takes an old piece of junk furniture and gives it a new life by stripping it down to its simplified state. There's nothing left on it, no varnish, paint, or hardware- just plain wood. I see the bare wood, but this artist "sees" a revived piece of furniture of great beauty and value. The Lord sees the messed up, broken pieces of our lives in the same manner, even when we can't.

At fifteen years old, I was one of the stars of my high school track team. I could run fast, first out of the blocks each race. I was also "fast" off the track- fast to say yes to the invitations of promiscuous activity, thus leaving me pregnant and scared for my future. My coach was having similar thoughts and encouraged me to have an abortion. I never ran again for that year or the next.

My life began to unravel in the very places I was having some form of success in, school and athletics. Nothing mattered anymore for a long time. I had murdered my child. How could I go on?

A few years later when invited to a Women's of Faith conference, I heard that Jesus would forgive any lady that night who'd ever had an abortion. That day the Lord began to heal that loss, that pain. He breathed new life into my soul. He redeemed that portion of my life. He knew. I've given birth to five sons and adopted a daughter. By the grace of God, what I thought was impossible, He has raised up.

The Lord's Word is life. He can rebuild our broken-down pieces as we allow His Holy Spirit to reveal Jesus to us through the Word of Life. What places in your life are laying in ruins or have been set aside as "of no use anymore"? Allow the Lord to help you rebuild again and breathe new life into your soul.

Father, You are the Master Builder, the Giver of Life. You take the shattered pieces and create masterpieces. Breathe new life into me, Lord, for Your glory. Amen.

Picture This - Look at the "bones" of your journey that need new life.

Ask This - How do you imagine Jesus can renew and rebuild those bones?

Pray This - Father, You know what can and should be rebuilt in my life. Please be my Architect and breathe on me to build me up again. Amen.

Words of Comfort for Rebuilding

"I believe we could paint a better world
If we could learn to see it from all perspectives."
~Pablo Picasso

Shell-Shocked

Rebecca Grambort

"I am the vine; you are the branches. If you remain in me and I in you, you will bear much fruit; apart from me you can do nothing."

~John 15:5 NIV

Loss is shell-shocking, isolating, and paralyzing. Like a blackout, loss can short-circuit our systems, causing us to feel disconnected from the world around us – the comforts of what we once had suddenly stripped away. Those around you may attempt to comfort you, but can leave you feeling even more misunderstood.

Whether or not your grief stems from death, divorce, relocation or change, it does more than alter our circumstances … it changes who we are.

In this scripture, Jesus uses the metaphor that He is "the vine." Vines are connected to water – a life resource that we cannot live without. His power never goes out. There are no blackouts with Jesus. In fact, His power works greater in our weakness and in the darkest of nights. It is also where He can do some of His finest work, where allowed.

When you gave your life to Jesus, your faith in Him is what grafted you to The Vine (Romans 11:17). All believers are branches in the family tree . . . an extension of Him – made in His image. This heritage is found in great biblical names such as Job, Abraham, Sarah, and Rahab! Yes, even Rahab! She was engrafted into the lineage of Jesus through her faith, as well (Matthew 1:5)! The Bible pays tribute to them all. Yet, no tribute came without tribulation. They all faced great trials and they each bore much fruit by wholly relying on and staying connected to Him.

We, too, should be bearing fruit. We can think about what kind of fruit we might be able to bear by staying connected to the Vine. Everything we need – He is – and is supplied in Him!

Jesus, help me to know that staying in close communion with You is the most vital aspect of my life. Thank You that You have provided me with all of the resources I could ever need for the journey ahead. Amen.

Picture This - Picture having every endless resource at your fingertips being available to you. What are some of the kingdom resources that you will need for your journey?

Ask This - In what ways can I practice staying connected to the Vine?

Pray This - As I stay close to You, thank You for always remaining in me. Apart from You, I can do nothing!

Words of Comfort for Rebuilding

"There is not enough air in the room but you are breathing. There is nobody here but you are held. You have broken and the world is breaking and we will always rebuild. Do you hear me, love? We will always rebuild."
~Jeanette LeBlanc

The New Road I'm On

→ Traci Weldie

"Therefore, as God's chosen ones, holy and dearly loved, put on compassion, kindness, humility and patience; bearing with one another and forgiving one another."

~Colossians 3:12-14 CSV

Have you ever been in a car in a third world country? I have to laugh as I think back to our time in Ethiopia, traveling through the capital of Addis Ababa and believing if I survived this trip, I would never complain about a tiny pothole or a gravel driveway. Road signs? Stop lights? Lane markers? Who needs those tools? The adventure lies in just trying to beat someone else through an intersection. I truly grew to appreciate paved, organized roads on that trip.

My life was on a steady highway. Flatly paved with clear yellow lane markers and exact signs telling me which way to go all leading to a nice, comfortable drive. Imagine my surprise, when like the roads in Addis that just end, and literally fall a foot into a pit, my nice Sunday drive road just ended…and fell. This was not what my life was supposed to look like! Adoption was supposed to bring joy and happiness and sunshine and unicorns. Instead, I fell into a gravel pit and my car was greatly damaged in the process.

Once the dust settles and the fog clears, I can see I'm not actually in a pit, but rather a new road. This road is full of twists and turns, ups and downs, but it IS a road none-the-less… a road I must now travel on. So, I rebuild. I start moving forward.

Paul's letter to the Colossians has a beautiful passage that urges the believer to rebuild, and move on. Paul calls us, as set apart and greatly adored children to literally put on, get dressed in, characteristics that will change our outlooks.

We don't have the power to offer compassion and kindness, gentleness and patience unless we forgive; let go and move on. When I actually stop and think about all my son has been through, and how difficult his life will be living with a disability, I can't help but want to bear with him his burdens. When forgiveness is freely offered, I have the power to rebuild the broken car and get back on my new road, ready for what exciting adventures await.

Dear Lord, help me to freely forgive others and instead, clothe myself with compassion and kindness. May my life be a picture of the strength that comes from humility.

Picture This - Consider how each characteristic of compassion, kindness, humility and patience can help you rebuild your life.

Ask This - What does it mean to you to bear one another's burdens? How can forgiveness play a role in your healing?

Pray This - Read Matthew 11:28 and give your burden to Jesus.

Words of Comfort for Rebuilding

"Clearing the debris from the aftermath is a great first step.
It enables you to start with a clean slate so you can rebuild exactly
what you desire. Where can you begin?"
~Susan C. Young

Rebuilt On His Promises

» Victoria Dreckman

"Bring all the tithes (the tenth) into the storehouse, so that there may be food in My house, and test Me now in this," says the Lord of hosts, "if I will not open for you the windows of heaven and pour out for you [so great] a blessing until there is no more room to receive it. Then I will rebuke the devourer (insects, plague) for your sake and he will not destroy the fruits of the ground, nor will your vine in the field drop its grapes [before harvest]," says the Lord of hosts. 'All nations shall call you happy and blessed, for you shall be a land of delight,' says the Lord of hosts."

~Colossians 3:12-14 CSV

What happens when your little next egg is smashed to pieces like Humpty Dumpty falling off the wall? Not once, but several times over a couple years? Our family experienced this exact disappointment. What was all our faithful tithing for if it was all going to be taken away from us again and again? We began doing the responsible things to make ends meet, yet I found myself searching for change in the couch, in my car, and in the laundry room just to buy a gallon of milk.

It was awkward.

It was work.

Grocery shopping one day, after those couch and car cushion searches, I had one kid in a stroller and one toddler in the cart. The store was full. It was rush time. ALL I HAD was milk (it was all I *could* get). The cashier was young and here I was I was counting out spare change that I was digging out of my purse to be able to get this one tiny necessity. People were waiting behind me with full grocery carts of food for their family.

I was embarrassed.

The young lady gave me my receipt and I dashed out to the car, wanting to get home and bury my head in the sand. Humiliated and embarrassed, I slumped into my car and turned on the radio and that's when the announcer read the Bible verse of the day . . . Malachi 3:10-12.

We hadn't stopped tithing, but I had forgotten His *promise*.

My spirit ignited. "Thank you, God!"

Slowly and incrementally, we saved and rebuilt what the enemy stole from us . . . not just our earnings, but our faith in God's promise. You see, all of God's promises are true. Every last one.

I challenge you to stay faithful to what His promises are saying to you. Even though the enemy may try to steal, kill, and destroy what you have worked hard to attain, the God of all faithfulness will keep His promises to you.

Lord, I ask You to assemble the broken pieces of my life and fill my heart with gratefulness to receive Your blessings to overflowing. Amen.

Picture This - Picture a time of rebuilding in your life. Describe the differences between then and now.

Ask This - Identify three or more scriptures that relate to rebuilding and God's promises.

Pray This - May the God of all faithfulness open His storehouses upon you so that your arms will not be large enough to contain what He blesses you with in this life. May His favor surround you as a shield and His blessings pour out so abundantly that you don't have enough room to receive it. It's in Jesus' name we pray, Amen.

Words of Comfort for Rebuilding

"We cannot snatch back what is lost, from the brutal hands of time. We can only start building something even better now."
~Drishti Bablani

Master Rebuilder And Chief Cornerstone

» Kimberly Krueger

"They will rebuild the ancient ruins. They will restore the places destroyed long ago. They will renew the ruined cities, the places destroyed generations ago."
~Isaiah 61:4 GW

Have you ever tried to rebuild something that was completely destroyed? My friends own a large pig farm in Iowa that was devastated by a tornado. Their home and almost all of their outbuildings were destroyed. Debris was everywhere and most of their 10,000 pigs were found roaming around the wreckage either panicked or stunned. They had to get to the task of rebuilding . . . fast. There wasn't much time for emotion. There was just too much to do!

When I saw pictures and heard the story, I remember thinking how much my own life seemed to have been ravaged by a different kind of tornado. After a night of violence ended my first marriage, our safety, security, and family as we knew it were destroyed. We lost our sense of joy. We were shell-shocked. My children and I roamed through each day panicked and stunned, searching for a place of emotional security and for life to make sense again.

In a weird way, it has always given me comfort that, throughout God's Word, His people endured a lot of destruction. Well, it's not so much the destruction part that comforts me, but the rebuilding. It's that God took the time and attention to weave stories about the rebuilding of ruins into His Word. The rebuilding has always given me hope! Anyone whose life has been in ruins can relate to that! And whose among us hasn't? God knew that tornadoes of all sorts would be part of the human experience and that we would all, on some level, be able to relate to a story about a pile of rubble that He promised to turn into something great once again.

The tornadoes in my life have had many names: divorce, abuse, betrayal, addiction, persecution, death, failure, loss. But today I sit atop the ruins in a renewed and restored place. I have a new life, which God helped me to rebuild one brick at a time. It was not easy, and, at times, it felt like it was going to take forever. But I can look back now and assure you that for every brick I picked up and put in place, God Himself picked up and added three more. The rebuilding isn't on us, alone. Yes, we need to show up to work. Yes, we'll sweat (a little) and cry (a lot). Our hands may even get a few blisters. But the God who says, "they will rebuild the ancient ruins," is the God who never calls in sick. The "they" who will rebuild in this verse is Jesus and us. Remember? He is a Jewish Carpenter! He even got promoted in Heaven to the Master Builder and Chief Cornerstone.

Friend, your burden is on Him. And He'll know just what to do! You just have to be ready to hand Him some rubble.

Lord! We are so blessed that You are the God who rebuilds! No matter who does the destroying, You are always the Master Builder. Come into our ruins and have Your way today. Thank You for making beauty from my ashes and for turning my rubble into something great. Amen.

Picture This - You already know what your ruins look like. What would you like them to look like after they are rebuilt? Describe what that means for you and your life.

Ask This - Are you ready to hand your rubble over to the Master Builder so He can make something great that will glorify His Name? Why or why not?

Pray This - Write a prayer inviting Jesus to be the Chief Cornerstone (the foundation) and the Builder of your new life. Offer all of your ruins and rubble to Him as you express your trust in His Wisdom as the Master Builder.

Words of Comfort for Rebuilding

"Everybody's constantly being destroyed and rebuilding themselves, some more drastically than others."
~Michael Shannon

Be A Companion

⋙

Instead of,
"Don't you think it's
time to move on,"
Try,
"I don't know how to make
this better, but I'll stay
close if you need me."

⋀

With Words Of Comfort

You may not be able to give them acceptance.
But you can love them through it.

The Eleventh Stage

A C C E P T A N C E *(noun) – according to your companions*
[ak-**sep**-t*uh*ns]

1. Total surrender to God and admission that He has a perfect plan in all of it
2. Relinquishing all individual will

*What does "**acceptance**" mean to you:*

Your Ticket Out

> Luanne Nelson

"For I am convinced that neither death nor life, neither angels nor demons, neither the present nor the future, nor any powers, neither height nor depth, nor anything else in all creation, will be able to separate us from the love of God that is in Christ Jesus our Lord."

~Romans 8:38-39 NIV

We lost our business, our house, and nearly lost our minds.

My husband and I had visited a wonderful little town that we adored so much, we ultimately honeymooned there, visited it again, and even took the kids there eventually. Everybody loved when we came to town and we decided to pick up and move there. As new professionals in a small town, though, we weren't accepted by locals who had worked with the same people their entire lives. We'd never struggled in business before, but an organized complaint campaign sent a message, loud and clear; we were welcome to be tourists spending our money there, but we were not part of their family. Some townspeople threw in a death threat just to make sure we were leaving. Not only did we lose everything, financially, we had lost a place that had once meant joy for us.

We finished packing our condo, and I realized that I couldn't find my passport, anywhere.

I laid on living room floor and screamed.

I said, "If I stay, I'll die here."

My husband came over and prayed with me. Just like that I found my passport. It was as if Jesus answered, "Here. Here's your passport. Here's your ticket out."

We got out. We drove four thousand miles back home; back to the place we knew. We escaped.

My dear husband David and I sped away in separate cars, but pointed in the same direction, with our little corgi tucked away securely in his car hut. Good thing, because I am hearing impaired and I blared soulful and Holy Spirit-filled CDs practically the whole time. I sang praises as loudly as I could. Thanksgiving in June.

Living there was painful; leaving was joyful. Acceptance means that you take the direction God has given you, and follow that road with peace in your heart.

We continue to pray for those who need their tickets away from pain.

Trust Him.

Jesus Lord God Almighty, please bless us and transform us out of our own weakness into a useful tool for Your service. You will not let enemies kill us nor let our own doubts destroy us. In Jesus' holy name we pray. Amen.

Picture This - Can you identify times in your life when you've not been welcomed; when you've been hated, blamed or shunned? Compare that to the unconditional acceptance of God.

Ask This - Do you believe that absolutely nothing is able to separate you from the love of God that is in Christ Jesus our Lord?

Pray This - Dear Lord Jesus, when I am smack dab in the middle of trouble, please remind me of Your words, "If people don't welcome you, leave their town and shake the dust off your feet as a testimony against them." (Luke 9:5) Thank You for delivering us. Amen.

Words of Comfort for Acceptance

The first step toward change is awareness.
The second step is acceptance.
~Nathaniel Branden

Losing Emery

→ Heather Taylor

"For God so loved the world that he gave his one and only Son, that whoever believes in him shall not perish but have eternal life."

~John 3:16 NIV

I will never forget the look on my daughter's face when she came running down the hall from the courtroom she had just exited. Her face was paler white than usual and her green eyes were splashing tears through her red hair as she ran.

"Mom, Mom?" she said in a breathless whimper. She was gasping for air but it wasn't because of the sprint she had just endured to reach me. It was because the news she was just given was completely unexpected and completely tragic. "Mom, they are taking her!"

I could barely hear her words through the tears and the heavy breathing, but somehow, they made it through to my brain. My daughter was about to lose her daughter, a daughter we had helped to raise from birth, because of lies that her soon-to-be ex-husband shared while he was stuck in his own pain. He accused her of being unfit. I knew that he had come home from the military damaged, but this was too far. So much hurt would be in our lives with my grandbaby taken away.

My head started pounding. "No!" was all I could say. I ran to the attorney who had assured us this could never happen and begged him for the punchline. This child, my beautiful grandbaby, had been with me since the minute she was born . . . since before she was born. We had done everything, given everything. How could this happen? They don't even know her! They haven't held her while she slept, spent endless nights in hospital rooms singing to her and praying for her. Why would this happen? Why? I was in complete denial, along with my entire family.

It took years for me to be able to say her name without completely breaking down, or to keep from running off when I looked at her picture or saw another child with wild red hair and big blue eyes. We had to grieve her loss, even though she wasn't truly gone – just gone from us.

God and I were in a timeout during this season of denial. I didn't understand how He could let this happen. I didn't want to understand. I was mad. I was hurt. I was grief stricken.

How could He do this to us? To her?

One day, while I was alone in my office staring at a picture of her, I heard a quiet whisper in my ear, "I do know how you feel, I have lost someone too."

As I heard those words, the hairs on my neck stood at attention. Whoever was speaking to me had to be standing right beside me with their lips pressed up to my ear. "I know the pain you are suffering because I too have lost someone I love. My Son."

Tears fell from my eyes. I knew this voice, I knew this person's Son. "But He died for a reason," I whispered. "There is *no* reason for this!"

"My reasons are not always for you to understand but if you trust Me I will make this loss matter. Will you trust Me?" I knew what my Father in Heaven was asking me.

I knew that He was promising me, just like his Son's death made a difference, someday even this could be used for good. I fell to my knees and started to weep. "I will trust You, because You always make beauty from ashes."

Lord, I pray that, during times of grief, You would comfort us from our pains and help each person reach for You and not turn away from You. Thank You for making all things be used for Your glory. Amen.

Picture This - If you've had something you love taken away from you without knowing why it has happened, imagine that loss playing a part in a bigger picture of love and joy.

Ask This - How can you better accept that sometimes we don't know why bad things happen, but God can bring beauty from our pains?

Pray This - Lord, I ask You to make the tragedies in our lives have silver linings. I pray that You will use our pains to bring glory to You somehow. In Jesus' name, Amen.

Words of Comfort for Acceptance

The animals are not grieving with us. They're very accepting. They're not lying there thinking 'How could you do this to me? Why aren't you keeping me going?' They come and go with great acceptance.

~Jon Katz

Here I Am

→ Linét Lewerenz

"I revealed myself to those who did not ask for me;
I was found by those who did not seek me.
To a nation that did not call on my name,
I said, 'Here am I, here am I.'
All day long I have held out my hands
to an obstinate people,
who walk in ways not good,
pursuing their own imaginations—
a people who continually provoke me
to my very face,
offering sacrifices in gardens
and burning incense on altars of brick…."

~Isaiah 65:1-3

Burdens are anything but convenient. We find no wanting of the grief they bring. Women are often the family caretakers; we bring our support and take on the burdens of our loved ones. Struggling to make sense of her life, my daughter needed me. I show up in her adult life, unbidden and unwelcome, to discover an aura of hurt and sadness enveloping her. It reached out to me and touched me. I felt her pain, but she was angry with me and those who brought me. I wasn't asked into her life. Her decisions, though, had caused harm to herself that she unknowingly cloaked in deceit. Faking it had become her "norm" and she found it easy to feign cooperation. Feeling I had done my work, I was vulnerable to the lie, wanting to return home to my husband, her father. So I chose to believe her burden had been lifted. I had invested time, money, and heartfelt support. I had shown her a better path and was optimistic she understood.

Not long after I returned home, though, my daughter called me for help. This time, I was welcomed. There was honesty in her need.

"Here I am."

Now, several months after my daughter asked me back in her life, I, too, see things anew. Why I named my daughter's need a "burden" was selfish. In fact, this "burden" is fragile and—at the same time—harder than any tempered steel. I must treat it gently. There is no doubt this is Jesus being revealed . . . giving me a way to help my daughter to walk in the ways of God and turn away from the false gods of modern life.

She thought she was calling to her mother and I answered, "Here I am," when—in fact—Jesus called to her: "I am here."

Today I pray – Jesus, thank You for calling to my daughter and me. We are grateful for Your presence in this hour of our need. We know Your goodness will give us strength and ease our struggle as we work through the burdens of this life. I know You called me and my daughter with the gift of Your love. I am in awe of Your gift. I love You, Jesus. I know You are here. Amen.

Picture This - Envision replacing your anger with faith in Jesus. How can this help to renew the damaged soul left behind by the grief and burdens of this world?

Ask This - God, please give me inspiration through faith, family, and friends to continue to motivate the recoveries of those who desperately need You and Your love.

Pray This - Jesus, empower me to see damaged souls as fragile lives which must be healed with Your love. Help me to see past the façades that are worn on top of hurt, including those built with anger. Thank You for always answering, "Here am I." Amen.

Words of Comfort for Acceptance

"Acceptance doesn't mean resignation; it means understanding that something is what it is and that there's got to be a way through it."
~Michael J. Fox

I Am More

» Victoria Dreckman

"Many women do noble things, but you surpass them all. Charm is deceptive, and beauty is fleeting; but a woman who fears the Lord is to be praised."
~*Proverbs 31:29-30 NIV*

Sitting in my comfy chair, with my fuzzy socks and baggy clothes, I drink my morning coffee while reading my devotions. The sun slowly rising as I stop reading to stare at my reflection in the window.

In my twenties, I wanted an hourglass figure. In my thirties, I wanted a toned rear-end, no saddlebags and fewer wrinkles. In my forties, the list got even longer. I gaze at the reflection of a woman who is bombarded every day by women who don't seem to age through the scope of television and internet filters.

'I can't compete with this!' The silent cry of my heart pleads, *'Lord, help me accept who I am. Help me to see what you see in me.'*

In that still quiet moment I hear Him say, *'Proverbs 31.'*

I quickly page through the chapter looking for some ounce of inspiration and encouragement. A familiar chapter, yet, nothing. That is, until I read verse 29. "Many women do noble things, but you surpass them all. Charm is deceptive, and beauty is fleeting; but a woman who fears the Lord is to be praised."

Did you see that? Charm and beauty are fleeting traits that don't last. Saddened by decades wasted worrying about my appearance, trying fad diets, and tackling every exercise I could in an effort to gain back a little bit of my youth, I find comfort in hearing His words. God says a woman who fears the Lord is to be praised. Accepting these words as truth into my life ushered in a brilliance and immeasurable beauty that no one can contest because I am the daughter of the King of Kings.

Father, as we honor and revere You, the Almighty God, give us eyes to see ourselves as You see us. Forgive us for being vain and looking for our self-worth through this world's eyes. Show us the wonder and beauty in ourselves and others so that we can share Your love with those around us. Amen.

Picture This - What does acceptance in the midst of your grief look like to you?

Ask This - What is the Lord speaking to your heart about this moment?

Pray This - Father, help me to accept Your Word as truth into my circumstances and life. Amen.

Words of Comfort for Acceptance

"Acceptance looks like a passive state, but in reality it brings something entirely new into this world. That peace, a subtle energy vibration, is consciousness."
~Eckhart Tolle

Healed And Whole

⇛ Traci Weldie

"And not only that, but we also rejoice in our afflictions, because we know that affliction produces endurance, endurance produces proven character, and proven character produces hope. This hope will not disappoint us, because God's love has been poured out in our hearts through the Holy Spirit who was given to us."

~Romans 5:3-5 CSV

I clearly remember driving home one rainy afternoon talking to my husband about how this life is not at all what we expected. We thought we would parent our children and then launch them out to live on their own, have jobs, get married, live the American dream. Now, it looks like we could very well have one of our children living with us the rest of our lives. We have a son who will be a perpetual third grader. We will have to drive him everywhere, budget his money, make sure he takes his medicine; NOT living the American dream.

My husband stopped us from complaining any further and said, "But Traci, one day we will see him in heaven and he will be whole! He will have clarity of thought and he will no longer battle mental illness! Imagine the joy of seeing our son healed and whole." I was undone.

It is difficult to read a verse like the one Paul wrote to the Roman church and genuinely say that I celebrate my suffering. It's as if I can make a little check list of the afflictions in this family: disease, disorder, illness, misery. Yet, God calls us more than once in His Word to rejoice in that checklist.

Someone once asked me, "What would your life look like if God would have taken away your suffering the first time you asked him to?"

I paused and thought. If God had done that, I would be standing here a proud, arrogant woman. You see, living for a decade in a place of hardship has actually been a beautiful thing! I am on my face before a Holy God wholly dependent on Him to sustain me. I am a humble woman who has great compassion for other moms and caregivers. There is nothing in this world that satisfies my soul anymore, only being in the presence of my Savior brings me peace and comfort.

So yes, I rejoice! I thank my God that I have . . . and still am in . . . a season of trials. I am not the same woman I was before. I look at the list of characteristics that acceptance brings: endurance, proven character, and eventually hope. Don't miss that this hope is not dependent on us, for it is from God whose hope will never disappoint or forsake or leave. Because of Jesus Christ, we know God's love is more powerful than any brokenness.

Father, as we honor and revere You, the Almighty God, give us eyes to see ourselves as You see us. Forgive us for being vain and looking for our self-worth through this world's eyes. Show us the wonder and beauty in ourselves and others so that we can share Your love with those around us. Amen.

Picture This - How has God allowed trials in your life to lead you toward endurance, proven character, acceptance, and hope?

Ask This - What can you thank God for today that came as a result of afflictions in your life?

Pray This - Read the following verses and write a prayer to the Lord about rejoicing in your suffering:

Acts 5:41

Colossians 1:24

James 1:2-3

I Peter 4:12-13

Words of Comfort for Acceptance

"Understanding is the first step to acceptance, and
only with acceptance can there be recovery."
~J.K. Rowling

Simple Faith

⇒ Lisa Danegelis

"This is the day the Lord has made; we will rejoice and be glad in it."
~Psalm 118:24 NKJV

God told me to "Just be."

'What? Are you kidding? You can't expect a self-described performance-based maniac to "Just be."'

Yet that is exactly what He had been telling me for some time, though it had fallen on deaf ears. I had strived to prove to God I was worthy of His love. Now, here I was bedridden and suffering from extreme withdrawal symptoms.

God was using a megaphone this time . . . "Just be!"

My dear friend had told me earlier in my journey, "The hardest thing for you to do, is to do nothing, and that's just what God wants." She always was a step ahead of me!

So, I did nothing. I was forced into what felt like a straightjacket of acceptance as I lay there month after languishing month *doing nothing* but "just being." That's when I learned to lament.

Lamenting is defined as: "A passionate expression of grief or sorrow", or, "A song, piece of music or poem expressing sorrow."

I wailed, moaned, rocked, and muttered. It was not pretty. In fact, it was downright primitive at times. I questioned Him. I screamed at Him. I sat before Him in silence wondering how on earth He was okay with the mess He saw before Him who was doing nothing. Then, in time, I began to accept the seclusion as my place of metamorphosis, and I started falling more in love with my King.

Through the gradual acceptance, moments of rejoicing thrilled me as they sprung up during my lamenting. I was beginning to experience blessed freedom from the performance mentality that had enslaved me. David learned the discipline of rejoicing as he danced in abandonment before the Lord. I can almost see him reciting the verse above as he twirls around in jubilation! Let us model ourselves after David the worshipper as we accept this day from our Creator's hand.

Rejoice with me today, fellow sojourners, it is but preparation for the big dance party awaiting us in eternity!

Ever faithful Father, give me the grace needed to accept my circumstances and see You in the midst of them. May the simple belief that You will never leave me nor forsake me give me reason to rejoice, and . . . maybe even dance! Amen.

Picture This - What does stillness look like in your life?

Ask This - What do you think goes on inside of you when your outside is still.

Pray This - God, thank You for turning my mourning into dancing and for working on me even when I'm not doing any "work."

Words of Comfort for Acceptance

"Wisdom is knowing what you have to accept."
~William Stegner

This Isn't So Bad

→ Maria Notch

"In this you greatly rejoice, though now for a little while you may have had to suffer grief in all kinds."

~1 Peter 1:6 NIV

There came a point in my journey when grief became like an old familiar friend. I recognized that I grieve really well, meaning I know how to communicate how I'm feeling, what I'm losing, and how I'm choosing to respond. My toolbox for coping consisted of my husband, a tight circle of women I could lean on, some fabulous essential oils, key breathing and relaxation techniques, my Priests and church family, and a Christian therapist. Mostly, acceptance came as I recognized all the good gifts the Lord had given me.

My greatest gifts have been my husband and our children - our son Jacob, who is six years old, and our four saints in Heaven, Mickey, Moriah, Providence, and Hope. As difficult as it has been to let go of our four babies, I thank God every day for my amazing husband, for the gift of our son here on Earth, and for the opportunity to carry four other souls and birth them into eternity! We've grown incredibly close through the losses and have come to appreciate and love each other more fully than I think we would have had we not experienced such profound loss.

The eternal gift the Father gave me through this suffering is that He's allowed me to share in His pain and in the pain of Mary, the Mother of Jesus: the pain of losing a child. There's an intimacy to my faith relationship with the Father through this pain; I also relate to the pain of His chosen mother of Christ, Mary. The feelings of closeness with God and relatability to His people have been strengthened as God has allowed me to share in a parent's grief. God weeps with me when I weep and rejoices with me in my rejoicing.

Additionally, Jesus' suffering continually points us to the relentless love of the Father, and He models trust in God's will, even when it requires laying everything down to the point of death. We witness to God's love, mercy, and goodness when we carry our cross with joy and obedience. When we suffer as Christ did, we have the opportunity to point others to the Father's love, as well. In this, I have come to rejoice at the opportunity to suffer and thank God for it!

Heavenly Father, thank You for allowing us to share in Your suffering and the suffering of Your Son, Jesus. Lord, help us to carry our crosses humbly, with joy and obedience as You did, knowing that there is a beautiful intimacy with You to be had amidst the pain.

Picture This - Clench your fists and imagine that you're tightly holding onto your pain, grief, and suffering. Notice the tension and the discomfort in your hands and forearms. Now open your palms and release all the hurt to God. Accept that He is in control, and promises to work all things for your good.

Ask This - What will help me accept my current situation, thank the Lord for the opportunity to suffer, and trust in His plan?

Pray This - Cling to Romans 8:28 and "know that in ALL things, God works for the good of those who love Him."

Words of Comfort for Acceptance

"Accept your past with no regrets,
handle your presence with confidence,
and face your future with no fear."

New Life

→ Reji Laberje

"They can't understand the truth. They are separated from the life of God. That's because they don't know him. And they don't know him because their hearts are stubborn. They have lost all feeling for what is right...But that is not the way of life in Christ you learned about. You heard about Christ and were taught about life in him. What you learned was the truth about Jesus. You were taught not to live the way you used to. You must get rid of your old way of life....You were taught to be made new in your thinking. You were taught to start living a new life. It is created to be truly good and holy, just as God is. So each of you must get rid of your lying. Speak the truth to your neighbor. We are all parts of one body."

~Ephesians 4:18-25 NIRV

When I finally came to Christ as an adult, there were two distinct realizations that followed my baptism: 1 – *'How have I been missing out on this reality all my life?'* and 2 – *'Wait a minute . . . what about the rest of my loved ones . . . they aren't all here with me now and won't be with me in eternity, for Christ is the only way.'*

In reading Paul's letter to the Ephesians, I see two people. There are "they" who don't know about God and live for themselves, or some other false God or idol, such as materialism, fame, desire, prideful thinking, or earthly legacy. I was part of that "they." Then, there is "you" who lives the new life in Christ. The bridge from "they" to "you" comes when "what you learned…" and "you were taught…" occur. Long before I could bridge my way to "living a new life created to be truly good and holy," I needed motivation to get there. I needed a reason to hear the learning and accept the teaching. I know where that point was for me. I don't know where it is for the people in my life who still don't know Christ. This has been one of the hardest things to accept and I grieve it often, feeling loss, not for what has passed, but for what is yet to come.

One thing I discovered, long after my baptism by water, and then by the Holy Spirit, is that there were people – many people – praying for me: my in-laws, my best friend who introduced me to church, my husband, and even distant relatives who had spent years in prayer. None of these prayer warriors had control over when I would soften my stubborn heart to God's truth, but they prayed anyway. They prayed in hope of my new life in Christ, and accepting that they did not know when or if they would personally be able to see my transformation. They accepted my free will given by God, even when I used that free will to deny Him.

When Paul tells us that "we are all parts of one body," he means all of us. Every man and woman was made by and for God and He wants them all to come back to Him. There was a time that I did not know I was part of Christ, but loved ones spoke truth and prayed on. I, too, must accept that new life will come to my loved ones in their time . . . and in time.

Thank You for the prayer warriors in my life, including those I never knew about. I ask You for help in accepting the journeys taking place outside of my control, as well as reminders to pray on for them, even though I don't know when they will be willing to learn of Your Truth. I pray this in Your Son's matchless name, Jesus Christ. Amen.

Picture This - Imagine the changed life of a nonbeliever you care about. Write down the promises God has given you for that person.

Ask This - List the joys in your life that came when you committed or recommitted your life in Christ. What other positives, when reflected on, are a result of your full life in Christ? List those gifts, as well.

Pray This - Ask God to reach the nonbelievers in your life and soften their hearts to the possibility of a transformed life through Christ.

Words of Comfort for Acceptance

"The only way out is through."
~Robert Frost

Open Your Hands Wide

→ Kimberly Joy Krueger

"Pour out all your worries and stress upon him and leave them there, for he always tenderly cares for you."

~1 Peter 5:7 TPT

Acceptance, as it relates to grief, is a bit ironic. Acceptance in most other circumstances means we will receive something. We accept an invitation to a party, a marriage proposal, an offer on our house, and a promotion. In all of these cases, acceptance means saying yes to something, opening our hands and taking hold of it. And then there's grief—as we work through this gauntlet called grief, acceptance has an opposite meaning. Accepting that we have lost something we so desperately want or need means we must open our hands…and let go.

There was a Christian college student whose professor passionately encouraged his students to let God do everything for them in every area of life. "Let Him supply! Let Him bless! Let Him heal!" He said. The student was so moved, he came back to his tiny apartment, pulled out six blank note cards and began to write one letter on each card until the cards spelled L-E-T G-O-D. He taped them to the wall over his study table as a reminder and then he set out to let God… well, be God. He tried with all his might to trust God with and for everything; but nothing seemed to change. Frustrated, he sat looking at the note cards, and finally prayed. He told God that he was trying so hard to "let Him", but it was not working. He asked the Lord to show him what he was missing.

Almost immediately, a strong wind came through the nearby window and knocked one of the cards right off the wall. It was the letter D. The cards now spelled L-E-T G-O. The student believed this to be Heaven's reply to his prayer. He finally realized what had been missing! In order to let God, he must first, let go.

And so it goes with acceptance. In order to accept what we've lost, what we cannot change, or what may never be, we must first let go. When we relax our grip on the things we hold so tightly, we are allowing God to be God in our lives. If there is one thing grief has taught me, it is that I NEED God to be God in my life! Do you? Do you need His provision in your loss? His healing for your brokenness? His infilling for your emptiness? His answers for your questions? Today, I encourage you to open your hands wide…and let go.

Father God, we need You to be God for us today. We need Your provision in our loss. We need Your healing in our brokenness. We ask for Your infilling in the place of our emptiness. We have struggled to open our hands and let go. Today, we ask for the grace to relax our grip and allow You to do what only You can do in our lives. Amen.

Picture This - What are you struggling to accept? Close your eyes and picture it in your hands. What is it? Now imagine letting it go. What are you thinking and feeling?

Ask This - What might be holding you back from letting go and practicing acceptance?

Pray This - Lord, it is so difficult to imagine letting go. But Your Word says that You are gentle and that you tenderly care for me. Would you be gentle with me today, as I follow your lead and trust in Your Love? I choose to let go and let you be God in my life today. (Now write your own prayer of letting go, to God.)

Words of Comfort for Acceptance
"What you choose also chooses you."
~Kamand Kojouri

I Accept, But ....

→ Neesie Cieslak

"He Himself is before all things, and in Him all things hold together."
~Colossians 1:17 NRSV

Have you ever stated, *'I just won't accept that?'* or *'I just can't accept that?'*

Accepting our current situation and looking it in the face leaves room for us to rest in God. When my brother took his own life in 2013, there was much that I just could not accept at first. I couldn't and wouldn't accept that I'd done enough for him, I couldn't and wouldn't accept that I wasn't part of the reason for his suicide. It was excruciatingly painful to accept that he was truly gone. I was incapable of accepting my reality until I allowed Jesus to come in fully, and trust fully in his character.

It is HE that was before all things, will be after all things, and holds it all together. I needed Jesus to be in the center of this tragedy. I had to abide in His love, remembering He knew. He knew and He knows. For every circumstance, all the time, for everything and everyone, all things are held together. With the Lord holding my heart, I was able to accept the facts of my brother's untimely death. Greater still, I was able to accept the beauty of the grace Father God was desiring to extend to me. I needed to open my hands and ease the guilt, blame, and unacceptance in order to bestow upon me grace, love, peace, and eventually joy again.

Acceptance didn't mean I was forgetting my brother, or that it was unimportant. It simply meant, I accept it. Not accepting a grievous situation doesn't change the situation, it just prolongs the grieving process. You can face your loss and hurt with Jesus. He will hold you and walk with you. He can help you accept it, because you've accepted Him as your Savior.

Lord, it is difficult to accept the hurtful, pain-filled life events. We need Your assistance, Father. Help me to accept that You do all things well, and that You were walking with me. In Jesus' name. Amen.

Picture This - Imagine your grief as a real person and look it in the face.

Ask This - Ask yourself what part of that "grief person" is a surprise to God.

Pray This - Abba, Father with You by my side I can face any situation that arises in my life. You will hold me together. Thank You. Amen.

Words of Comfort for Acceptance

"There are things we don't want to happen, but have to accept,
things we don't want to know, but have to learn, and
people we can't live without, but have to let go."
~Nancy Stephan

The Beauty Of Sorrow

» Susan Brozek

"Sorrow is better than laughter, for by a sad countenance the heart is made better."

~Ecclesiastes 7:3 NKJV

Did you know that sorrow carries within it a certain type of beauty? We typically don't view sorrow as anything other than sadness and misery. Those are primary elements of sorrow, to be sure. But if we peel back those layers, residing within the emotion of sorrow is also a kernel of beauty. If we can accept that and embrace it, it will draw us ever closer to the heart of our Savior, Jesus Christ. He was known as "a Man of Sorrows", according to Scripture. Does this mean that Christ was melancholy? I don't necessarily think so. But He suffered much sorrow while He walked this earth those 33 years. His sorrows, though, clearly drew Him closer to His Abba Father.

There is a beauty within the human heart when we express sorrow over a loss. We get in touch with a part of ourselves that many of us try to run from instead of accept. When we accept the sorrow our heart is experiencing, we approach a new depth of emotional capacity. Our hearts deepen to take in the emotion of sorrow. We gain experience in how to approach sorrow as a natural part of our existence, rather than an emotion to be swept aside or avoided. The depth of the pain that we allow ourselves to experience through sadness, grief, and mourning happens to equal the height of the joy that we will also be able to partake in. If we stop running, avoiding, numbing out, distracting ourselves, addicting ourselves, and hiding when pain strikes…what waits for us on the other side is a level of joy that we may not have otherwise had the privilege of knowing. If we stuff all of our painful emotions, we also limit our capacity to truly enter into the positive ones. By trying to numb out and not feel, we may fill in the valleys, but we also shear off the mountaintops.

When the time is right for you in your loss; accept, embrace, and begin to take small steps forward on your journey. Along the way, don't forget to approach sorrow with less trepidation; it just might serve to be a friend, not a foe.

Remember: The height of a mountain is best appreciated after the depth of a valley.

Today I pray – Strengthen those who fear their negative emotions such that they might allow themselves to feel those emotions and not run away from them, Lord. Help them to know that You, Man of Sorrows, will hold their hand as they bravely walk this path of grief with You. Amen.

Picture This - What comes to mind when you envision a heart filled with both sorrow *and* joy?

Ask This - Seek God today as you continue to process your grief. Are there elements of your loss that you feel you might be starting to accept?

Pray This - Lord Jesus, thank You for Your faithfulness to us throughout the journey of our lives, and the paths we must walk when we grieve. Remind us that the hearts You created within each of us are designed for the capacity to experience and express both the mountaintops of joy along with the valleys of sorrow. Amen.

Words of Comfort for Acceptance

"Just knowing you don't have the answers is a recipe for humility, openness, acceptance, forgiveness, and an eagerness to learn - and those are all good things."
~Dick Van Dyke

Standing On What We Believe

» Amy Sikkema

"I keep my eye always on the Lord. With him at my right hand, I will not be shaken. Therefore my heart is glad and my tongue rejoices; my body also will rest secure, Because you will not abandon me to the realm of the dead, nor will you let your faithful one see decay. You make known to me the path of life; you will fill me with joy in your presence, with eternal pleasures at your right hand."

~Psalm 16:8-11 NIV

I sat there and watched his every breath – my head propped gently on his chest, my soul memorizing the beats of his heart. Reality would hit me again and again, over and over, each morning I would awake. I could not accept what was happening. How could this be our reality? I could not wrap my mind around what was to be. God was calling him home. I believe, with all my heart, my husband was the first to accept this. He knew where he was going. He knew that he would not be abandoned in the realm of the dead.

Fighting was all I did until just hours before his death; finally accepting that this was his time to go home. When his breathing became so labored, like a fish out of water, when He struggled to choke down the fluid that was seeping up in his esophagus from his lungs, it was then and there that I begged God to heal him. I accepted what the scripture had told us and told my husband it was ok. We would be ok.

"Go home," I gently whispered.

It wasn't until we both could accept what was happening that we could let go. We did not accept a terminal diagnosis since God is in the miracle business – and yes, we witnessed so many of those miracles during his battle. We did not accept eighteen months as a survival. We fought and he had a beautiful twenty-three after diagnosis. We did not accept fear; we did not accept no; we did not accept giving up.

We do accept God's will. We do accept His plan. We do accept and look forward to a new beginning. A new Heaven and a new Earth where all is restored and made new. For You will not let your faithful one see decay. You surely do make known the path of life and we, as Your children, accept and praise You for that!

My prayer is that when we find ourselves in a place that is hard to accept, God will graciously give us peace and understanding. Amen.

Picture This - What would total acceptance and complete surrender look like right now?

Ask This - In what way would God like to heal my pain if I were to accept painful circumstances in my life?

Pray This - Dear Lord, thank You for never leaving or abandoning me. Thank You for all of the promises You speak over our lives as Your children. Help me to understand and accept my circumstances and to know that, through it all, You are faithful and You are good. You have promised to never leave us in those lonely places. Instead, may we find joy in Your presence as we seek Your will for our lives and honor You in all that we do. In Your name we pray. Amen.

Words of Comfort for Acceptance
"For after all, the best thing one can
do when It is raining, is let it rain."
~Henry Wadsworth Longfellow

Be A Companion

With Words Of Comfort

Instead of,
Bible verses and platitudes,
Try,
Companionship and comfort.

You may not be their source of hope.
But you can point them to it.

The Twelfth Stage

HOPE *(noun) – according to your companions*
[hop]

1. Desirous expectation of renewal and or restoration
2. The belief that good is attainable regardless of how bad things have been
3. Deep trust, with confidence, in our best future from God
4. Expecting the impossible to become possible

*What does "**hope**" mean to you:*

Glimpse Of A New Day

⇒ Linét Lewerenz

"From inside the fish Jonah prayed to the Lord his God. He said: 'In my distress I called to the Lord, and he answered me. From deep in the realm of the dead I called for help, and you listened to my cry. You hurled me into the depths, into the very heart of the seas, and the currents swirled about me; all your waves and breakers swept over me. I said, 'I have been banished from your sight; yet I will look again toward your holy temple.' The engulfing waters threatened me, the deep surrounded me; seaweed was wrapped around my head. To the roots of the mountains I sank down; the earth beneath barred me in forever. But you, Lord my God, brought my life up from the pit."
~Jonah 2:1-6 NIV

She is my lifelong friend, and I hurt for her. Her daily routine is fueled by grief. It consumes her every thought and action and it is as if she dwells among the dead. She weeps; she cries out; her pain is like no other. She has given birth and endured illness, but this . . . this is like drowning and—at the same time—burning. Her husband is gone now.

'Why can't I join him,' she wonders. *'Where is God. Is He listening? I don't want to wake up. I want to be done with it all. I can feel my heart in flames, my grief fueling it.'*

But the day came when she shared a new waking. She opened her eyes and felt a fleeting moment of peace. She is alive. She prayed. Not that she hasn't prayed before, but this was a different kind of prayer. It wasn't a prayer asking to remove the grief, to end it all . . . or to end herself . . . but a prayer of thanks for a new day. Just for that day, she started with a thankful prayer rather than burning despair.

It was just a moment, and then her grief pulled at her once more . . . and she wept.

I know that my friend will have more glimpses of hope amidst the weeping in more of her new days. May we all take the brief moments of peace and recognize them with gratitude until God pulls us from the pit of anguish.

Today I pray – Please, God, give me strength. Let the light of each new day show me a way. I need Your strength to climb out of this living death. I need to want to welcome each new day. I don't ask that my grief be gone, only that it not consume me. God, hear my plea. Amen.

Picture This - Imagine a sunny morning after an overnight rain. What emotions greet you as you open your front door to the fragrant smells of the outdoors?

Ask This - How can you step out into the sunshine today?

Pray This - Lord give me strength to open the front doors of my life and step out into Your light.

Words of Comfort for Hope

"Carve a tunnel of hope through the dark mountain of disappointment."

~Dr. Martin Luther King, Jr.

Extravagant Hope

⇢ Annabelle Ahlers

"The Spirit of the Sovereign Lord is on me, because the Lord has anointed me to proclaim good news to the poor. He has sent me to bind up the brokenhearted, to proclaim freedom for the captives and release from darkness for the prisoners, to proclaim the year of the Lord's favor and the day of vengeance of our God, to comfort all who mourn, and provide for those who grieve in Zion—to bestow on them a crown of beauty instead of ashes, the oil of joy instead of mourning, and a garment of praise instead of a spirit of despair. They will be called oaks of righteousness, a planting of the Lord for the display of his splendor."

~Isaiah 61:1-3 NIV

The promises of the Lord are very extravagant, such is Isaiah 61. In this passage of scripture, we find a cluster of earth rocking promises. From turning our mourning into joy, to praise instead of despair, we learn that our God has promises for us that are worth contending for. We also discover in this passage the transformative nature of the Lord. He does not only want to deliver us from depression, heartache, or shame, but also deliver us to a reality far better.

After going through a season of constant heartbreak or trouble, when we get to the place of normalcy, we may feel that this is where it ends. However, the Lord has a far better plan for us. The place of comfort or safety is not a final destination, but a launching pad. Jesus takes us to a place of peace in order for the real healing to begin and healing, in the Lord's definition, not only means coming to terms with the loss, but actually getting back what was taken. Jesus is the Lord of the double portion – He has much to give to those who seek what He has. Yet, to get to the place of delighting in our recovered booty, we must first trust in the promises of God and press on to receive a healing that is complete.

At the end of this verse, there is another key insight in the heart of God. We learn that we, as children of the Lord, are then put on display for all to see His great work in us. Jesus wants to turn your mourning into joy, He wants to give you the garment of praise instead of mourning and much more, and He wants us to then go out to the world as a sign, and wonder of his greatness. How amazing that the Lord uses broken and hopeless people, and transforms us through His love to be a sign to all those still in suffering.

Knowing this truth, let us press on to receive the fullness of what the Lord has for us, and in us. We get to trust in the Lord while he is the one who restores us in our brokenness and emptiness.

Thank You, Jesus, that Your promises are good and trustworthy. Amen.

Picture This - What was taken from you during your loss? What have you grieved, mourned, and despaired over that you would like God to turn to joy, beauty, and favor?

Ask This - What would it look like for you to receive healing in this area? What does it look like on the other side of the healing from those areas of loss?

Pray This - I pray that the eyes of your heart may be enlightened in order that you may know the hope to which He has called you, the riches of His glorious inheritance in His holy people, and His incomparably great power for us who believe (Ephesians 18-19). What things do you need to surrender to receive God's healing; we can get accustomed to grieving and mourning. Say this prayer: "Lord, help me release my grief and move to a place of rest in Your promises, so that I may receive all that You have for me. I know You are a good God and You have so much to launch me toward. Amen."

Words of **Comfort** for Hope
*"Find the seed at the bottom of your
Heart and bring forth a flower."*
~Shigenori Kameoka

Hope Lives On

⇝ Amy Sikkema

"May he give you the desire of your heart and make all your plans succeed. May we shout for joy over your victory and lift up our banners in the name of our God. May the LORD grant all your requests. Now this I know: the LORD gives victory to his anointed. He answers him from his heavenly sanctuary with the victorious power of his right hand."

~Psalm 20:4-6 NIV

Hope is the great expectation. It's where our faith rests and so can our soul. When our world is crashing around us, it is easy to lose sight of where hope once might have existed. Maybe putting our hope in the wrong place or in the wrong things is setting us up for disappointment. Maybe hope got lost in a broken relationship or unkept plans. Where can we find hope? Where is she now?

A lot of the grieving after my husband's funeral looked like standing still in the middle of a storm. I couldn't move forward with anything. I would wait for him to walk through the door. I would want to call him when an event happened, or to work with him to handle a parenting situation. Smelling the aroma of the dirt that he would have on him when he was home from a greenhouse or the smell of fire after battling a house fire was a common expectation, but those scents didn't come. It numbed me to know that his presence was no longer here. I still had to care for the kids, get them to and from school, to doctor's appointments, and up in the morning. I also had to care for my children's grief before I could tap into my own; feeling nothing at all was the easiest choice. After the Novocain of my husband's death wore off and while life had continued going on around me, I looked about to see the rubble that was left. The chatter in my head on constant repeat; "how am I going to do this alone?" "He is gone, how am I going to do this?"

There were so many unknowns, so many broken expectations of our future together . . . our children's futures with their dad. All the dreams we had, the trips we planned, and anniversaries we had yet to celebrate were gone. Gone also were celebrating together all of the milestones with our kids: the birthdays, driving, graduation, marriage, grandkids. All of that . . . gone.

Hope – the hope that we have in Jesus Christ – the hope that GOD IS VICTORIOUS, and He gives victory to his anointed; that is what's still here. No matter how the battle ends, he wins the war. We have the hope and expectation of a brighter tomorrow. We have the hope that He is good, and He will never fail us. We have the hope that all of his promises are true. We can always cling to that hope and to the only One from whom it's freely given.

I pray that all who feel hopeless will lean into the everlasting love of God and the hope of goodness and eternal life that is only found through Him! Amen.

Picture This - Where have you seen God bring hope to a lost place in your life?

Ask This - Is there any area of your life that you may be expecting God to bring hope and new life to?

Pray This - Dear Father, thank You for being a God who seeks after us no matter how lost or hopeless we feel. Thank You for bringing hope to this broken world and for the power and victory that only comes through You. May the desires of my heart align with Your will for me, Lord. We look forward to the day of complete restoration when You return. Amen.

Words of Comfort for Hope

"Hang onto your hat. Hang onto your hope.
And wind the clock, for tomorrow is another day."
~E.B. White

Hope In The Dark

→ Heather Taylor

"I have told you this so that my joy may be in you and that your joy may be complete."

~John 15:11 NLT

I have experienced death; a type of death that leaves you unaware of your current circumstance (you've been murdered). Sure, you are walking, talking, maybe even smiling but inside you are dead. This has been caused by a medication that has been prescribed to help you, not kill you.

After months of unexplainable joint pain, I went to a doctor who came highly recommended to me. He felt I had Fibromyalgia. There wasn't a test to diagnose Fibromyalgia, but he seemed sure so I decided to listen and started taking a Class V Gabapentinoid. That was a mistake! My pain didn't go away, not really, just the desire to care.

I lived in a hollow, lonely shell for almost two years because I didn't know how to save myself. I couldn't find my voice. My daughter was planning her wedding, and I didn't care. My husband was becoming unhappy in our marriage, and I didn't care. My children said I was different, and I didn't care. I didn't care about anything. I started to fantasize about death, maybe even plan it. I didn't feel anything other than misery and bleakness. I wasn't living, rather I was dying, or maybe I was already dead. I had once been filled with joy; always laughing and loving life, yet now I was alone, unhappy and there was no joy. There was no hope. I tried to claw my way out of the bubble, but the drug was too powerful. My life was falling apart, and I couldn't do anything to fix it.

Then, through a friend, I remembered that I had one thing on my side. I had God! God to me meant there was hope, and I needed hope. I prayed, and I cried, and I prayed some more. I reached out to my friend and asked for help. She recommended I get off of the drug I was on.

'Of course! Why didn't I think of that? That's right I wasn't able to think clearly!'

The class of drug I was on can't just be stopped, you have to wean yourself off of them because of the effects they have on your brain and in my case the CNS. I didn't care. I wanted them out of my body, so I did the worst thing I could do and stopped cold turkey. The pain was at times excruciating; my body felt like it was on fire. Just one touch set my nerves on an endless shooting dance of fire daggers all through my body. I didn't care. I was overwhelmed with delusions, uncontrollable fear, irrational thoughts and behavior, but I didn't care.

Through all of this I had HOPE, finally, and that was all I needed. I knew that at the end of this agony there would be joy again. I held on to the promise that Jesus gave us in John 15:11: His joy will be in me and my joy will be complete! Hope! Through this dark night there will be a dawn, and that dawn will begin with me laughing, smiling and loving again.

It took several weeks, maybe even months to withdraw from that poison, but in the end, I came back. Hope in Jesus brought me back to life and back to my family.

Jesus, I pray that anyone reading this who needs hope to get through the next seconds, minutes, hours or day will turn to You and let you take their yoke from them. I pray, Lord, that You will give them HOPE. Show them that through the darkness the sun will once again shine and bring a new day.

Picture This - Envision being placed in a bubble where everything you thought and did was lacking emotion.

Ask This - Have you disconnected from the rest of your family and friends? Are you living your life to the fullest?

Pray This - I ask that you will help me to recognize the areas in my life that I am allowing to harm me. I pray Lord that you will expose any lies and help me to live with joy.

Words of Comfort for Hope

"Hope is a renewable option: if you run out of it at the end of the day, you get to start over in the morning."

~Barbara Kingsolver

Wiped Away

→ Karen Bruno

"He will wipe every tear from their eyes, and there will be no more death or sorrow or crying or pain. All these things are gone forever."

~Revelation 21:4 NLT

After my husband's suicide, the hardest people to face were my children. Witnessing the grief, loss, deep sorrow, and pain in their eyes was devastating. Wiping it away was a daily desire for anyone that encountered their pain. People tried to comfort them and console them to instill a glimmer of hope. Most of the efforts were helpful but all of them temporary.

There is only one permanent, complete fix to the brokenness of this world. It comes at the hand of God. Envision His hand reaching out to wipe our last tears as a mother does for a crying child. With one tender touch of His hand He will eliminate the pain, suffering, and grief completely and forever. We will no longer recall the sorrows of this world. This is true for all believers.

Not another grave will be dug, never again will a parent bury a child, mental illness will not wreak havoc on a family, physical ailments won't destroy lives. We will not lose loved-ones, jobs, homes, pets, hopes, dreams, life-styles. There will be no more famine or war. All human atrocities will cease. Nothing that would cause us to cry will remain.

It's hard to imagine the earth released from its bondage to death and decay. The beauty of it all is overwhelming. Although it is a future hope, we can rest our heart's troubles on the truth that His children – my children – our children will all experience Him wiping away the tears of this world forever.

Thank You, Lord, that I can find hope in knowing You will wipe away all our sorrows, crying and pain forever. Amen.

Picture This - Draw, day-dream, or write about what you picture when you think of the "new earth."

Ask This - What comfort can you gain from knowing God will wipe away our tears forever?

Pray This - Lord, I yearn for the day Your hand stretches out to wipe the final tears from the world and restore it completely.

Words of Comfort for Hope

"Hope is passion for what is possible."
~Soren Kierkegaard

She's Right Here

» Ava Olivia Willett

"'Do not let your hearts be troubled. You believe in God; believe also in me. My Father's house has many rooms; if that were not so, would I have told you that I am going there to prepare a place for you? And if I go and prepare a place for you, I will come back and take you to be with me that you also may be where I am.'"

~ John 14:1-3 (NIV)

I reflected on the town that became a home for me. My first job brought me to a place that was always lit up brightly and decorated so beautifully. Each street corner had a memory linked to it. Each little business had owners who knew me from my choir programs or from family. Although there was never a whole lot to do here, it was my home.

I remember packing up my suitcase and sitting inside my closet that overlooked my bedroom. I was counting down the days until I moved back to where I grew up as a child. It felt like I was ready to move on from these amazing things that had happened in my little home. I knew I must move on from all of it, though.

God gave me a heart full of hope. It's as if it ached from overflowing with hope. God works in mysterious ways that make us wonder how it's possible to feel such a deep sadness mixed with such joy. But that is how I grieved my childhood home. God promised me that, as I stepped my foot into my adult life and away from my youth, He would remind me of His Promise. Wherever He leads my feet, wherever the pain may settle in my bones, He's there every step of the way.

And with a hopeful heart, I began my journey as a woman of God, independent and working to support myself. One day in early May I stopped in the middle of my waitressing shift and overlooked the various people and atmosphere surrounding me. I thought to myself, the strong woman I'm destined to be isn't someone I need to keep looking forward to. Looking deeply ahead trying to imagine what I'd look like, speak like, think like - she's right here, standing in a glimmering restaurant with a waitress apron around my waist; awed by people and their beautiful, intricate lives; opening wine for women in jeans and heels; pouring champagne for the generation who will soon step back and watch us take on the nation ourselves.

I am empowered.

Jesus, You are hope. Light a fire within my soul to burn bright for the whole world to see Your goodness and Your love. Let [my] conversation be always full of grace, seasoned with salt, so that [I] may know how to answer everyone (Colossians 4:6). Blessed be Your name. Amen.

Picture This - What have you specifically done or can begin doing in order to apply what God has gifted you with to empower those around you?

Ask This - What characteristics do you have that were born out of grief and how do those characteristics bring you hope toward your better future?

Pray This - Lord, stand beside me as I journey through this life You've given to me. I am free because of Jesus. Let this Good News be my flame of hope! Amen.

Words of **Comfort** for Hope

"Part of being optimistic is keeping one's head pointed toward the sun, one's feet moving forward."
~Nelson Manela

Deep Roots

⇒ Traci Weldie

"I will heal their waywardness and love them freely, for my anger has turned away from them. I will be like the dew to Israel; he will blossom like a lily. Like a cedar of Lebanon he will send down his roots; his young shoots will grow. His splendor will be like an olive tree, his fragrance like a cedar of Lebanon. Men will dwell again in his shade. He will flourish like the grain. He will blossom like a vine, and his fame will be like the wine from Lebanon."

~Hosea 14:4-7 NIV

I was crying a lot when I got an email from my mentor telling me to read Hosea, the whole book. She knew I was grieving the loss of a dream of what my family would be. She knew I now had a son who didn't return any form of love or affection toward me, and that had completely broken my heart. "Read Hosea. Pay special attention to the last chapter." So I read, and as I did, the Holy Spirit ministered to my heart saying, "This is what redemption looks like. This is what restoration looks like. Don't stop pursuing your son."

To be honest, Hosea was one of the books of the Bible that I naively thought was of no use to me. I mean, I was sure I was not in an adulterous relationship, and I couldn't possible reconcile what God was teaching *me* in that book. However, when we brought our son home, I did find myself in an adulterous relationship. Here I was being asked to love someone who was unlovable and feeling that way, myself. What is most amazing about the last chapter of Hosea is that God doesn't call us to love the unlovable and then leave it at that. There is a promise that will be fulfilled by God's love. The hope is in Hosea's story. The fact that there's a book in the Bible that so clearly addresses how we are to love, even when somebody doesn't return that love to us, has been so encouraging and has given me a lot of hope. I don't feel alone in this. People have to make a choice in an adulterous relationship, whether or not to fix what's broken. I'm that way with God. He lovingly continues to pursue us and bring us back. I feel like part of God's plan is for us to learn how to love ourselves and know that God will see us through. At the end of the book, when men will come under his branches and be blessed; that's what I pray for George. He's going to have deep roots in the lord. When he's a man, he's going to bless others.

Hosea ends with this endearing chapter of hope and life and pure love. God promises that He will…not us. He heals our waywardness and loves us freely. In the dark moments of despair over my new normal, God gently showed me how I was so often distracted away from Him. I chose Facebook or reality TV or a brownie over spending time with God. Yet God is the one who pursues, the one who will heal and the one who will love. The result of this love is astonishing! When we are loved and made whole by God, we will blossom into something beautiful. Our lives will be restored; we will possess strength with deep roots. Roots are pretty amazing, and the deeper the root, the more stable and healthier the tree. God's love encourages our roots to dig in, to hold on tight when the grief comes in waves. The beauty is that we won't only "hold on", those roots will cause the tree to grow and flourish, and Hosea adds that "men will dwell again in his shade." We can actually become a blessing to other people. Only with God can we turn our grief into hope again.

Lord, thank You for being the One who will. You will heal. You will love. I pray my roots would dig deep and I would grow in order to begin being a blessing to the people You have put into my life.

Picture This - What is the benefit to a tree that has deep, strong roots? What benefit is it to your life to have deep, strong roots?

Ask This - How is God continually pursing you? Who has He put into your life that is demonstrating the love of God?

Pray This - Ask God to show you how you will be a blessing to other people because of the trial you have endured.

Words of **Comfort** for Hope

"This new day is too dear, with its hopes and
invitations, to waste a moment on the yesterdays."
~Ralph Waldo Emerson

A Miracle Minute

→ Lisa Danegelis

"God, who gives life to the dead and calls those things which do not exist as though they do"

~Romans 4:17 (NKJV)

The years upon years of desperate prayers seemed to have been answered with silence. Did the numerous passionate discussions and the tear-stained letters I sent him mean nothing at all? My dad was near death's door, close to ending his grueling battle with Parkinson's disease. What was even more heart-wrenching for me, though, as I stood at his bedside, was the life-long internal battle he had fought. At the tender age of twelve, his father's sudden death had shaken him to the core.

His fragile trusting heart seemed to have broken in all the wrong places.

My grandma told us he had locked himself in his room for days, and emerged changed. This phrase from the Simon & Garfunkel's song, "I Am A Rock" describes the transition: "I touch no one and no one touches me, I am a rock, I am an island." This former altar boy left an "angry God" behind and became an agnostic. To him, God was not "good" anymore.

As my own faith grew, so did my awareness of my dad's doubting shattered heart. His sad eyes spoke volumes. I had shared my faith passionately with him for years; yet he had remained cold and resolute . . . until now.

He was near comatose when my ten-year-old son, David, said, "Grandpa, I want to see you in heaven. You need Jesus."

In a miracle minute, he turned his head, opened now soft tear-filled eyes, and said, "I believe in His goodness," as he pulled my son close.

This hardened seventy-nine-year-old cynic met Jesus that day. Decades of questions were answered in that moment. The joy! Oh the joy I felt! My daddy was going to heaven!

God gives life to the dead places. He called faith up and out of a dry well that day. A lifetime of pleading prayers can come to fruition with one breath of the Spirit. That is our God, friends; never let your flicker of hope fade.

Father, help me to trust You through all the seasons of my life. I know that You are a God of miracles! I ask that You renew my hope and breathe life into all the dead places. Amen.

Picture This - What is the thing or person in your life that you feel is beyond God? Imagine God's miracle intervening.

Ask This - Who do you want with you in Heaven who does not know God and believe in His goodness?

Pray This - Write a prayer to God, with the innocence of a child, asking Him to soften the hearts of the unbelievers in your life. Mention them by name and pray for Jesus' goodness over their lives.

Words of Comfort for Hope

"The miserable have no other
medicine, but only hope."
~William Shakespeare

The Light At The End Of The Tunnel

→ Neesie Cieslak

"In hope of eternal life, which God, that cannot lie, promised before the world began."

~ Titus 1:2 KJV

Two stupendous words: "in hope." Straight away, they say *'there's a light at the end of the tunnel,'* and not just any tunnel, but this tunnel called life. Eternal life is the Great Hope, a promise by a God who cannot lie. I was so grateful of this promise when I sat reflecting on the heinous murder of my little brother twenty years ago.

Michael was nineteen, an artist, gentle. He also became a runner for a drug dealer, a choice that took his earthly life. I was shocked upon receiving the call that he was found dead on the street with a bullet in him. There was a bit of a maternal reaction in my heart, for I was the oldest sibling. I would care for him on my own for much of my young life. Then as a follower of Jesus, had I witnessed to him enough? Did I tell him about Jesus? Guilt and despair threatened to suck the life out of me. The Spirit reminded me that I'd indeed shared the gospel with my brother, on more than one occasion. He also reminded me of His love for my brother and His mercy, and where Hope gave me peace. Hope in the mercy of God, hope in the love of God, and hope of eternity. There is a hope that I will see Michael again, because I have the "Great Hope" of eternal life.

The Lord didn't just drum up the idea of eternal life. He promised it "before the world began". He can't lie. We can trust Him to take us through life's tunnel and into the Light of Eternity- Heaven. Therefore, we don't mourn as the world mourns.

Jesus, thank You for giving your life so that I can have eternal life. You are our hope. Your promise is sure and true. Help us to look to You when it seems all hope is gone, and place our trust in You. Amen.

Picture This - Picture yourself standing at the beginning of a dark tunnel with a light shining at the end of it.

Ask This - Is the mercy of God big enough to get your loved one to the light at the end of the tunnel? YES! How can you begin or continue to allow the light of Jesus to shine through you to those who need it?

Pray This - Father, guide me through, I place my hope in you. Amen.

Words of **Comfort** for Hope

"Hope is a verb with its
shirtsleeves rolled up."
~David Orr

For Our Good Even When We're Not

→ Rebecca Grambort

"And we know that all things work together for good to those who love God, to those who are the called according to His purpose."

~Romans 8:28 (NKJV)

In one of my darkest seasons of suffering, a few of my Christian friends would attempt to encourage me with this scripture. *'He works all things together …'* they would say.

I questioned what they said, and wondered if the latter parts of the verse revealed some requirements that I just couldn't measure up to. *'Did my love for God fall short of the bar? 'Was I really called? What if God wouldn't work things together for my good because I fell short of the mark?'* These questions caused me fear and doubt.

I learned that I couldn't trust myself to figure it out on my own. I had to put my faith into something bigger and someone bigger. My own strength couldn't make a way out. And the same was true of what other people could do for me.

Going back to the roots of the faith instilled into me as a child by my earthly father, I concluded that if there was a way out of my suffering, my only Hope would be Jesus. And so, I went all in and banked on Christ. With persistent effort over time, I started to see the faithful fingerprints of God throughout my entire life. I noticed that He was there well before the death of my husband, and had strategically pre-arranged people in my past, pre-arranging a solution for my present storm. He was working it together for my good even before I loved Him or had ever served Him! Because of this, I fell wholeheartedly, reciprocally in love with the King.

Shortly after putting my trust in God, I heard His voice for the first time; as He called me out on assignment. That is where He began to use me . . . by helping single moms in need. Coming alongside these women served a purpose not only for them, but also for me . . . I discovered that I was healing as I helped them. My pain had a purpose, just like Jesus' pain had a purpose when He went to the cross to redeem His people.

God works all things together for our good. He sees our future-selves instead of looking at our past, no matter how sordid it may be. The Father has full assured confidence in who we will become, and is not challenged by who we once were. There is a new you on the horizon. God uses everything. The enemy never wins! With Him, not a drop of our suffering is ever wasted. He works all things together for our good and for His Glory!

Father God, I trust You that my pain has a divine purpose. Thank You for working all things together for our good and Your Glory! Amen.

Picture This - Imagine a *new you* on the horizon? Write down what you envision. Does this bring you hope?

Ask This - What kind of purpose do you think your pain can prove to become useful?

Pray This - As you thank the Lord for working things together for your good, pray gratitude for the future you trust He will bring you.

Words of Comfort for Hope

*"Let your hopes, not your hurts
shape your future."*
~Robert H. Schuller

The Rainbow After The Storm

≫ Maria Notch

"Now faith is being sure of what we hope for and certain of what we do not see."

~Hebrews 11:1 NIV

No one likes to wait. Waiting is hard. It takes patience and I don't ever seem to have enough. Waiting is when growth and preparation happen, when one must remember that God's delay is not God's denial. Hope is when, in the midst of waiting, we cling to the promises of God for us and for our future.

What does waiting look like for a miscarriage mommy? There was waiting for that first full cycle until I got a "normal period," waiting for my hormone levels to regulate, waiting for my body to stop "feeling" pregnant, and waiting to get over the fact that I was "supposed to be pregnant" but I wasn't . . . not anymore. As it pertains to waiting in hope, I feel I've become an expert. There are two simple steps I've trained myself to follow.

First, I have faith in God's promises, believing in what I cannot yet see. My mentors in business always say "what you speak about you bring about." Why would I practice anything different in an area of my life that I cared about even more than my business? I began making it a practice to talk about our future children! "If God blesses us with a girl, I'm gonna LOVE watching you melt, every day," is an example of something I say to my husband.

Secondly, I now use my imagination and make up the best, most wonderful scenarios of welcoming another baby into our lives. I think about the baby shower, imagine the people in our lives who will be eager to celebrate new life in our family, and picture my son or daughter's baptism one day.

In circles of miscarriage mommies, I've heard women say, "I don't want to get my hopes up," and I like to ask, "what are you afraid of?" I think, for a miscarriage family, the answer is obvious. "I'm afraid of losing another baby." I get it, but—when we serve a big God who promises to give us whatever we ask for in His name—why not get our hopes up? Because we're afraid of getting hurt? Our God is the Master Healer! He can bring miracles – yesterday, today, and forever!

I've come to a place where I know, with the grace of God and the support of those around us, we could get through anything . . . even another miscarriage. I mean, we've handled four losses. It's been harder than words can possibly express, but I've grown into the woman God needs me to be because of it. He may deem it the right time for us to have another little one; in the meantime, it's my job to cling to His promises to and hope for what He has in store for us! I will hope for, dream about, and talk about that rainbow baby (a rainbow baby is the baby born after a loss). Until His plan is revealed, I'll wait expectantly and praise God when he or she arrives!

Heavenly Father, You are a big God who is in all the little details. Increase our faith that You can bring to fruition what we hope for and bring to light what we cannot currently see. We claim Your goodness for our future and wait in joyful hope to see it come to fruition! Amen.

Picture This - Imagine what you dare to hope for coming to fruition. How will you thank praise the Lord? How will you celebrate? Who will you tell? What will you feel?

Ask This - What's holding me back from being hopeful? Is it fear? Is it doubt?

Pray This - Lord, increase my belief. Help my unbelief!

Words of **Comfort** for Hope

"You are not here merely to make a living. You are here in order to enable the world to live more amply, with greater vision, with a finer spirit of hope and achievement. You are here to enrich the world, and you impoverish yourself if you forget the errand."

~Woodrow Wilson

Conjuring Up Hope

→ Kimberly Joy Krueger

"May the God of hope fill you with all joy and peace in believing, so that by the power of the Holy Spirit you may abound in hope."

~Romans 15:13 ESV

No one likes to wait. Waiting is hard. It takes patience and I don't ever seem to have enough. Waiting is when growth and preparation happen, when one must remember that God's delay is not God's denial. Hope is when, in the midst of waiting, we cling to the promises of God for us and for our future.

Although I have suffered and lost much, somehow hope has remained intact; except for once. My newest baby, my eleventh born, was just a few weeks old. My first born and oldest son was seventeen (and there were nine others in between). He had been getting into a lot of trouble. I had a feeling something very bad was coming. One day, as he was bringing the garbage cans up after school, three squad cars pulled in and police officers jumped out and began to surround him. They handcuffed him and read him his rights. I stared out the kitchen window incredulously as my son, my baby, was being treated like a criminal. Soon the story unfolded, and I learned that he had, in fact, committed some crimes. And since he was seventeen, instead of writing him tickets and fining him, he was charged as an adult and taken to jail. My heart was broken.

From the time I was a young mother until that day, I prayed, "Lord, please don't let me wreck my children." The day they came for him was the day my worst fear became my reality. His day of doom was also the day that sealed my ultimate failure. All I ever wanted for my children was for them to stay on the straight and narrow. My dream was dead. My hopes were crushed. And into the pit of hopeless despair I sank.

A few weeks later, a dear friend came over. She said she was extremely worried about me; that she'd never seen me like this. "I've never been like this," I replied robotically in my daily "uniform" of sweat pants and a t-shirt. She said, "I think you have lost your hope." Yes, that was it—it resonated with me. But the thought of finding it again was…exhausting. Did God expect me to? The idea didn't even appeal to me. I succumbed to my hopeless existence while rocking my newborn baby. My friend promised to pray for me.

Just a few days later, Romans 15:13 crossed my path; it was my divine intervention. As I heard the words "may the God of all hope fill you…so that you may abound in hope," it hit me! Hope comes from God. He created it, and He fills us with it. It can't be conjured up, forced or faked. If you have it, it is because God filled you with it. If you don't have it, then He is the only place to get it! I was so relieved. God did not expect me to "be hopeful." And He wasn't mad at me for being hopeless. He was lovingly offering to fill me with hope once again.

Before I knew it, hope was alive in me again. It started small and grew. And that new hope was enough for me to face my (perceived) failure, my shame, and my new reality…with grace.

God of all Hope, will You fill us with Your hope yet again? You see and feel our hopelessness. It breaks Your heart to know that we are in such a dark place. Thank You for being the origin of all hope and for never running out. May we abound in Your hope today. Amen.

Picture This - Close your eyes and imagine you are bringing your aching hopeless heart to Jesus right now. What does that look and sound like? What is He saying and doing back?

Ask This - Have you felt pressure to somehow work yourself out of hopelessness and conjure up hope? If not for yourself, maybe for the people around you? If so, describe how Romans 15:13 is a relief to you.

Pray This - Now, ask the God of all hope to fill you with hope for your future today. Write your prayer here.

Words of **Comfort** for Hope

*"Hope itself is like a star – not to be seen in the sunshine of
prosperity, and only to be discovered in the night of adversity."*
~Charles Spurgeon

Meet Your Companions

FEW INTERNATIONAL PUBLICATIONS is *"An Extraordinary Publishing Experience."* We believe women were created to be an answer for the problems our world faces today. The Fellowship of Extraordinary Women (FEW) was born out of that belief and today FEW empowers women from all over the globe to live extraordinary lives and tell their stories. FEW Monthly Meetings develop women's understanding of their true identity in Christ and empower them to embrace their God-given destinies. When we see women begin to understand that they were created to be an answer, they cannot help but to make significant differences in the lives around them! FEW's Certified Women's Leadership Course (CWLC) for Christian women changes the way women see God, themselves, and others. It catapults women into their God-given destiny and purposes as leaders on the seven mountains of cultural influence. CWLC gives women unbridled confidence to be who God made them to be! FEW International Publications, an invaluable arm of the Fellowship of Extraordinary Women, is a #1 Bestselling Publisher (with a unique writer-coaching model) for women authors at all levels who are seeking more from telling their stories than just a printed project. We are privileged to watch authors connect, learn, and grow through the creation of written works that impact others and glorify God.

KIMBERLY JOY KRUEGER, owner and president of FEW and FEW International Publications, as well as one of the company's many #1 Bestselling authors, has overcome some of life's toughest struggles with beauty, dignity, and grace; her eyes always looking up and never looking back. She fell in love with running in 2014 and has since run more than ten 5Ks, half marathons, and full marathons. After being hit by a car in 2014, she ran a half marathon just eleven months later. Her favorite race to run is her race with God; and she runs it to win! As a third-generation entrepreneur, she has set her goals high and continues to reach higher, while helping women to see their true value and reach their God-given potential. Her mission is to empower women to live extraordinary lives and tell their stories. Through *The Fellowship of Extraordinary Women* (FEW) monthly meetings, FEW's Women's Leadership Course, and FEW International Publications, she is doing just that—by leaps and bounds. Kimberly says that her greatest accomplishment in life is being a wife, mother to twelve children, and "Noni" to five (perfect) grandchildren. Her closest friends will tell you that she is a mom to many and a friend to all. For fun, she transforms into a "Biker Chic," and rides alongside her husband, Scott, on her Harley-Davidson® Road King.

Visit *www.kimberlyjoykrueger.com* for more information on Kimberly and FEW.

REJI LABERJE is the **Writing and Publishing Coach to FEW International Publications**, but this is the first FEW book she's *contributed* to. It is her fiftieth book since the start of her professional writing career, including eight #1 Bestsellers (so far)! She's also helped dozens of other authors become #1 Bestsellers. In addition, Reji teaches, writes, edits, does layout, and markets for traditional and nontraditional publishers, classes, and authors of sports writing, biography, leadership, juvenile fiction, self-improvement, playwriting, and more. While in her third decade in the industry, her roles in the field pale to those of veteran, wife, and mother. With family and loved ones, she enjoys service, music, theatre, camping, and life in Wisconsin. Discover more at: *www.bucketlisttobookshelf.com.*

HEATHER TAYLOR's writing career started at the age of sixteen when she first became published. She has since become an Amazon #1 Bestselling Author as well as Producer and Co-host of the *"Coffee with Kim"* Podcast. Most recently, she attained the title of **Lead Ambassador for** FEW (the Fellowship of Extraordinary Women) due to her endless support, encouragement, and belief of FEW's mission to help women be extraordinary and tell their stories. Heather uses her in-your-face sense of humor to speak to women and teen girls who are trying to tackle obstacles like depression, self-esteem and relationship struggles. Her relatable personality and huge heart make

it easy for her to offer compassion and hope . . . with a side of laughter. Heather's first love is her family. She loves playing with her granddaughter, laughing with her three adult children, and her thirty years of morning coffee dates with her husband, Terry. For booking information please contact: *hjtenterprise@gmail.com* and visit: *alliknowis.net.*

AMY SIKKEMA is a widow and mom of two busy boys and one spunky little girl. Grand Rapids Michigan is where she resides and eagerly serves Jesus. Her passion for reaching out to the lost and hurting has led her to her calling. Writing, blogging, and speaking the good news of hope and God's promises are her mission. Amy serves on the board of the non-profit organization "Shields of Hope-West Michigan" where she walks alongside families who are battling cancer. In her down time Amy enjoys camping, sunsets over Lake Michigan, and gathering friends and family around bonfires in her backyard. You can follow Amy at *amysikkema.com* or on Facebook- search *Sikkemastrong.*

AVA WILLETT lives in northern Wisconsin and works as a barista at the local coffee shop. She's passionate about church, writing, her friends, and traveling. She plays piano for her church's worship team and helps teach at youth group. Ava had been writing stories and poems ever since she could pick up a pencil, and completed her first book when she was thirteen. *Comfort for the Grieving* is Ava's first published work. By the end of 2019, she plans on publishing her first solo-written book, a memoir titled *Lone Wolf.*

ANNABELLE AHLERS is a published poet, author, and student, currently residing in the South of Spain. Motivated by her experiences of Jesus meeting her in the darkest places of her life, Annabelle's writing is intended to reach the heart of the orphan and the widow who feel at their lowest. Her ministry includes participation in healing rooms, street evangelism, and intercession for trafficked women. Annabelle's passion is to make known the beauty of Jesus and to bring the Kingdom of God into every situation.

Annabelle Ahlers and Jessica Chase comprise one of three mother - daughter writing contributors to A FEW Words Of Comfort For The Grieving. The others are Reji and her mother, Linét, and Ava and her mother, Rebecca.

JESSICA CHASE is a creative people development professional, life coach, and devoted mother. Jessica's passion is coaching people to reach their fullest potential in every area of their lives. Having spent many years working to overcome childhood trauma, Jessica understands the challenges that can hinder personal, professional, and spiritual growth first-hand. She finds deep joy walking alongside people during their healing journey. Jessica enjoys spending time with the Lord, friends, family . . . and *Tito* (her pet beagle).

KAREN BRUNO was widowed at age forty after eighteen years of marriage to her high school sweetheart. Her husband's physical and mental health struggles ultimately led to his suicide leaving her and their four children to grieve and survive the devastation of their loss. She was serving her church as director of Women's ministry at the time sharing her passion for women to live fully and free in Christ. Ministry work has been her heart's home since her walk with Christ began in her early twenties. Karen has developed and implemented multiple discipleship and mentorship programs for woman of all ages. Having struggled through her teens she has a passion for coming

alongside teen girls helping them navigate those years of life. When speaking she utilizes humor and life's adventures coupled with the truth in God's word. Her teaching style is relevant, raw and relatable.

LINÉT LEWERENZ is a wife, mother, and grandmother. She has volunteered with AARP as a fraud fighter and believes strongly in equality for all. She has chosen to be a contributor to this body of work with a goal of enabling women to heal and move forward to peace and abundance. She enjoys seeing a good play, participating in a challenging game of duplicate bridge, and relaxing with a cup of coffee and an engaging book. She would encourage women of faith to find within this devotional a path that leads them forward to living their best life.

LISA DANEGELIS and her family live in the beautiful state of Wisconsin. She attended a culinary program where she fell in love with and married her instructor thirty-one years ago. Together, they own the prestigious Lee John's Catering. She is also a busy mom of five adopted children and a survivor of wrongly prescribed psychiatric drugs. She has her own YouTube channel and Facebook group to support others on this harrowing journey. In time, she hopes to use her home as a safe haven for those in need. Lisa enjoys gardening, yoga, and writing. You may contact her at: *Bakingfever@yahoo.com*.

LUANNE NELSON is a motivational speaker, ordained minister, #1 Bestselling author, wife, and mother. She studied English Literature at Westminster College in Pennsylvania and Journalism at Marquette University. Her love of Jesus Christ and her enthusiasm for God's Word are apparent in both her writing and her joy-filled street ministries. She has been through many adversities and knows the healing grace of God. Her husband calls her, "a Force you can't ignore!" Luanne was once included as one of the most interesting people in the city in *Milwaukee Magazine*. Her hobbies include gardening, piano composition, photography, and antiquing. She loves her corgi and her husband, Dave.

MARIA NOTCH is driven by her love for people and her love of the Lord. She walks with women experiencing infertility, miscarriage or loss of a child, as well as those growing their families. Her blog educates people about challenges in these areas while focusing on supporting couples walking through a difficult time. Maria serves on staff at her church in music ministry and as the director of the Milwaukee Mercy Choir. Maria is married to her high school sweetheart, Jacob, and is mommy to LJ, MaryAnne, and four babies in Heaven. For more information visit: *Hopeandhealing.blog*.

NEESIE CIESLAK resides in Phoenix , Arizona with her husband, children, and grandchildren. Growing up in poverty, dysfunction, and much loss, she desires to share the love of God and the reality of His healing power. Neesie has experienced God's comfort in her life numerous times and prays she can comfort others, as He's comforted her. She has been able to speak and encourage thousands of people on their journeys. Neesie has homeschooled her children for twenty years; she enjoys reading, journaling, praying, and worshipping with her family. Reach her here: *https://m.facebook.com/Neesie-Grace-Cieslak-1911585768903526*.

REBECCA GRAMBORT resides in Merrill, Wisconsin and is one of the many #1 Bestselling female authors with FEW International Publications. She is also a marathoner and enjoys challenging herself by training year-round for long distance races. Her other interests include downhill and cross-country skiing, kayaking, and spending time with her four children. Her current contributions with FEW include: *The Ah-Ha Effect*, *The Miracle Effect*, and *A FEW Words on Becoming Holy, Whole, & Fit*. For more information please visit her website at **www.mahmonline.com**.

SUSAN BROZEK, M.S.W., L.C.S.W., is Director and Founder of Healing Word Psychotherapy Services, LLC (***www.healing-word.com***). Her heart is to help people who are hurting. She has been a Licensed Clinical Christian Psychotherapist for nearly twenty years and she has spoken at many conferences. She hosts a monthly TV broadcast on the The NOW Network (www.thenownetwork.org), and a bi-weekly Radio Broadcast called *The Way of Healing*, which can be heard on Blog Talk Radio. She is a #1 Bestselling Author, and her books include: *A FEW Words on Becoming Holy, Whole and Fit*, and *HEALING WORDS: 30 Devotional Word Studies for Emotional and Spiritual Healing*. Susan and her husband, Jeff live in Mequon, Wisconsin.

TRACI WELDIE is high school Learning Specialist, teacher, coach, and small group leader. Traci is a co-founder of an adoption and foster care conference, *Refresh*, for women located in Upstate South Carolina. She has six children, two of whom are adopted, which has led to a desire to encourage and equip women who have made the decision to care for the fatherless. Traci has written with vulnerability and honesty what it has been like to adopt children with special needs. Married to her best friend for twenty-two years, Traci enjoys sitting on the back porch with Joe.

VICTORIA DRECKMANN is a fitness instructor, author, and speaker. Her desire is to mentor and encourage women in their daily walk as they tackle life's F-words - Faith Family Fitness Food. Her willingness to show truth, authenticity, and raw vulnerability through her writing speaks to the hurt woman in all of us. She resides in Delafield, Wisconsin with her husband and two of her three children. You can follow her on Facebook at ***https://www.facebook.com/LiveVictoryUs/*** *"We must be willing to get rid of the life we've planned, so as to have the life that is waiting for us."* Joseph Campbell (1904-1987)

An Invitation To Receive The Comforter

→ From Kimberly Joy Krueger

We know that, at one time or another, every woman's heart will experience grief and the need for comfort. The good news of the Gospel is that we can not only find comfort in Jesus, but we can invite The Comforter to dwell in our hearts permanently!

The promise, made by Jesus, for those who have been saved by grace through faith, is that saying "YES," to Him means that we will receive the Holy Spirit (The Comforter, Helper, Advocate).

I don't know about you, but I need all of that in my life and heart—on bad days – and good.

Have you said "YES," to The Comforter making His home in your heart? If so, then you can also be assured that He is the ultimate Companion on your journey. He will not only comfort you, but He will begin to heal and make you whole.

If you are not assured of your salvation in Jesus Christ, you can be today by receiving His free gift.

You are invited to pray the prayer on the next page, today.

Begin your journey with the Comforter, Himself, by inviting Him into your heart.

Father, I believe that your Son, Jesus, lived on this earth to ultimately die for me.

I know I've sinned; I've missed the mark many times and I cannot save myself.

I know that no amount of good deeds can wash me clean – but Your blood can!

Today, I choose to place my trust in the price you paid on the cross. I now turn from my own ways and toward You.

I ask you to make me new and fill me with your Holy Spirit today!

Thank You for dying for me and giving me the gift of eternal life.

Thank you for sending The Comforter to live in my heart, to guide me, and to heal me, now and always.

Amen.

Enjoy some of the many other inspirational titles from FEW International Publications. Most FEW books are sold on Amazon and almost all FEW authors are available to present to your church or organization. Refer to their websites listed in the biographies of this book. OR – reach out to FEW International Publications Founder and President, Kimberly Joy Krueger, at www.kimberlyjoykrueger.com.

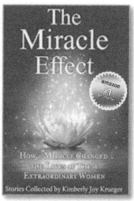

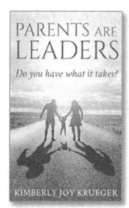

And, available soon, enjoy the latest in the "Effect Series!" "The Breakthrough Effect" is coming on November 26th, Cyber-Monday 2018!

Currently seeking women authors of all levels and experience who wish to have an extraordinary experiential writing journey in a book that glorifies God. Interested? You could be our NEXT #1 Bestselling Author. **Email: Kimberly@thefewwomen.com.**

34221563R00154

DUBSTEP
GRAPHICS

Editor: Katriona Feinstein
Art Direction: Joshua Hibbert

Published in 2014 by Graffito Books Ltd.
32 Great Sutton Street, London EC1V 0NB, UK.
www.graffitobooks.com

© Graffito Books Ltd. 2014.
ISBN 978-1909051119

British Library cataloguing-in-publication data.
A catalogue record of this book is available at The British Library.

Printed in China.

DUBSTEP
GRAPHICS

GRAFFITO

ABOVE *Photograph of Tiki Taane. by Jono Hislop.*

CONTENTS

INTRODUCTION 7

ASHES57 8

CAIGE BAKER 16

BUNGO DESIGN 22

ANTONIO CAMPOLLO 28

CDXVM 36

ZEKE CLOUGH 40

COOLKATZ MEDIA 46

JAMIE DEAN 50

HARDGORE 58

JONO HISLOP 64

HYPERVISION 70

PAWEL JANCZAREK 78

LACZA DESIGN 82

MIKE LAMBO 88

RICHARD LOCK 94

MICHYBAPS 100

MONSTA 106

SAMUEL MUIR 112

MICHAEL REICH 118

RYAN EL 122

TANSOMAN 128

TANT 136

THAT BANANA MEDIA 142

VECTOR MELDREW 150

APPENDIX 158

ABOVE *Photograph of FWD at Fabric.* by ASHES 57.

INTRODUCTION

DUBSTEP is everywhere. If it's not filling arenas for Skrillex, it's popping up in beats by Snoop Dogg, Rihanna and Britney Spears. It's loud, it's intense and it's the global phenomenon that's made history as the first type of electronic dance music to storm the US charts without the help of radio play or promotion. A dedicated army of bass music fans have ensured its takeover of college campuses, festivals and club nights across the country. And if you're still wondering what the fuss is about, I challenge you to keep still when the sub-bass kicks in on a mind-blowing drop!

The first time I heard dubstep, I was a young designer trying to make it in New York. Legendary DJ Dave Q asked me to work on a flyer for Dub War - America's first ever dubstep night. Watching DMZ play was unreal - I was instantly hooked. The scene was still pretty underground and small but it was filled with the spark of something new and exciting. There was an amazing sense of community among us bass addicts, with many people coming from far and wide to listen to the rare dubplates being played. Since those early days, I've watched dubstep's popularity explode and with it, the call for great dubstep graphics, as each artist and record label works to define their own style. I've now been fortunate enough to design for some huge acts like Wu-Tang Clan, who chose to take the path originally laid by the likes of El-B, Hatcha and Skream, by making dubstep music.

If you look back to its European roots, you see the massive range of influences that created dubstep. It was both a product of, and reaction to, drum and bass, garage, grime and dub in late 90s South London, and this heady mix spawned what remains a hugely eclectic genre of music. The sparse sounds of Burial are every bit as much dubstep as Bassnectar's face-melting explosions. The challenge to visually represent this range of styles is what makes dubstep graphics special. On album covers, posters and live projections you will find dark, urban imagery or eye-popping, twisted cartoons, minimal, trippy designs or two-fingers-up, witty graphics. And there is dubstep's amazing typographic innovation, one way it has always led the way visually.

Now that dubstep mania has taken root on US soil in a way never seen before, the world looks to the States to see what will come next. Whether it's minimal, heavy or "brostep", the sounds and styles of this mighty genre are evolving and paving the way for a new musical future.

ASHES57

ASHES57

Real name: Delphine Ettinger
Originally from France. Moved away fourteen years
ago and now based in East London, UK.
A true heavyweight of the dubstep graphics scene.
Her clients include Wu-Tang Clan, Exit Records,
Loefah, Tectonic, Hyperdub and Public Enemy.
Was involved in the underground NYC dubstep
scene from the start, after designing a poster for
DMZ.
Creating a logo for Loefah changed her life, and
she is now the in-house designer for his record
label Swamp 81 and DJ crew Teklife.
Likes to use Posca pen on paper and sketches
over it until it looks right.

LEFT
Like 2 Party.
for REPS.
Digital.

RIGHT
Artwork. for
Swamp 81.
Posca pen.

ABOVE Cover design, for Kryptic Minds. Digital.

ABOVE *Enter the Dubstep.* for Wu-Tang Clan. Posca pen and digital.

LEFT Ashes 57 at work
RIGHT *Swamp.* for Swamp 81. Posca pen.

RIGHT
I Don't Give
for DJ Rash
Photograph
digital.

BELOW
What You N
DJ Spinn/T
Photograph
digital.

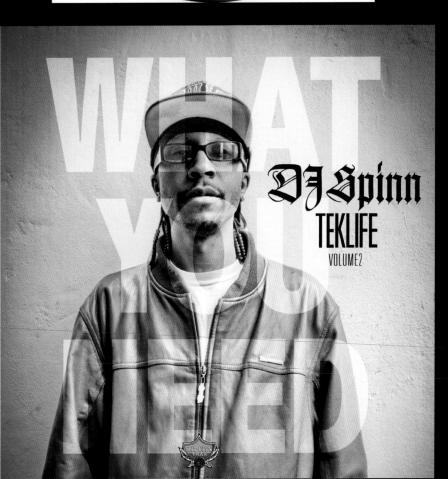

CAIGE
BAKER

AKA: The Third One.
Based in Calgary, Canada.
A young prodigy, he's just graduated high
school and has already been working as a
designer for 3 years.
His career took off when his unique style
was recognised by artist collective Dubstep
Designs.
Has done artwork for several DJs including
Reid Speed and Subsidize.
Originally inspired by the mind-bending
graphics of Alex Pardee.

ABOVE *Gathering What We Can.* personal work. Digital.
LEFT *Our Twin Ate Us.* personal work. Digital.

ABOVE *What's in the Box.* personal work. Digital.

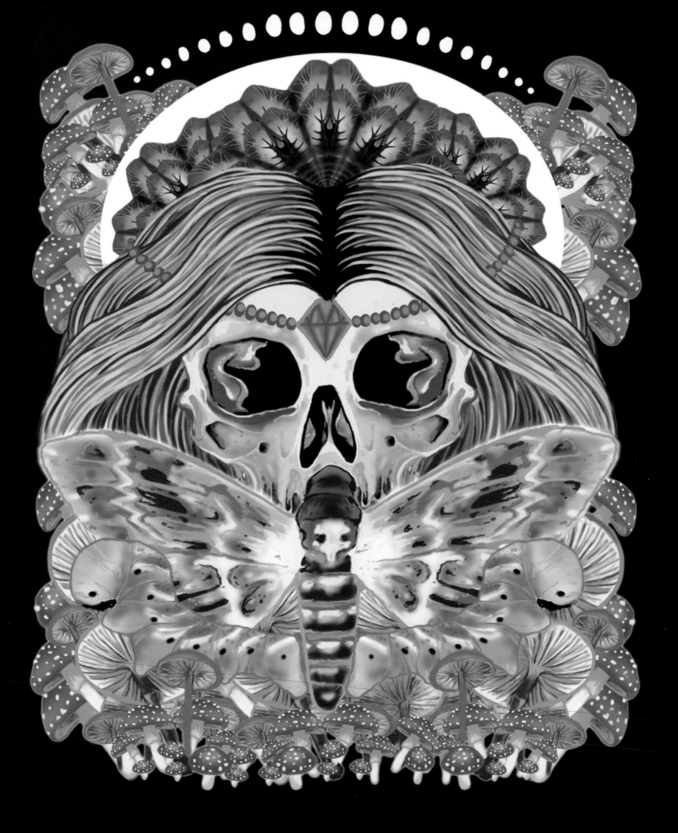

ABOVE *Just Transcendence.* personal work. Digital.

BUNGO DESIGN

Real name: Edmund Maier.
From Oxford, UK. Now based in Brighton.
A love of drum and bass got him into designing graphics for music.
His long list of clients includes Ergh, Substep, Modu, Blur and JME.
Says demand has risen steadily for underground music designs to be pieces of art.
Puts his presence in the music and design scene down to attending club nights instead of lectures at university. .

MOVEMENTS 26/05/12
WAREHOUSE CLUB

ABOVE *Movements.* for New Generation Takeover. Digital.
LEFT *ERGH.* for Ergh. Pencil and digital.

ABOVE *Mix Tapes.* personal work. Digital.

RIGHT *Mosaic.*
for Roy Green &
Protone. Digital.

BELOW *Fox Mask.*
personal work. Pencil and
digital.

BELOW RIGHT *Suburban.*
for Suburban Moscow.
Pencil and digital.

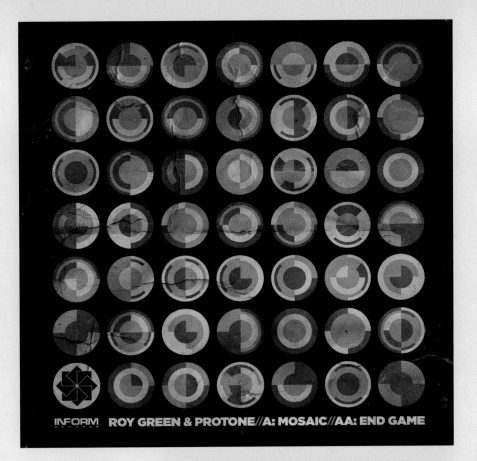

INFORM **ROY GREEN & PROTONE//A: MOSAIC//AA: END GAME**

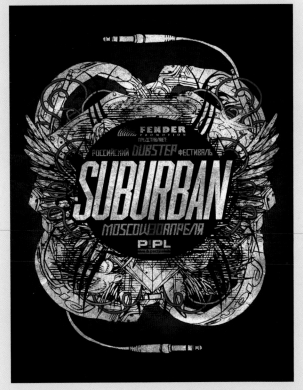

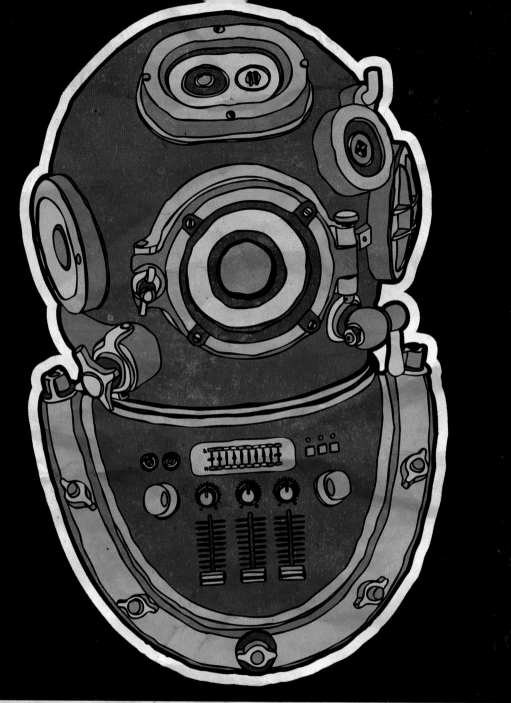

DUB POLITICS PRESENTS SKRILLEX
29TH JANUARY 2011 · THE BULLINGDON

ABOVE *Sub-head.* for Dub Politics. Digital.

MODU
TIMELAPSE
WINDOW SEAT

INFORM

MODU - TIMELAPSE / WINDOW SEAT - INFORM009

ABOVE. *Modu - Timelapse*, for Modu. Digital.

ANTONIO CAMPOLLO

AKA: Plaga.
Based in Antigua Guatemala, Guatemala.
Completely self-taught motion and graphic designer.
Loves textures and likes to experiment with 3D elements. Cinema 4D and Photoshop.
Has designed for many clients around the world, including MonsterCat, PlayMeRecords Kill the Rave and Quartus Saul.
Enjoys the liberty and fun of doing what he wants.
Would like to try his hand at DJ-ing.

ABOVE *The Chillers Logo.* for The Chillers. Digital.
LEFT *Lifted.* for K-lix. Digital.

ABOVE Preliminary sketch for Quartus Saul's *Smash*. Pencil.

LOVE & WAR

ANTONIO CAMPOLLO

S M A S H
QUARTUS SAUL

ABOVE *New Smash.* for Quartus Saul. Digital.
RIGHT K-Lix Logo Artwork, for K-Lix. Digital.

ABOVE   *Beastmode.* for Quartus Saul. Digital.
LEFT   Bleak Logo Artwork. for Bleak. Digital.

50CARROT
20K EP

CDXVM

Real name: Aaron Kirkby.
Based in Sheffield, UK.
Designing professionally for 3 years.
Wanted to combine his love of music and
design to create dubstep graphics, to cover
college costs.
Now works for artist collective Dubstep
Designs and clients including Tosti, 50 Carrot
and Lord of the Mics.
Doesn't like to look to other people's work for
inspiration; he just goes with what he thinks
will suit the specific piece.

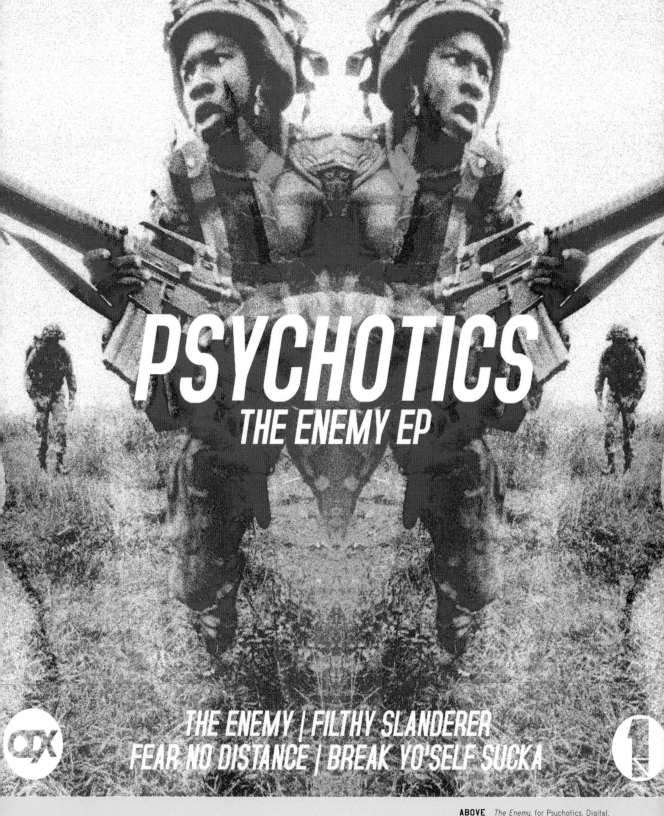

PSYCHOTICS
THE ENEMY EP

THE ENEMY | FILTHY SLANDERER
FEAR NO DISTANCE | BREAK YO'SELF SUCKA

ABOVE *The Enemy.* for Psychotics. Digital.
LEFT Cover art. for 50 Carrot Gang. Digital.

TOSTI
WASTE
MAN

ABOVE *Wasteman*, for Tosti. Digital.

ABOVE *The Test EP.* for Rilla Dubz. Digital.

C D X V M **39**

ZEKE CLOUGH

Based in Yorkshire, UK.
Was doing 'zines, comics and community art projects when dubstep pioneer Shackleton noticed his eye-popping designs and asked him to create sleeves for his record label, Skull Disco.
Other clients include Mordant Music, The Bug, *The Wire* magazine and *Resident Advisor*.
Uses pen, ink, acrylic paint and photocopied collages as well as digital media.
Is inspired by Japanese 'Ukiyo-e' artists and the gothic hills around his house.

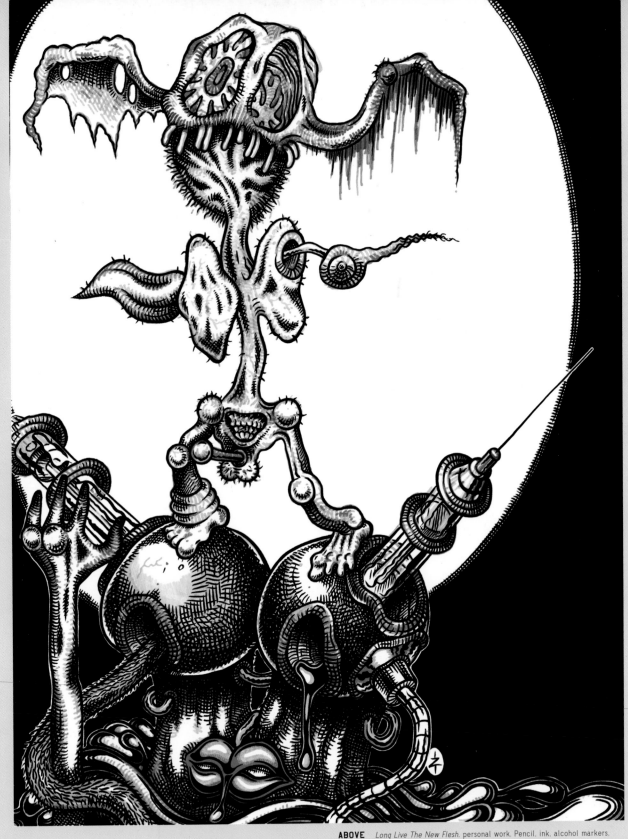

ABOVE *Long Live The New Flesh*. personal work. Pencil. ink. alcohol markers.
LEFT *Satan Cover*. for Skull Disco. Pen. white ink. photocopier. pencil. digital.

ZEKE CLOUGH **41**

SKULL DISCO
SOUNDBOY'S SUICIDE NOTE

ABOVE *Soundboy's Suicide Note*, for Skull Disco: lettering by crippaXXXalmqvist. Pencil, pen and ink, digital.
LEFT *Shackleton Portrait*, for Shackleton. Pencil, pen and ink, digital.

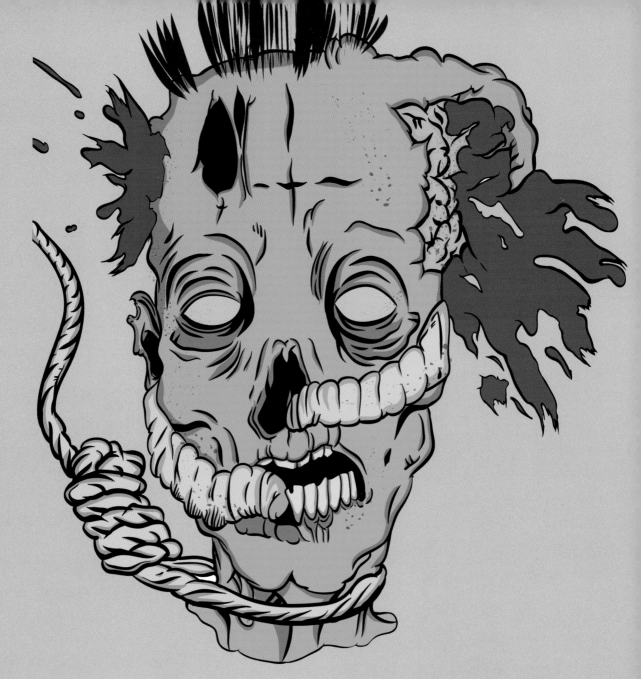

COOLKATZ
MEDIA

Real name: Christopher T. Wisnieski.
From California, now based in Kansas, USA.
Studied art in Korea and worked as a painter
before joining the US military.
For the past 3 years has worked on his insane
designs in his spare time "for beer money."
Clients include Getter, Barron, Fetch, Dead
Lights, Stoger and T-fresh.
Thinks dubstep graphics will continue to get
more gnarly as time goes on.

ABOVE *Queen of Skulls (B+W).* personal work. Digital.

ABOVE *Warrior.* personal work. Digital.

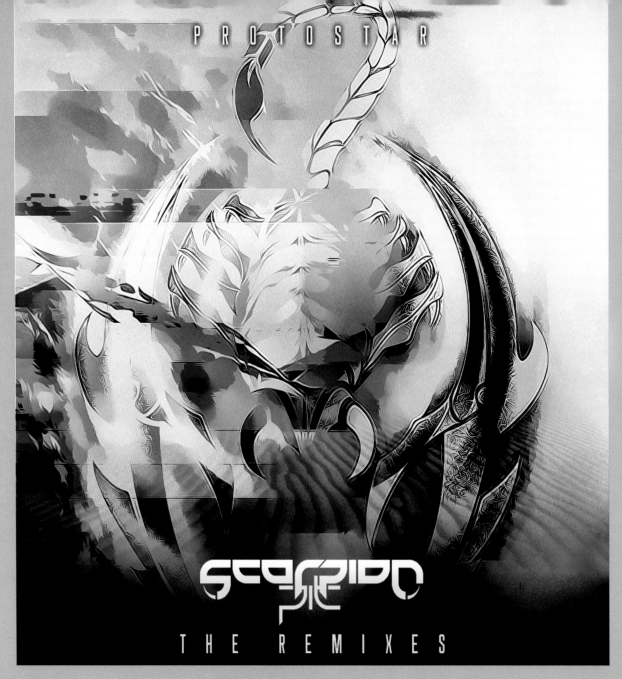

PROTOSTAR

SCORPION
THE REMIXES

JAMIE DEAN

AKA: DG Digital.
Born in London, now based in Cambridge, UK.
Designing professionally for 5 years.
Clients already include Getter,
Protostar, Monstercat Records, Prime Audio,
filth.fm, Dirty Deeds, 50 Carrot, and Kelly
Dean.
Listening to the music is a crucial part of his
process when designing for DJs.
Says the rise of dubstep means a lot of young
designers breaking into the scene.

PROTOSTAR & MAKO

NO FIRE FT RACHEL HIRONS

ABOVE *No Fire*. for Protostar and Mako. Digital.
LEFT *Scorpion Pit*. for Protostar. Digital.

PROTOSTAR

MYSTIC CAVE ZONE REMIX

ARTWORK BY DG DIGITAL. YEAH, EVEN THE DORITO.

BLVCK

JAMIE DEAN

HARDGORE

Real name: Brandon North.
From Blackburn, now based in Manchester, UK.
Studying Illustration at Salford University.
Has already had over 40 music industry clients,
including Dirt Monkey, Jantsen, 1UP, Davr, Dub-
All or Nothing and MrDubandBass.
Has loved dubstep since the first time that
powerful bass hit his ears and hopes it
continues to grow in the future.
Claims to know Banksy's true identity.

ABOVE *Ball'd At The End*, for Elonious. Digital.
LEFT *Panda-monium EP*, for Substep. Digital.

ABOVE *Rasta Ritual.* for Shawshank. Digital.

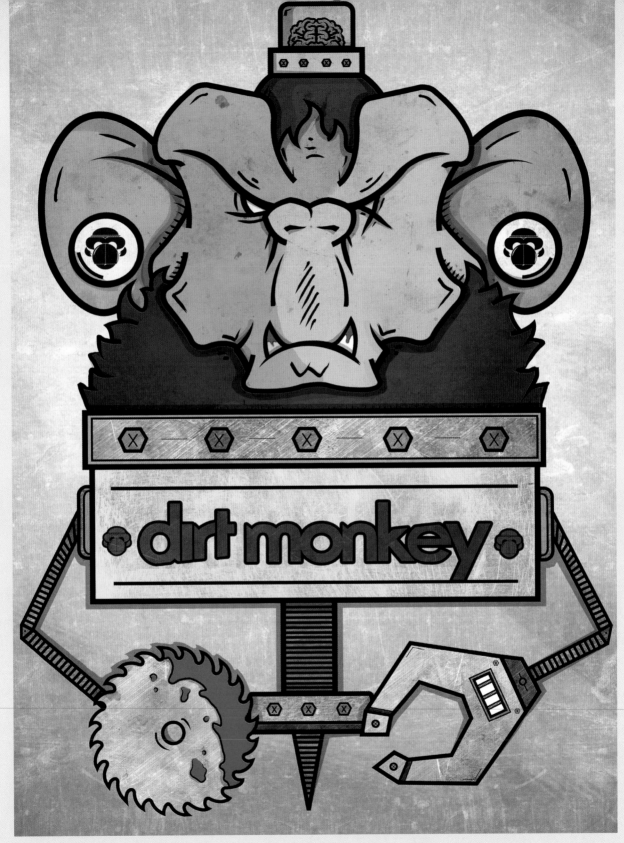

ABOVE *Don't Touch My Monkey,* for Dirt Monkey. Digital.

HARDGORE **61**

SKULLETONS EP.

ABOVE *Skulletons EP. for 1UP* (copyright Dub-All-Or-Nothing). Digital.

DIRT MONKEY JANTSEN

TOO DARN HOT

ABOVE *Too Darn Hot.* for Dirt Monkey & Jantsen. Digital.

JONO
HISLOP

AKA: Jono Kivex.
Originally from Auckland's North Shore, New Zealand. Now based in London, UK.
Started out as a 16 year-old flyer designer for club nights he got into with a forged driver's license.
Clients include Flux Pavilion, Circus Records, Tiki Taane and Dirtydub Records.
Has branched out recently into making music, motion pictures and live event visuals.
Sleep paralysis and lucid dreaming have helped him create design concepts.

Blow The Roof

FAR LEFT
Falinox
Conceptual Art.
for Falinox.
Digital.

LEFT
Blow the
Roof. for Flux
Pavilion. Digital.

ABOVE *Bloodstone*, for Tiki Taane. Acrylic and digital.

ABOVE *The Mystic.* personal work. Digital.

BELOW *Sprites*, personal pitch to SBTRKT. NASA Nebula photos and digital.

HYPƎRVISIØN

Based in Los Angeles, USA.
Designs for a range of high-profile clients
from multiple electronic music genres,
including hip hop and drum and bass.
Dubstep clients include Skrillex, 12th
Planet, Kill the Noise and record label
SubHuman.
Creates his works with Illustrator,
photoshop and by hand.

SKRILLEX PRESENTS
SWEET TREATS
VOLUME:001

01. **SKRILLEX & 12TH PLANET** - NEEDED CHANGE
02. **FLINCH** - WORLD ON FIRE
03. **ZEDD** - CHANGES FEAT. CHAMPIONS - ORIGNAL MIX

BLOOD COMPANY
MEDIA CONTENDER SMOG

ABOVE *Sweet Treats,* for Skrillex. Digital.
LEFT *The End is Near,* for 12th Planet. Digital.

RIGHT
Kill the Noise Logo, for Kill the Noise. Digital.

56
FUSION
ETHIO
FEATURING
LIMEWAX

ABOVE *Infiltrata Cover.* for Infiltrata. Digital.
RIGHT Logos. for various artists. Digital.

BORGORE

NVMBERNINE

MARK INSTINCT

Pain is a promise

SVBHVMAN

FOREIGN BEGGARS

CIRCLE MANAGEMENT
STEEZ PROMO & SERAPH

DUB NATION

PRESENTS

EXCISION

PHILLY:PA

ABOVE *Excision.* for Dub Nation. Digital.

SATURDAY OCTOBER 16TH

DUB NATION

PRESENTS

DIESELBOY

•BALTIMORE MD•

STEEZ PROMO & LIVE NATION PRESENT:

DUB NATION

• REVOLUTION LIVE - FT. LAUDERDALE, FL •
FRIDAY DECEMBER 10TH 2010

W/ SPECIAL GUEST
SMASH GORDON

NOV. 18TH
STEEZ PROMO & AK1200
PRESENTS
IT GETS HOT
FEATURING
MY NAME IS SKRILLEX
IN ORLANDO, FL
WITH SPECIAL GUEST
SMASH GORDON!
STEEZ PROMO
ROXY

PAWEL JANCZAREK

Based in Breslau, Poland.
His design company From The Trunk does art
direction and illustration for a range of music
industry clients.
Has done various posters for dubstep label
New Moon Recordings and club night My Head
is Dubby.

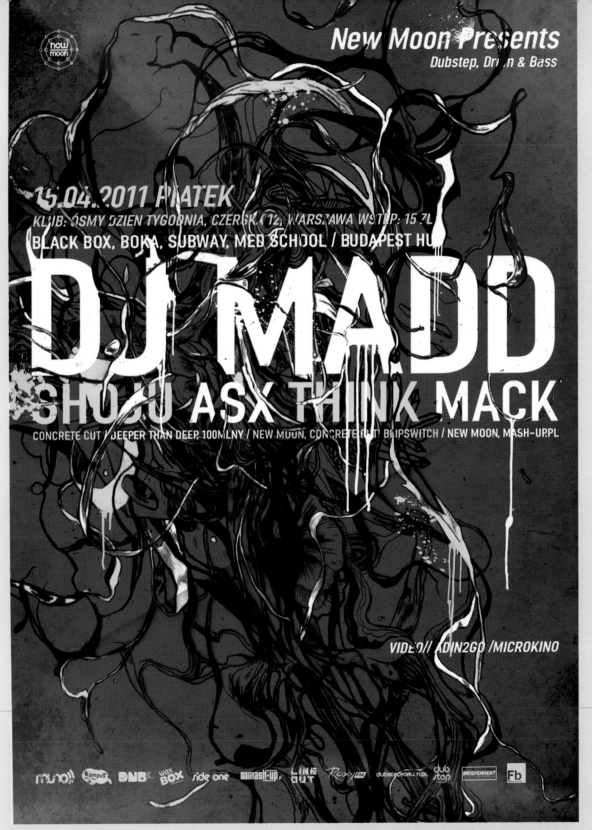

New Moon Presents
Dubstep, Drum & Bass

15.04.2011 PIATEK
KLUB: ÓSMY DZIEN TYGODNIA, CZERSKA 12, WARSZAWA WSTEP: 15 ZL
BLACK BOX, BOKA, SUBWAY, MED SCHOOL / BUDAPEST HU

DJ MADD
SHOJU ASX THINK MACK
CONCRETE CUT / DEEPER THAN DEEP 100MLNY / NEW MOON, CONCRETE CUT BLIPSWITCH / NEW MOON, MASH-UP.PL

VIDEO// ADIN2GO /MICROKINO

ABOVE DJ Madd poster, for New Moon Recordings. Digital.
LEFT Bristol poster, for Phaeleh. Digital.

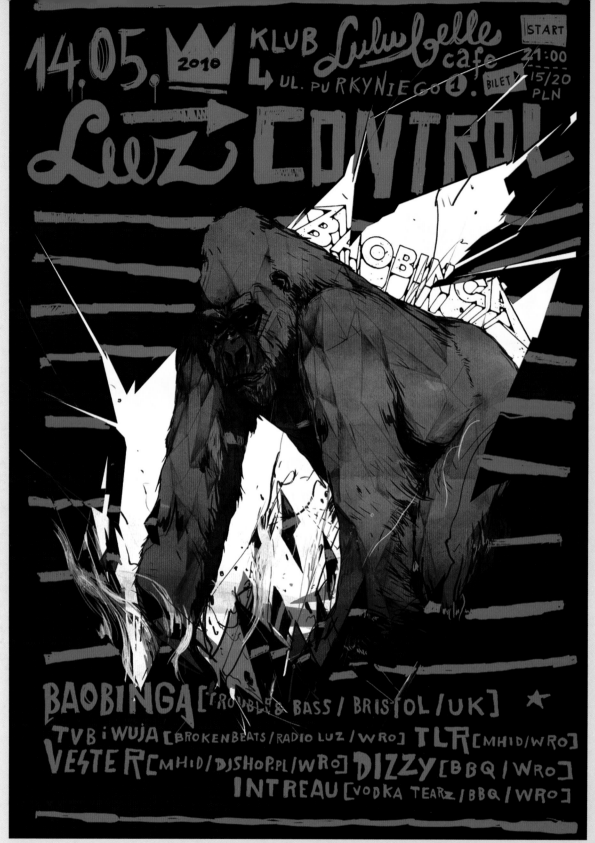

ABOVE *Klub Lulu Belle Poster,* for Luz Control. Digital.

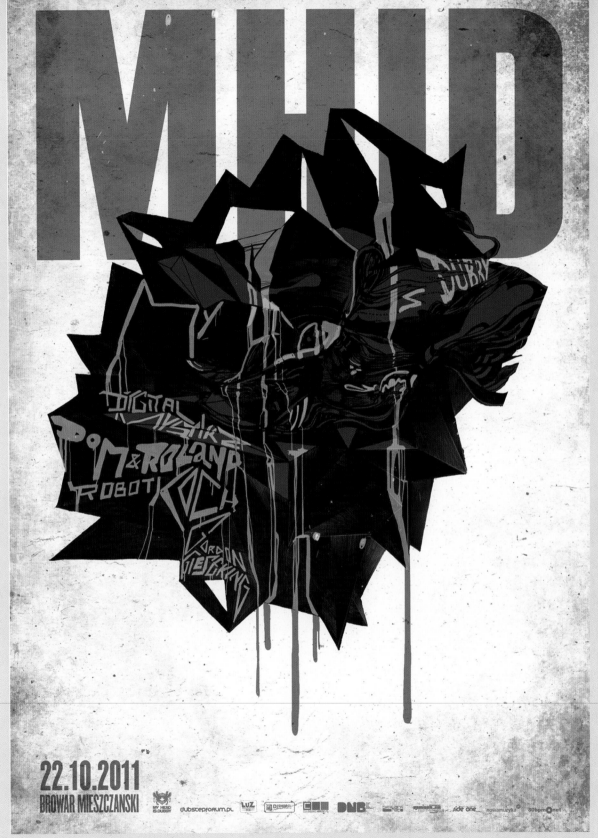

ABOVE *Digital Mystikz poster, for My Head is Dubby. Digital.*

LACZA
DESIGN

Real name: László Magyar.
Based in Dunaujvaros, Hungary.
Entirely self-taught in digital arts.
Gave up being a chef to design full-time.
Now works for artist collective Dubstep
Designs and various record labels like
Subterra, Hyperblast and Digital Empire.
Never set out to make dubstep graphics but
quickly got noticed for his perfect mix of
aggressive yet eye-catching shapes.

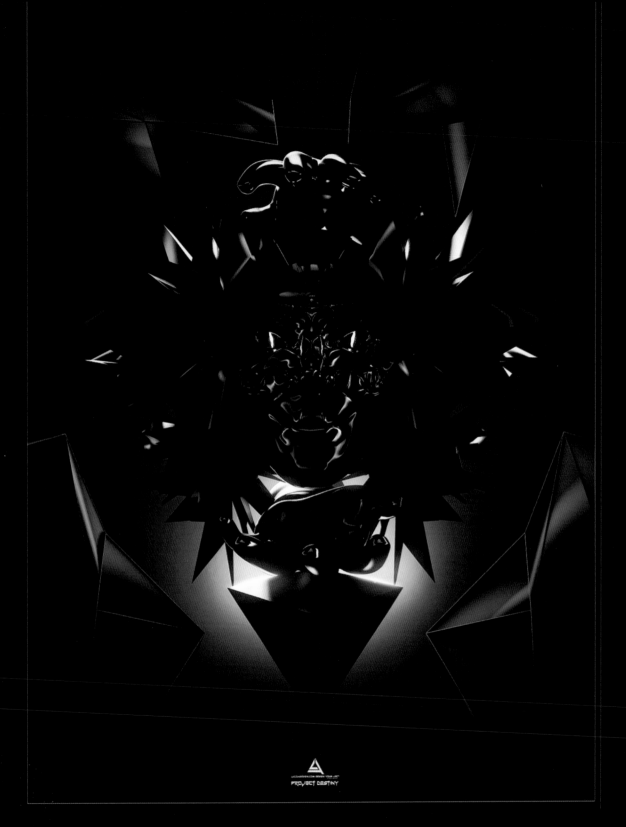

ABOVE *Destiny.* personal work. Digital.
LEFT *Gangster Slang.* for Miraflore. Photography and digital.

ABOVE *Sage Art.* for Sage Emerald. Digital.
RIGHT *Dex Logo Artwork.* for Dex. Digital.

ABOVE *What Am I.* personal work. Digital.

MIKE
LAMBO

Based in Brighton.
Visual Artist for Firepower Records.
Switched from a love of drum and bass to
dubstep after listening to Excision and Datsik
in college.
His clients include Datsik, Protohype, Getter,
Sub-Antix, D.K.S. and Excision.
His influences come from games like Mortal
Kombat, Halo and Tekken.
Signature touch: adding glowing eyes to his
designs.

ABOVE *Psycho EP.* for Getter (typography by DGDigital). Digital.
LEFT *The Massacre.* for Gunz for Hire. Digital.

ABOVE *The Monumental EP,* for Rise At Night. Digital.

ABOVE *Scum.* for Datsik. Digital.

ABOVE *Release Me.* for Datsik. Digital.

ABOVE *Can't Get Enough,* for D.K.S., Digital.

RICHARD
LOCK

Company name: Devolution Designs.
Based in Reading, UK.
Clients include Circus Records, Flux Pavilion,
Doctor P, Monsta, Nero and Fabric nightclub.
Designed for heavy metal and punk graphics
first before dubstep.
Says music and visual art are one and the
same, as they both must provoke a reaction.
Thinks the digital revolution has made dubstep
graphics less subtle, as artwork needs to be
bigger and bolder on iTunes than on a record
sleeve.

HORIZONS MUSIC

NITRI

UNDESERVING FEAT. AMELIA WEDNESDAY AA // STRANGE SIDE

ABOVE Cover. for Nitri. Digital.
LEFT *GT Logo.* for Gorilla Tactics. Digital.

AUDIO FALL
FT. STAPLETON BACK
AA AUDIO & INSIDEINFO RUST

ABOVE *Fall Back.* for Audio and Stapleton. Digital.

BHAGWAN
RECORDS

YOGA FLAME

SHC
SPONTANEOUS HUMAN COMBUSTION
HOUSE / ELECTRO / DRUM & BASS

ABOVE *Spontaneous*, for Yoga Flame. Digital.

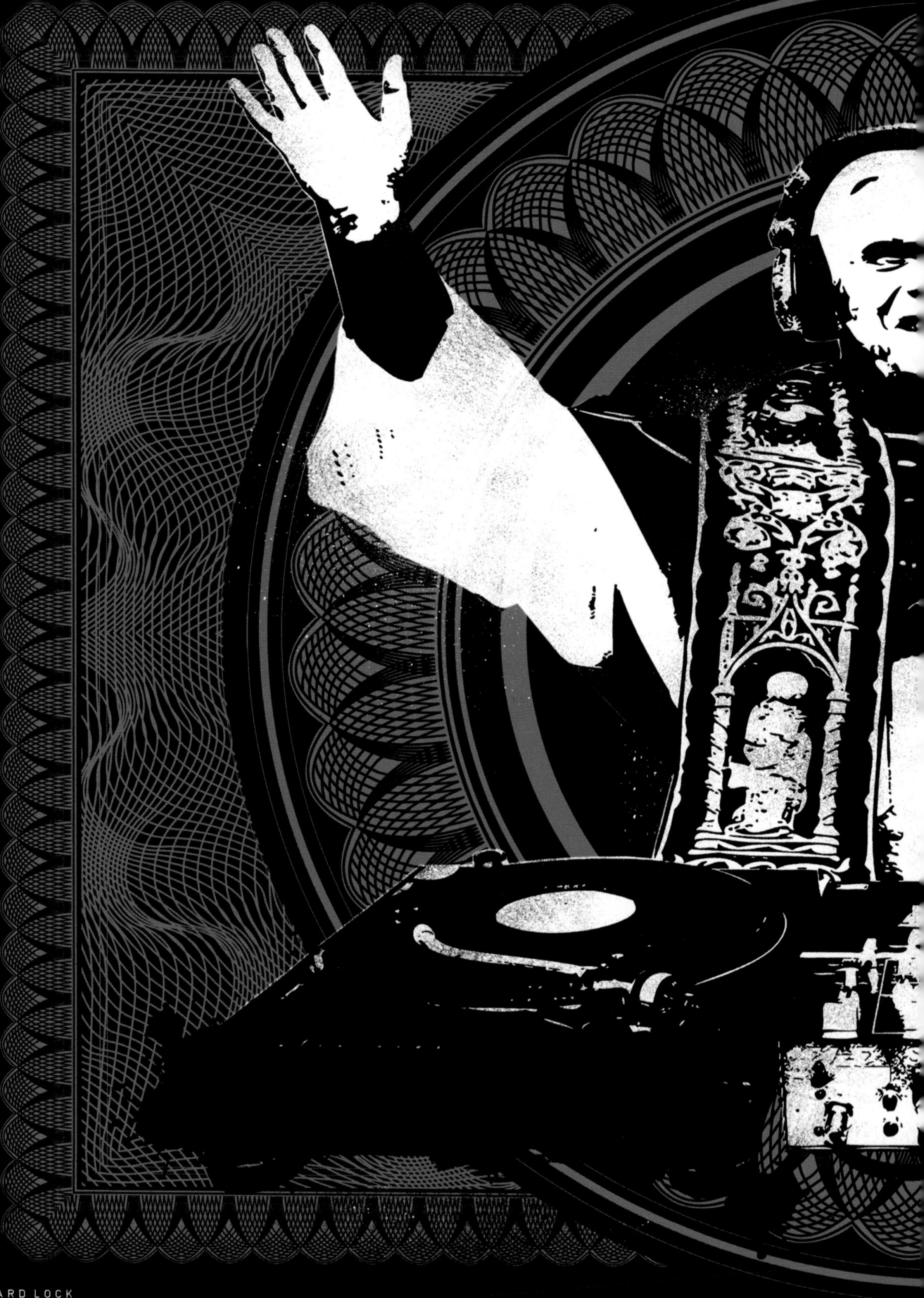

RIGHT
Pope DJ, personal work. Digital.

MICHYBAPS

Real name: Michael Douglas.
Based in London.
Has been designing for 4 years.
Does commission work for DJs and labels
through artist collective Dubstep Designs.
Accidentally got into dubstep graphics after
experimenting with 3D elements and realising
the grungy effect he'd got was just right.
Can't see that dubstep's audience will stop
growing any time soon.

HIDDEN WITHIN
NATURE WITH LIFE

ABOVE *Nature and Ice*, personal work. Digital.
LEFT *Virus*, personal work. Digital.

ABOVE *HD Wallpaper. personal work. Digital.*

ABOVE *Ice Poster.* personal work. Digital.

ABOVE *The Concept.* personal work. Digital.
RIGHT *The Light.* personal work. Digital.

BELOW
The Light.
personal work.
Digital.

THE LIGHT
FOURTH INSTALLMENT

MONSTA

Originally from Bristol, now based in
Cambridge, UK.
Designing professionally for 10 years.
Quit delivering parcels for DHL to concentrate
on his art.
His comical cartoons of drum and bass DJs
were spotted by Jungle music legend Goldie,
who asked him to design cover art for his
Rufige Kru alias.
Clients include Rinse FM, Dub Soldiers,
Metalheadz and Hospital Records. Was
responsible for the videos for dubstep icon
Caspa's live sets.
Owns record label Monsta Dubs.

ABOVE *Confused Forces.* for Fused Forces. Digital.
LEFT *Coffi - Gully Art.* for Monsta Dubs. Digital.

ABOVE *The New Development EP.* for Devilman. Digital.

108 MONSTA

ABOVE *Dubplates Knives & Forks EP.* for Skinzmann. Digital.

ABOVE *Malice in Wonderland.* for Rufige Kru. Digital.

ABOVE   *Yeah.* for Dead Players Club. Digital.

SAMUEL
MUIR

Based in London.
Has worked as a music-based designer for about 15 years.
Gets his inspiration from pop artists and illustrators from the 50s, 60s and 70s.
Clients include, Sony, Universal, MTA Records, Fly Eye, Ram and Metalheadz.
Notices dubstep graphics are beginning to look like older rave graphics and hopes they will not become too computerised and techy in the future.
Thinks dubstep will, at some point, return underground with a more subtle vibe.

LEFT
Revolt EP. for Kill
FM. Digital.

BELOW
Logos for Nero.
Must Die. Skism.
Loadstar. and
Gemini. Digital.

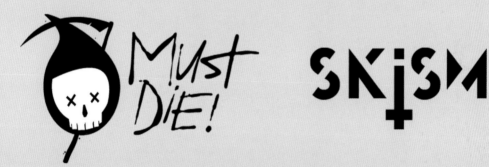

ABOVE   *Future Perfect.* for Loadstar. Digital.

ABOVE *Refuse To Love.* for Loadstar. Digital.

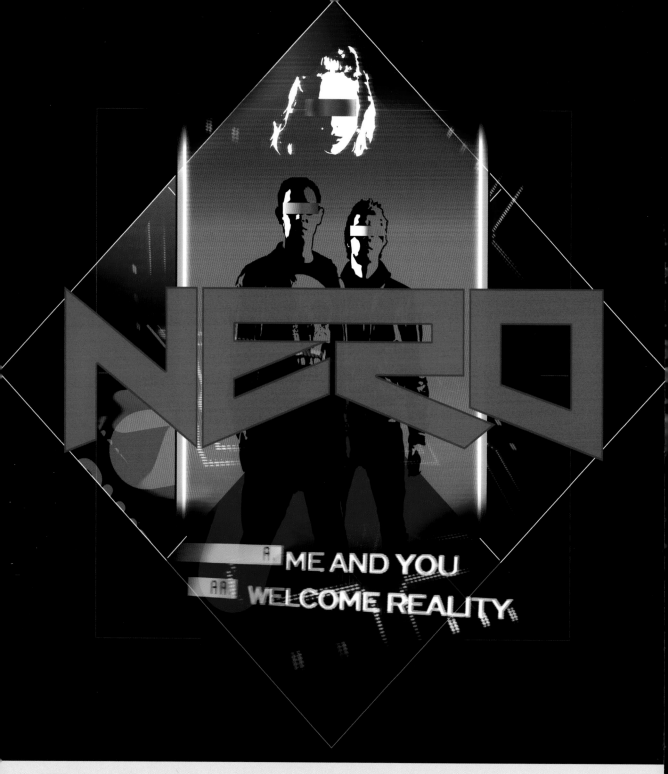

ABOVE *Me and You*, for Nero. Digital.

INNOCENCE
ELECTRON

MICHAEL
REICH

Company name: Reich Michael Designs.
Based in Munich, Germany.
Decided to create digital art after watching animations on TV.
Now works for artist collective Dubstep Designs and a range of labels and DJs, including Mosbit Records, Austrian Dubstep, UKF and RohTon.
When not producing designs for the music industry, creates websites for clients.
Says dubstep is constantly innovating and is therefore set to grow.

STATUES

ABOVE *Statues EP*. for Aaronic. Digital.
LEFT Cover. for Habstrakt. Digital.

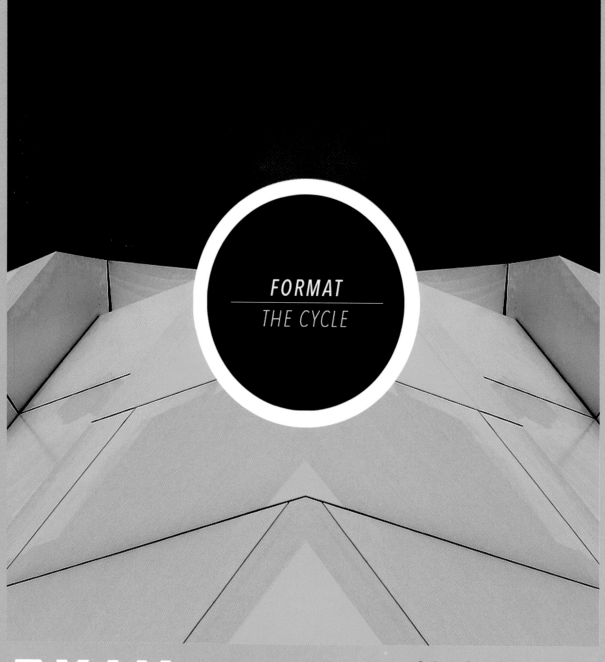

FORMAT
THE CYCLE

RYAN
EL

Real name: Ryan L. Lester.
Based in Louisville, KY, USA.
Has worked as a designer for 10 years.
Creative Director for record label Mindstep
Music, part of the creative team at Fokus FM
and a designer for Format, B9, Deafblind,
ARtroniks and many more.
The true sound of dubstep has been an
obsessive passion of his since 2009.
Sees his dubstep graphics as giving something
back to the music that's inspired him.

SUNSHINEINABAG
OFFICIAL LAUNCH PARTY

ABOVE
LEFT

BELOW Branding and logo design, for Dyad, Digital.

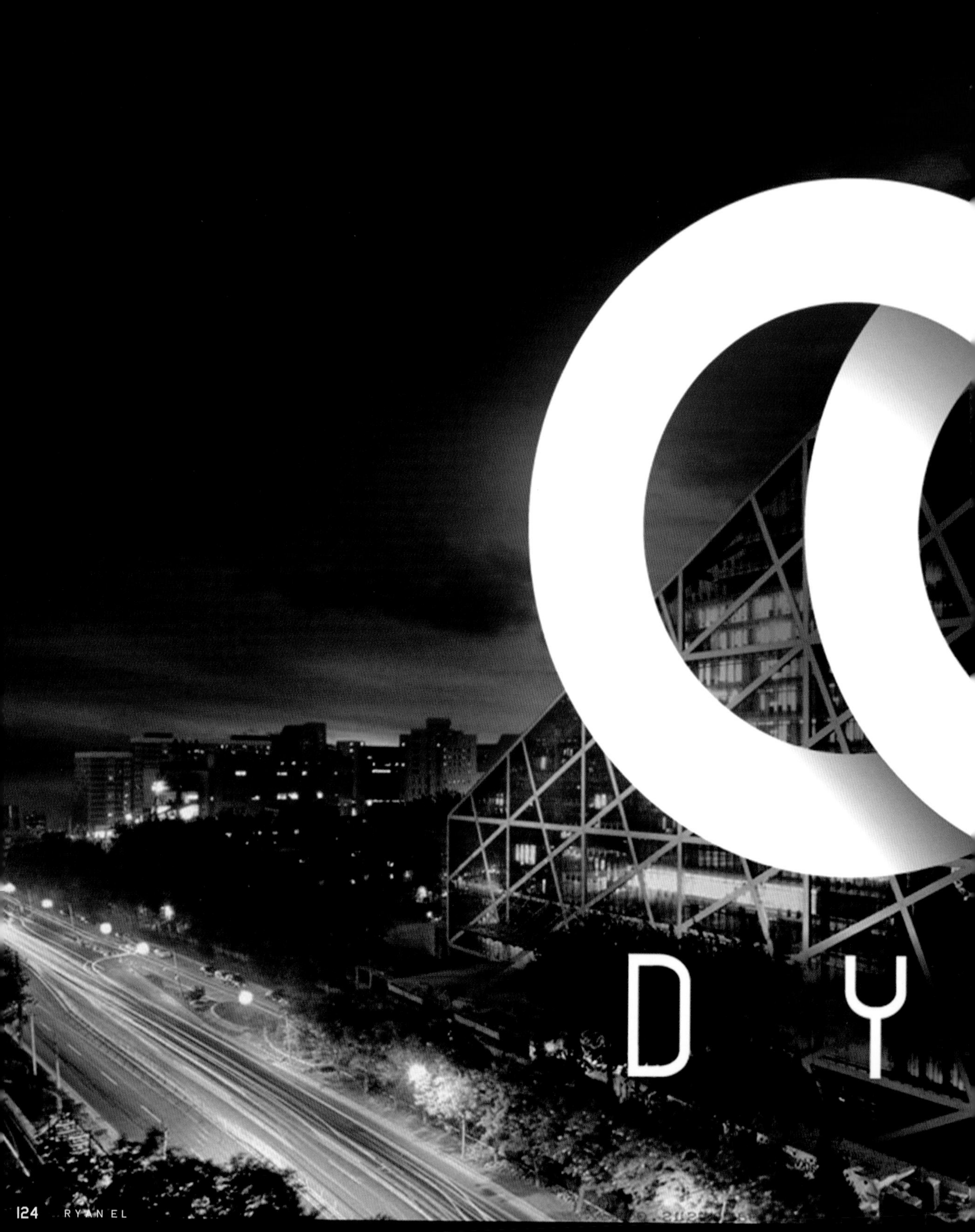

ABOVE Logo. for B9. Digital.
RIGHT Artwork. for Deafblind. Digital.

DEAFBLIND.

TANSOMAN

Real name: Ivan Silva.
Based in Pombal, Portugal.
Fell in love with making art using Photoshop and Cinema 4D when he was 16.
Completely self-taught and by age 19 had been picked up by artist collective Dubstep Designs.
Now works for a range of DJs and various record labels including Biosphere Recordings and Dank 'n' Dirty Dubz.
Is inspired by intriguing, unexpected or weird images in music videos.

ABOVE Logo for Epixz. Digital.
LEFT *Final.* free EP giveaway for Dubstep Designs.

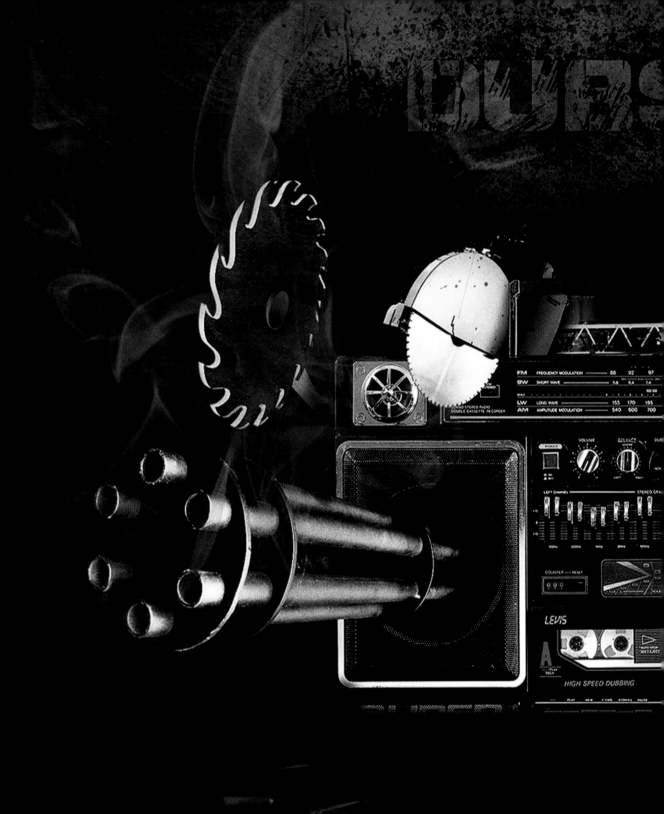

ABOVE *Dubstep. the Way it is.* personal work. Digital.

RED EYE & BROKEN FINGAZ PRESENTS

COTTI

U.K. DUBSTEP LEGEND

CITYHALL 9.4

TANT

Started as a street artist in 2005 in Haifa, Israel.
Re-thought his approach to design after a house fire
destroyed all his work.
Now has no base and spreads his street art across
the globe with the rest of world-famous collective
Broken Fingaz Crew.
Clients have included Rusko, Bar 9, Bare Noize,
Cotti, Circus Records and Chasing Shadows.
Still does all of his work by hand, only using
Photoshop at times for colour.
Says his crew members UNGA, KIP and DESO are
big influences, as well as "music, weed, porno,
psychedelic drugs, nature, old comics, porno, old
objects and folk art."

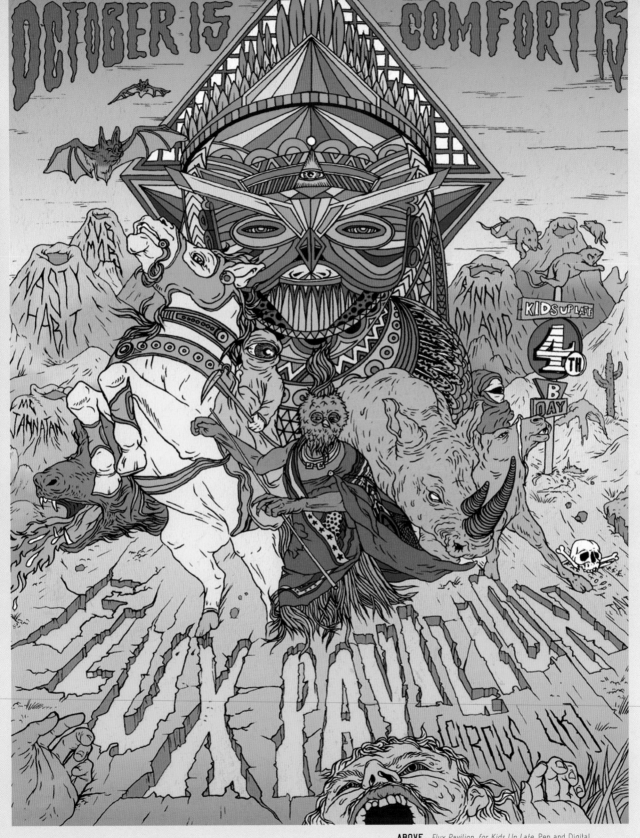

ABOVE *Flux Pavilion, for Kids Up Late.* Pen and Digital
LEFT *Cotti.* for Ghostown (typography by Desol. Pen and digital.

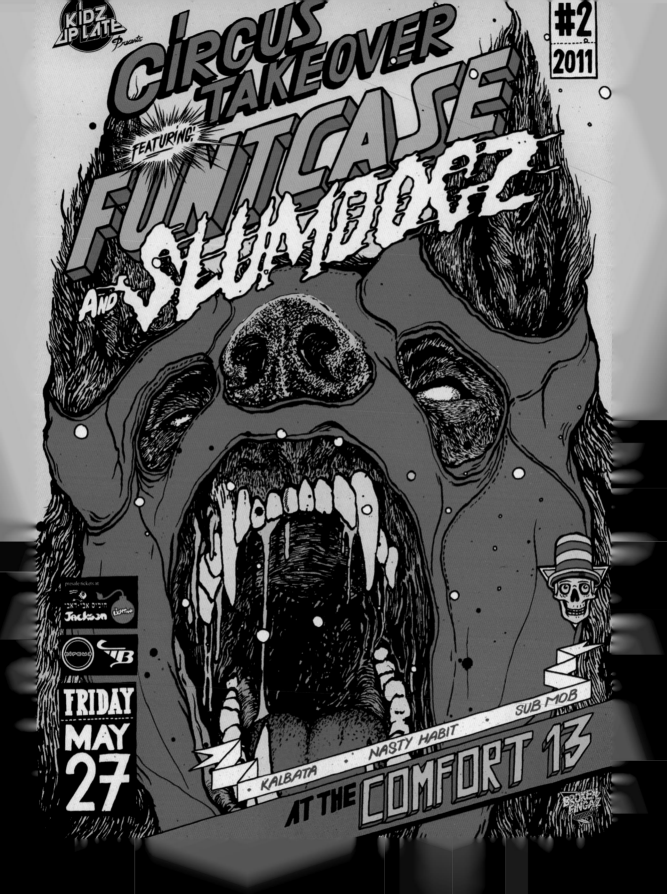

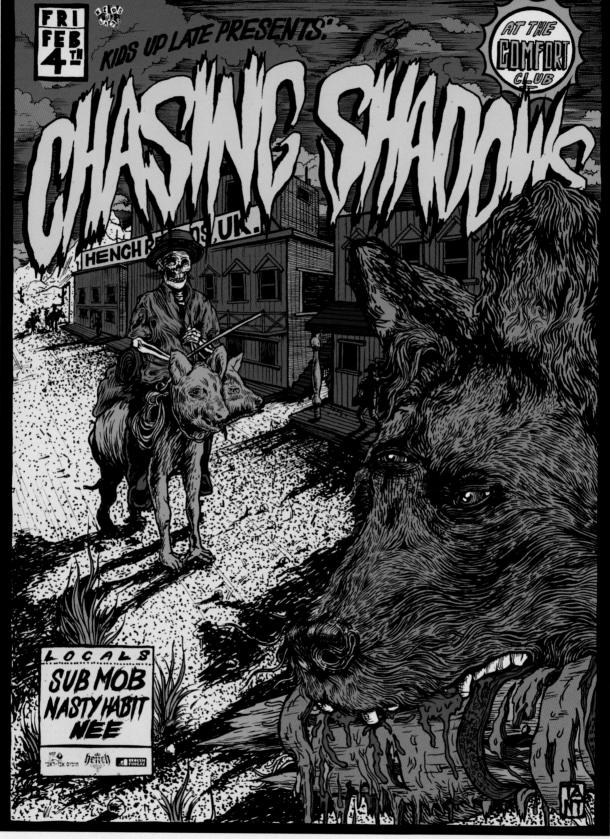

ABOVE *Chasing Shadows.* for Kids Up Late. Pen and digital.

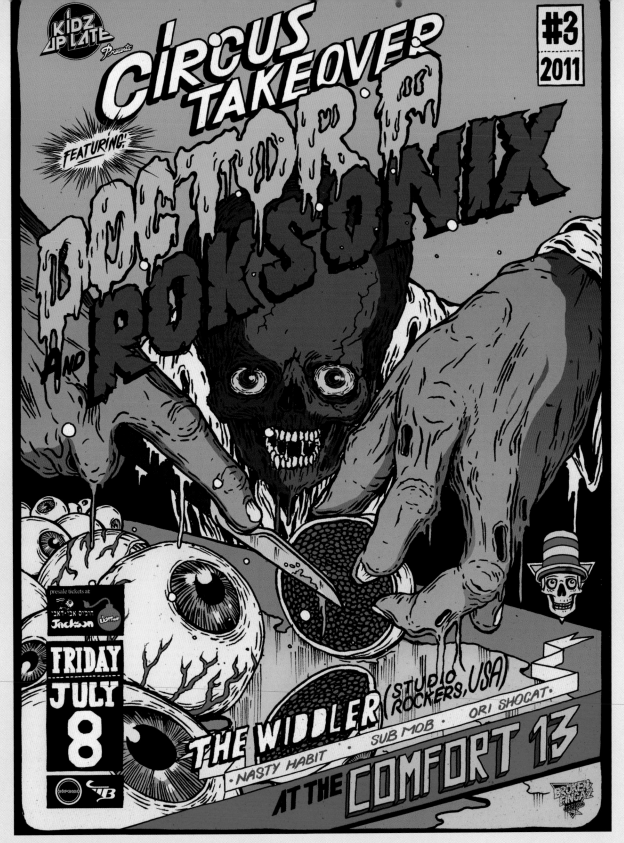

ABOVE *Circus Takeover with Doctor P. for Kids Up Late. Pen and digital.*

THAT BANANA MEDIA

Real name: Jeff Grqas.
Based in Levittown, New York, USA.
Demand for his work has been high after
doing a free design for Getter 2 years ago.
Other clients include Sluqqo, Mantis,
Cyberoptics, Sadhu and Dub all or
Nothing.
Says "most of my work is an agglomerate
of stupid ideas I decide to throw together."
Ended up being asked to teach digital art
classes in college whilst completing his
Psychology degree.

ABOVE   *Moving Fast.* for Sluggo. Digital.
RIGHT   *Sluggo Sticker.* for Sluggo. Digital.

OVERLEAF
LEFT   *DOOM.* for Getter (typography by DGDigital). Digital.
RIGHT   *Swine.* for Getter (typography by DGDigital). Digital.

ABOVE *Doominatti!!!!.* for Avacil. Digital.
LEFT *Cyber Sessions.* for Cyberoptics. Digital.

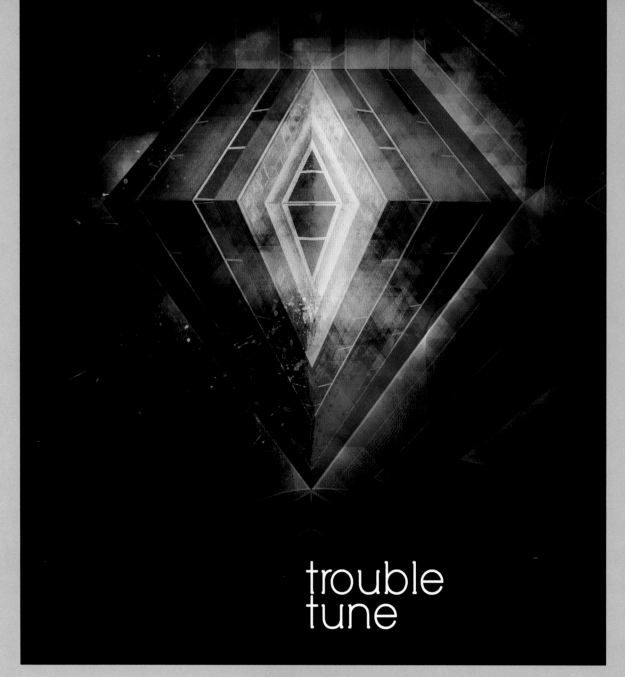

trouble
tune

VECTOR
MELDREW

Real name: Alex Donne-Johnson.
Based in South-East London, UK.
Used to design for UK garage legends Sticky,
Masterstepz and DJ EZ.
Grew tired of garage music's repetitive images of
champagne and girls in bikinis; welcomed the birth
of dubstep as a chance to experiment visually.
Became immersed in Bristol's thriving new dubstep
scene. Gained clients like dubstep pioneers
Pinch, Joker, Headhunter, Komonazmuk, 2562 and
Appleblim.
Comments that dubstep graphics are becoming
more like rave graphics from the late 90s.

ABOVE *Subloaded Flyer.* for Subloaded. Digital.
LEFT *Trouble Tune Flyer.* for Trouble Tune/London Southbank. Photography and digital.

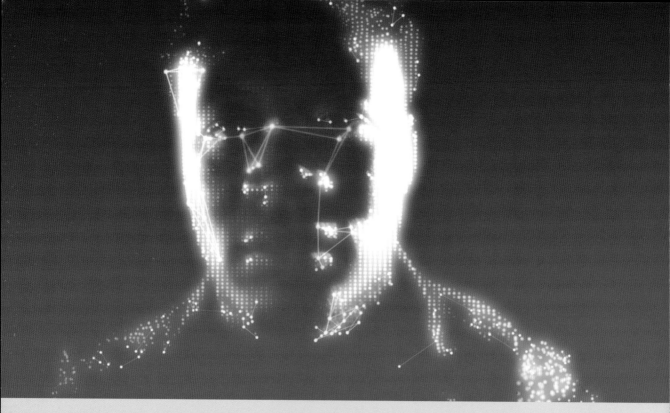

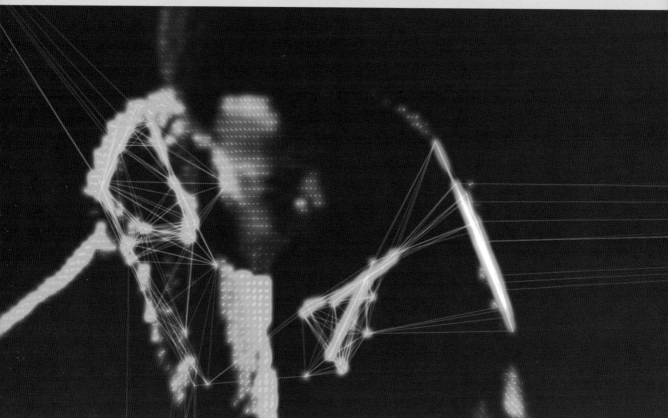

ABOVE *Komonazmuk*, for Hench. Digital.
LEFT *I Am Benga*, motion graphics for Red Bull.

ARTIST DETAILS

ASHES57
(Delphine Ettinger)
ashes57.com

CAIGE BAKER
(AKA The Third One)
FB: Caige Baker art.

BUNGO DESIGN
(Edmund Maier)
be.net/bungodesign
FB: Bungo Design

**ANTONIO
CAMPOLLO**
(AKA PLAGA)
FB: Plaga Studio

ZEKE CLOUGH
zekeclough.co.uk

CDXVM
(Aaron Kirkby)
codexarts.co.uk

COOLKATZ MEDIA
(Chris Wisnieski)
FB: CoolKatzMedia

JAMIE DEAN
(DG Digital)
behance.net/DGDigital

HARDGORE
(Brandon North)
behance.net/hardgore
FB: Hardgoredesigns

JONO HISLOP
(AKA Jono Kivex)
somethingfresh.co.nz

HYPERVISIØN
behance.net/hypervision
be.net/hypervision
vitrualghxst@gmail.com
IG: Virtualghxst
Twitter: Virtualghxst

**PAWEL
JANCZAREK**
behance.net/subgrafik
fromthetrunk.com

LACZA DESIGN
(Laszlo Magyar)
laczadesign.com
FB: laczadesign

MIKE LAMBO
behance.net/M1K3

RICHARD LOCK
(Devolution Designs)
devolutiondesigns.co.uk

MICHYBAPS
(Michael Douglas)
FB: MichybapsDesigns
behance.net/
MichybapsDesigns